# Campus Wide

東京大学教養学部英語部会 編
Department of English, The University of Tokyo, Komaba

東京大学出版会
University of Tokyo Press

Campus Wide
Department of English, The University of Tokyo, Komaba
University of Tokyo Press, 2006
ISBN 978-4-13-082119-3

[LISTENING] Elephants in Sri Lanka (photo by Naoko Irie)

Hopping

Following

Competing-1

Competing-2

[LIFE] Evolving Virtual Creatures (by Karl Sims)

[SOUND] Yaodong in the Yellow River region (photo by Ayumu Yasutomi and Yoko Fukao)

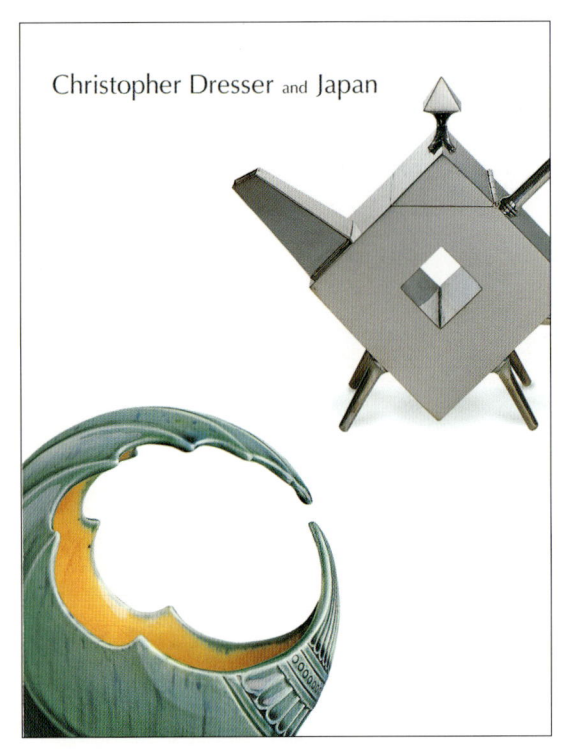

[ART] *Christopher Dresser and Japan* (Koriyama City Museum of Art)

[SCULPTURE] From *Leonardo's Horse* (by Jean Fritz [text] and Hudson Talbott [illustration])

Campus Wide

# まえがき

### このテクストの成り立ちと狙い

　本書は，平成 18（2006）年度以降，東京大学教養学部（以下「駒場」）の 1 年生全員を対象にした統一授業「英語 I」で使用される教科書で，先に刊行された *On Campus* の姉妹編（難易度はほぼ同じ）です。大学における英語の授業に新機軸を打ち出すべく 1993 年に開始された「英語 I」は，リーディング教材である教科書をマルチメディア教材と有機的に組み合わせることによって総合的な英語力を養成することを目標とするプログラムです。幸いなことに，「英語 I」の教科書としてこれまでに刊行された *The Universe of English, The Expanding Universe of English* とそれぞれの続編，そして *On Campus* は，駒場での授業という枠を超えて，一般の英語学習者にも広く受け入れられてきました。これは，多岐にわたる分野の最先端の題材を英語で読み解く力が自然に，そして着実に身につくような書物にしたい，と考えて制作者が凝らしたさまざまな工夫を，多数の学習者が評価して下さったことを意味するのでしょう。

　本書と *On Campus* の制作を担当したわたしたちは，先行する *Universe* シリーズのエッセンスを受け継ぎつつ，新たな発想も盛り込んでみたいと考えて仕事に取りかかりました。「英語を読む」のではなく「英語で読む」姿勢を読者が知らず知らずのうちに体得できるように，週 1 回の授業で読み切れる長さで，興味深いテーマを明晰に論じた文章を，多種多様な分野から精選し，それらに詳細な注を付すという *Universe* シリーズの特徴であった方針は，*On Campus* と *Campus Wide* でも継承されています。今回新たに編集方針に加わったのは，さまざまな分

野の第一線で活躍する人材を擁するという駒場の特性を活かすために，できるだけ多くの駒場の同僚に教科書制作のいろいろな段階でご協力いただくという発想でした。この編集方針は，一番目につきやすい形では，各章の Introduction の執筆を駒場の同僚にお願いしたことに反映されていますが，実際には，今回の 2 冊の教科書の制作過程全般にもっと広く深く関わるものでした。具体的には，それぞれの分野の最先端の研究テーマを扱った面白いテクストをご推薦（場合によってはご執筆）いただく，そうしたテクストを正確に読み解くための注の中で専門的な知識が必要なものをお書きいただく，テクストの理解に役立つ図版をご紹介（場合によってはご作成）いただく，駒場外の研究者も含む協力者をご紹介いただくなどです。

駒場の同僚を中心とする本当に多くの方々に惜しみのない全面的なお力添えをいただいたことにはいくら感謝してもしきれないほどですが，そのおかげで，それらの人々の力が結集されて，さまざまな研究分野への総合的な導入になりえているという意味で On Campus, Campus Wide というタイトルに恥じない，ユニークな英語教科書ができたのではないかと思っています。3 年半に及ぶ期間にわたって，（お話ししたこともなかった方々も含む）他分野の多くの研究者と力を合わせてこれらの教科書の制作に携れたことは，わたしたち制作班にとってこの上なく楽しく貴重な体験でした。本書と On Campus が，わたしたちと同じように読者が多方面からの知的な刺激を受けながら，本来の意味での英語のコミュニケーション能力を向上させるのに役立つ書物になりえていることを，わたしたちは心から望んでいます。

### 本文，注，Word Network List について

1. スペリングや引用形式に関して英・米いずれのスタイルを選ぶかは，文章内で統一されているかぎりは，原著者のスタイルにしたがっています。
2. 注の作成にあたっては，多くの辞書や事典を参照しましたが，特に頻繁に利用したものについては煩瑣となることを避けてその都度の出典の明記はしていません。それらの文献を以下にまとめて記して感謝申し上げます。*The Oxford English Dictionary* (2nd. ed.)，『平凡社 CD-ROM 版世界大百科事典』，『研究社 リーダーズ＋プラス』，『小学館 ランダムハウス英和大辞典』，その他，Web 上の『ウィキペディア（Wikipedia）』も折にふれて参照しました。
3. 注は *Universe* シリーズよりも多めにつけ，英語がそれほど得意でない人でもあまり躓かずに，あるいは内容に集中して読めるように工夫しました。辞書がなくても流れが追える程度の注が用意されていますので，それにひととおり目

を通してからテクストを読み始めてもよいかもしれません。いずれにせよ，コンテクストを意識しながら流れに乗って読み進むという経験が重要です。

4. 注をつけるにあたって，普通の意味でのイディオムではないけれどもよく用いられるフレーズ(複数の語の決まった組み合わせ)に注意を促すことを心がけました。そうすることが英文の理解に役立つと同時に「発信型」の英語力の養成にも貢献すると考えたからです。同じ目的で，テクストに現れた重要な語句や構文のさらなる使用例や関連する用例を，e.g. (for example) や cf. (compare) というかたちでかなり多く載せておきました。

5. 注については本書を通じて記述に重複があります。これは読者が必ずしも第1章から順番に読むとはかぎらないからですが，重要な語句や構文に注目してもらうためでもあります(適宜クロスレファレンスを指示しているのはそのためです)。

6. この「まえがき」の直後にある「Word Network List」は，本書に複数回現れるテーマやコンセプトやキーワードを相互にたどるための見取り図です。読む順序の参考にしていただければ幸いです。

### 謝辞

最初に，さまざまな形でご協力いただいた英語部会の同僚諸氏に深く感謝申し上げます。中でも On Campus と本書の全章を綿密にご検討下さり，詳細なコメントをして下さった鈴木英夫と Clive Collins の両氏には特別な謝意を表しないわけにはいきません。

各章のイントロダクションの執筆者および注作成の協力者(章の順で，敬称略)は，以下のとおりです。

1. 梅景正(精神衛生)
2. 池上俊一(西洋中世史)
3. Clive Collins(英文学)
   瀬地山角(ジェンダー論)
4. 開一夫(発達認知神経科学)
5. 西村義樹(言語学)
6. 池上高志(複雑系の科学)
7. 長谷川壽一(動物行動学)
8. 清水剛(経営学・経営統計)
9. 安冨歩(社会・生命のダイナミクス)
   深尾葉子(中国社会論)
10. 田尻芳樹(イギリス文学研究)
11. 今橋映子(比較文学比較文化)
12. 本村凌二(西洋古代史)
13. 岡山裕(アメリカ政治)
14. 古田元夫(ベトナム現代史)

このうち，西村，田尻，岡山以外は英語部会外からご協力いただいた方々であり，心から御礼を申し上げます。

さらに，編集の過程でさまざまな形で協力して下さった以下の方たちにも感謝申し上げます。

古賀裕章，設楽靖子，古川敏明，森仁志（以上，東京大学大学院博士課程），砂田恵理加（国士舘大学専任講師），佐藤元状（慶應義塾大学専任講師），有井秀子（東京大学事務嘱託）

中でも設楽氏には信じがたいほどの多大な時間を注作成の補助に割いていただき，適切な感謝のことばが見つかりません。英語I教材TAの皆さんにも有益なコメントをいただきました。

最後になりましたが，本作りに関して常に的確なアドバイスをして下さった上に，慢性的に遅れ気味の編集作業に優しく活を入れる(?)ために，制作会議にいろいろと差し入れまでして下さった東京大学出版会編集部の後藤健介氏に，心からの感謝の気持ちをお伝えしたいと思います。長い間本当にありがとうございました。

*On Campus* の「まえがき」にも述べられているとおり，わたしたち4人の制作班は，長期にわたって数えきれないほどの会議で侃々諤々の議論を重ねるうちに，本書のあらゆる部分に関して同等に責任があるという感覚を共有するまでになりました。したがって，本作りの常識に反するようですが，役割分担の明記はあえていたしません。驚くほど学ぶことの多かったこの有意義な仕事の成果に対する読者からのご意見やご批判を全員で楽しみにしています。（YN）

丹治　愛／ホーンズ・シーラ／矢口祐人／西村義樹

# WORD NETWORK LIST

This word network list has two main purposes. First, it is designed to enable readers to explore the way in which the meanings of apparently simple terms vary in subtle ways according to context. By tracking a single word as it appears and reappears throughout this book, readers will be able to see how context-dependent its meaning is, and how it makes sense differently in different contexts. The term 'space,' for example, which appears in six different chapters, shifts its meaning almost every time, asking us constantly to rethink what it means. Reading along, we move from cognitive space to national space to global space, from the spatial dimensions of a baseball field in Colorado to the spatial acoustics of a valley in China, from space as an abstract category of knowledge to the tangible spaces explored by babies to the 'memory spaces' inhabited by computer-generated lifeforms. In each case, 'space' means something slightly different, and as readers we have to constantly resituate ourselves and rethink our understanding of what 'space' means.

The second reason that we have included this word network list is that we wanted to make easily visible the way in which certain themes surface and resurface throughout the text. We hope that the word network list will in this way show how texts which at first sight seem to be firmly situated within distinct academic disciplines or traditions, located at a distance from each other, are in fact 'networked,' engaged in implicit conversation, and approaching shared concerns from different perspectives. In this sense, we hope that the word network list will function as a metaphor for the creative potential of interdisciplinary collaboration, for us one of the most exciting aspects of life on campus.

（抄訳）この「ワードネットワーク・リスト」には主にふたつの趣旨があります。まず，ひとつの英単語や語句が，いかに多層的な意味を持ちうるかを理解するための手がかりを示すものです。たとえば「space」という言葉は，単純に「空間」と和訳されがちですが，その意味は文脈によって実に多様です。またこのリストは，ある種のテーマが本書で頻出していることを示す指針にもなっています。一見すると，それぞれのレッスンは異なる学問分野の話であると思われるかもしれません。しかしこのリストから，学問全体に通底する学際的なテーマがあることがわかるでしょう。いろいろな分野に興味を抱き，積極的に知の枠組みを広げていくためのヒントとしてください。

| | |
|---|---|
| animals（動物） | biology, listening, sound, empire |
| art/artistic（芸術，芸術的） | art, sculpture, eurocentrism |
| artificial intelligence/life（人工知能，人工生命） | babies, life |
| biology（生物学）<br>biologist（生物学者） | biology, life, listening |
| brain（脳） | biology, babies, language |
| communicate/communication（伝達する，コミュニケーション） | biology, food, nationality, babies, language, listening |
| creativity（創造力） | biology, food, art, sculpture |
| death（死） | biology, life |
| ecology（生態，生態学，エコロジー） | babies, listening, life |
| empire/imperial（帝国，帝国の） | empire, eurocentrism |
| environment(al)（環境（の）） | babies, listening, life, baseball, sound |
| food, cooking, cuisine（料理（法）） | food, life, sound |
| grammar（文法） | nationality, language |
| history/historical（歴史，歴史的な） | babies, language, sound, art, sculpture, eurocentrism |
| [the] Industrial Revolution（産業革命） | art, eurocentrism |
| (im)/migration, citizenship, [to] move overseas（市民権・公民権）(移民，海外への移動) | food, nationality, empire, sculpture, eurocentrism |

| | |
|---|---|
| interdependence, fusion（相互依存，融合）<br>emergentism（創発主義） | biology, food, babies, life, empire, art, sculpture, eurocentrism |
| language（言語） | nationality, language, listening, law |
| orient(al)/occident(al)（東洋(の)，西洋(の)） | art, sculpture, eurocentrism |
| politics（政治(学)） | food, sound, law, eurocentrism |
| reading（読書，読むこと） | nationality, empire, law |
| research（調査，研究）<br>observation（観察） | biology, babies, life, listening, baseball, sound, art |
| rules（規則，決まり，法則） | language, life, baseball, law |
| social activity/socialization（社会的活動，社会化） | biology, babies, sound |
| sound, hearing, acoustics（音，音響，聞く，聴く） | nationality, language, listening, sound |
| space（空間，スペース） | babies, life, baseball, sound, empire, eurocentrism |
| 'The East'/'The West'（「東」「西」） | art, sculpture, eurocentrism |

\* 上記の日本語は厳密な「和訳」ではありません。それぞれの英単語・語句の意味を適切に捉えるためには，各レッスンを参照し，前後の文脈の中で考えてみてください。

# TABLE OF CONTENTS

## 1 • BIOLOGY ................................................................. 2
Introduction by Tadashi Umekage
"My Life in Science," by Sydney Brenner

## 2 • FOOD ...................................................................... 14
Introduction by Shunichi Ikegami
"The Nobu Matsuhisa Story," by Nobuyuki Matsuhisa

## 3 • NATIONALITY ...................................................... 26
Introduction by Clive Collins
"Miyon," by Kaku Sechiyama

## 4 • BABIES ................................................................... 40
Introduction by Kazuo Hiraki
"Deciphering the Infant World," by Philippe Rochat

## 5 • LANGUAGE ............................................................ 52
Introduction by Yoshiki Nishimura
"Language, Mind, and Grammar"

## 6 • LIFE ....................................................................... 68
Introduction by Takashi Ikegami
"The Artificial Life Workshop," by Christopher G. Langton
"Artificial Life," by Jeff Elman

## 7 — LISTENING · · · · · · 82
Introduction by Toshikazu Hasegawa
"Four Ears to the Ground," by Allan Burdick

## 8 — BASEBALL · · · · · · 94
Introduction by Takashi Shimizu
"Atmosphere, Weather, and Baseball," Frederick Chambers, Brian Page, and Clyde Zaidins

## 9 — SOUND · · · · · · 108
Introduction by Yoko Fukao and Ayumu Yasutomi
"Yangjiagou Soundscape," by Junko Iguchi

## 10 — EMPIRE · · · · · · 120
Introduction by Yoshiki Tajiri
"The Landscapes of Sherlock Holmes," by Yi-Fu Tuan

## 11 — ART · · · · · · 132
Introduction by Eiko Imahashi
"The Pleasures of Exhibition Catalogs," by Eiko Imahashi
"Christopher Dresser and Japan," by Angela Jeffs

## 12 — SCULPTURE · · · · · · 144
Introduction by Ryoji Motomura
"Leonardo's Horse"

## 13 — LAW · · · · · · 156
Introduction by Hiroshi Okayama
"The Constitution of Fear," by Frederick Schauer

## 14 — EUROCENTRISM · · · · · · 168
Introduction by Motoo Furuta
"The Myth of the West," by Ella Shohat and Robert Stam

## 出典一覧

Grateful acknowledgment is made for permission to reprint excerpts and figures from the following publications:

### TEXTS

1. BIOLOGY: "My Life in Science," by Sydney Brenner, from *My Life in Science* (BioMed Central, 2001). Press Release from The Nobel Assembly, cited from http://nobelprize.org/medicine/laureates/2002/press.html. Interview "Worms and Science," reprinted by permission from Macmillan Publishers Ltd: *European Molecular Biology Organization Reports* (*EMBO Reports*), 4, 224–226 (01 March, 2003), copyright (2003).
2. FOOD: From *Nobu: The Cookbook* by Nobuyuki Matsuhisa. Published by Kodansha International. Copyright © 2001 by Nobuyuki Matsuhisa. Reprinted by permission. All rights reserved.
3. NATIONALITY: 瀬地山角『お笑いジェンダー論』(勁草書房，2001年) より。
4. BABIES: Reprinted by permission of the publisher from *The Infant's World* by Philippe Rochat, Cambridge, Mass.: Harvard University Press, Copyright © 2001 by Philippe Rochat.
5. LANGUAGE: Notecard 1, Noam Chomsky (1991) "Linguistics and cognitive science: Problems and mysteries," in Asa Kasher, editor, *The Chomskyan Turn* (Blackwell). Notecard 2, Michael Tomasello (1995) "Language is not an instinct," *Cognitive Development*, 10, pp. 131–156. Notecard 3, Rodney Huddleston (1976) *An Introduction to English Transformational Syntax* (Longman). Notecard 4, Noam Chomsky (1955) "Semantic considerations in grammar," Monograph No. 8, pp. 141–153 (The Institute of Languages and Linguistics, Georgetown University). Notecard 5, Noam Chomsky (1977) "Questions of form and interpretation," in Chomsky, *Essays on Form and Interpretation* (Elsevier North Holland, Inc.). Notecard 6, Noam Chomsky (1979) *Language and Responsibility* (Pantheon). Notecard 7, Ronald W. Langacker (1991) *Foundations of Cognitive Grammar*, Vol. 2. (Stanford University Press). Notecard 8, Ronald W. Langacker (1987) *Foundations of Cognitive Grammar*, Vol. 1 (Stanford University Press). Notecard 9, Ronald Langacker (1988) "An overview of cognitive grammar," in Brygida Rudzka-Ostyn, editor, *Topics in Cognitive Linguistics* (John Benjamins).
6. LIFE: "The Artificial Life Workshop," by Christopher G. Langton, from "Preface," of Christopher G. Langton, editor (1989) *Artificial Life: Proceedings of an Interdisciplinary Workshop on the Synthesis and Simulation of Living Systems, Los Alamos, 1987* (Addison-Wesley). "Artificial Life," by Jeff Elman from "Connectionism, artificial life, and dynamical system: New approaches to old questions," in W. Bechtel and G. Graham, editors (1998) *A Companion to Cognitive Science*, Oxford: Basil Blackwood (Blackwell Publishing, Ltd.).
7. LISTENING: From Allan Burdick (2002) "Four Ears to the Ground: For an Ele-

phant, the Foot may be a Powerful Listening Device," in *Natural History* (American Museum of Natural History), April 2002. Reprinted by permission of the anthor.
8. BASEBALL: From Frederick Chambers, Brian Page, and Clyde Zaidins (2003), "Atmosphere, Weather, and Baseball: How Much Farther Do Baseballs Really Fly at Denver's Coors Field?" in *The Professional Geographer*, 55(4), 491–504.
9. SOUND: 井口淳子「村の音環境」(深尾葉子・井口淳子・栗原伸治『黄土高原の村：音・空間・社会』古今書院, 2000 年, 所収) より。
10. EMPIRE: From "The Landscapes of Sherlock Holmes," by Yi-Fu Tuan (1985), *Journal of Geography*, 84(2) [March-April], 56–60.
11. ART: "The Pleasures of Exhibition Catalogs," by Eiko Imahashi, 今橋映子(編著)『展覧会カタログの愉しみ』(2003 年, 東京大学出版会) より。"Christopher Dresser and Japan," from "World's first industrial designer creates a stir," by Angela Jeffs, first appeared in *The Japan Times*, May 20, 2002.
12. SCULPTURE: "A Long Shot Pays Off," by Nancy Mohr, from "Leonardo's Horse: A Long Shot Pays Off" in *Smithsonian Magazine* (September 2002), reprinted by permission of the author. Buon Viaggio, Gala Send Off, cited from http://www.leonardoshorse.org/buon_viaggio.asp. "The Horse Arrives in Italy," by Jean Fritz, from *Leonardo's Horse* (G. P. Putnam's Sons, Penguin USA, 2001). "Sculptor's Statement," by Nina Akamu, cited from http://leonardoshorse.org/nina.asp.
13. LAW: "The Constitution of Fear," by Frederick Schauer, from *Constitutional Stupidities, Constitutional Tragedies*, edited by William N. Eskridge, Jr. and Sanford Levinson, New York University Press, 1998.
14. EUROCENTRISM: From *Unthinking Eurocentrism*, by Ella Shohat & Robert Stam, (Routlegde, 1994). Copyright © 1994 by Ella Shohat & Robert Stam.

## FRONTISPIECE

"Elephants in Sri Lanka," photo by Naoko Irie.
"Evolving Virtual Creatures," by Karl Sims. Reprinted by permission of Karl Sims, from http://www.genarts.com/karl/evolved-virtual-creatures.html
"Yaodong in the Yellow River region," photo by Ayumu Yasutomi and Yoko Fukao.
"*Christopher Dresser and Japan*,"『「クリストファー・ドレッサーと日本」展カタログ』(郡山市立美術館, 2002 年)。
"From *Leonardo's Horse*," by Jean Fritz [text] and Hudson Talbott [illustration], published by G. P. Putnam's Sons, 2001.

## PLATES

1. BIOLOGY: "Sydney Brenner," cited from http://nobelprize.org/medicine/laureates/2002/brenner_speech_photo.jpg. "A pair of *C. elegans*," 飯野雄一 (1998)「線虫 *C. elegans* の性と生殖」『蛋白質核酸酵素』(共立出版) 43(4), 365 ページ。
2. FOOD: Cover photograph of *Nobu: The Cookbook*, Kodansha International, 2001.
4. BABIES: Cover photograph of *The Infant's World: Sandra*, © Hans Samson. "Professor Kazuo Hiraki in his office," photo by Sheila Hones.
5. LANGUAGE: Cover photographs of Noam Chomsky (2004) *The Generative Enterprise Revisited* (Mouton de Gruyter), ノーム・チョムスキー(福井直樹・辻子美保子訳)『生成文法の企て』(岩波書店, 2003 年), Michael Tomasello (1999) *The Cultural Origins of Human Cognition* (Harvard University Press), マイケル・トマ

セロ（大堀壽夫・中澤恒子・西村義樹・本多啓訳）『心とことばの起源を探る』（勁草書房，2006年），Ronald W. Langacker (1987) *Foundations of Cognitive Grammar*, Vol. 1: Theoretical Prerequisites (Stanford University Press).

6. LIFE: "A grid for a cellular automaton," from the original article (p. 499, Figure 38.4).
7. LISTENING: "Elephants in Sri Lanka," photo by Naoko Irie.
8. BASEBALL: "Coors Field home runs per at-bat, 1995–2002," from the original article (p. 501, Figure 5). "Coors Field," presented by Denver Metro Convention and Visitors Bureau.
9. SOUND: "*yaodong* in the Yellow River region" and "Local musicians playing *suona*," photo by Ayumu Yasutomi and Yoko Fukao.「牌楼」「大鐘」いずれも馬師元（画）。
10. EMPIRE: "At the Reichenbach Falls," by Sidney Paget (1893), reprinted from *The Life and Times of Sherlock Holmes* (Bracken Books, 1993). "The Sherlock Holmes Museum, Baker Street, London," photo by Yoshiki Tajiri.
11. ART:『「ジャポニスム」展カタログ』（国立西洋美術館［東京］，1988年）。『「クリストファー・ドレッサーと日本」展カタログ』より（郡山市立美術館，2002年）。
12. SCULPTURE: "Leonardo's Horse in Milan,"（中川亜希撮影）。"The sculptor Nina Akamu with a model of Leonardo's Horse," cited from http://www.leonardoshorse.org/graphics/photogal/e7.jpg
14. EUROCENTRISM: "*Bird of Paradise* (1932)," Directed by King Vidor, Allied Artists Classics (CAT# 4033), 1994. Cover photographs of Raymond Williams (1976/Revised Edition 1983) *Keywords: A Vocabulary of Culture and Society* (Oxford University Press), Edward W. Said (1978) *Orientalism* (Vintage Books), Ella Shohat and Robert Stam (1994) *Unthinking Eurocentrism: Multiculturalism and the Media* (Routledge).

# 1
# BIOLOGY

## Introduction
### Tadashi Umekage

In the last half century, molecular biology has not only gained in popularity but also made tremendous advances. Sydney Brenner has been one of the groundbreaking contributors to this golden age. He was awarded the 2002 Nobel Prize in Physiology or Medicine, with John Sulston and Robert Horvitz, for their discoveries concerning the "genetic regulation of organ development and programmed cell death."

Sydney Brenner was born in South Africa in 1927 and started his university studies in medicine at the University of Witwatersrand, Johannesburg when he was fifteen. His enthusiasm for research work took him next to Oxford, where he investigated bacteriophage resistance. In 1956 he joined the Cavendish Laboratory, at Cambridge University, where he went on to found the MRC Laboratory of Molecular Biology. During his time as director of the laboratory, from 1979 to 1986, he established the existence of messenger RNA and played a key role in deciphering the genomic code. His scientific interest was also directed at this time toward determining how genes control the division of cells and the development of organs. To develop his understanding of this issue, he focused his attention on a tiny worm, nematode *C. elegans*. It was his work on this specific model organism that laid the foundation for his Nobel Prize.

In the last ten years, Sydney Brenner has also concentrated on the Japanese pufferfish, *fugu*, having taken it up for study as an ideal model for the vertebrate genome. Still looking into the future, and with his enthusiasm for research undiminished, Professor Brenner is currently continuing to work energetically in the fields of human biology and medicine.

- [1] **molecular** [məlékjələr] **biology:**「分子生物学」(cf. molecule [málıkjuːl] 分子)。
- [1] **gained in popularity:** gain in ... は「...が増す」(e.g. In recent years, this problem has been steadily *gaining in* importance in philosophy.)。
- [3] **groundbreaking:**「新しい分野を切り開く」「開拓者的な」(cf. 本文 [122])。
- [5] **John Sulston:** イギリスの分子生物学者(1942– )。MRC 分子生物学研究所([13] 参照)で，シドニー・ブレナーの研究グループに参加し，線虫の全細胞系譜を明らかにした。また，世界初の多細胞生物ゲノム地図を完成させた。2001 年ナイト爵の称号を授与されている。
- [5] **Robert Horvitz:** アメリカの分子生物学者(1947– )。「プログラム化された細胞死（programmed cell death)」，すなわちアポトーシス（apoptosis [æ̀pə(p)tóusəs]）が厳密に遺伝子によって制御されていることを解明し，その機構を明らかにした。
- [7] **programmed cell death:** 生体中の不要となった細胞が死滅するよう「あらかじめプログラム化された細胞死」のこと。このプロセスは遺伝子によって制御されている。
- [11] **bacteriophage** [bæktíəriəfèɪdʒ] **resistance:**「バクテリオファージ」とは，語源的に「バクテリアを食べるもの」の意味だが，バクテリアのなかにはそのようなファージにたいして耐性をもつものもいる。bacteriophage resistance とは，言い換えれば，phage-resistance in bacteria のことで，「バクテリアのファージに対する耐性」を意味する。
- [13] **the MRC Laboratory of Molecular Biology:** ケンブリッジにある MRC（医学研究評議会）の分子生物学研究所。
- [15] **established:** この場合の establish は「確証する」「立証する」。
- [15] **messenger RNA:**「メッセンジャー[伝令] RNA」。リボ核酸（ribonucleic acid＝RNA）の一種で，DNA 上の遺伝情報を伝令する働きをもつところから，この名がつけられている。
- [16] **played a key role in deciphering the genomic code:** play a key role in ... は「...で重要な役割を果たす」。decipher the genomic [dʒənámık] code は「遺伝暗号を解読する」(cf. genome [dʒíːnoʊm])。
- [20] **nematode *C. elegans*:** nematode は「線虫」の総称。*C. elegans*（C.＝Caenorhabditis）はその一種で，体長 1 mm ほどの小さな土壌動物。全発生過程で 1090 個の細胞ができ，そのうち 131 個は決まった時期に「プログラム化された細胞死」を起こして消滅していく。
- [21] **laid the foundation for ... :** lay the foundation(s) for ... は「...の基礎を築く」と言う場合の決まった言い方。

# My Life in Science

## Sydney Brenner

*Sydney Brenner is currently Distinguished Research Professor at the Salk Institute, La Jolla, USA. Here, in two extracts from his book* My Life in Science, *Brenner talks about his skills as a scientist and about scientific creativity:*

I think my real skills are in getting things started — that's gone through my whole life. In fact that's what I enjoy the most, the opening game. And I'm afraid that once it gets past that point I get rather bored and want to do other things. So being a permanent post-doc is really very attractive to me, and I think the exciting part of intellectual life in science.

The other thing I'm rather good at is talking. When Fred Sanger was asked to give me a recommendation I was told that he said, "Oh, Brenner, the man who talks a lot!" So I believe that keeping up the conversation is one of the important roles one can have in science. The whole idea that science is conducted by people working alone in rooms and struggling with the force of nature is absolutely ridiculous. It is a social activity of the highest sort. And so keeping up the conversation, doing experiments with words, is very important. I'm fascinated by that, and I think that's how ideas emerge. Most of what I say is rubbish, but amidst the stream of unconsciousness, if I can coin a phrase, there is the odd idea that can be developed into something.

Sydney Brenner

[28]　**the Salk Institute:** アメリカ・カリフォルニア州ラホーヤにある Salk Institute for Biological Studies のこと。1963 年，ポリオ予防用のソーク・ワクチンの開発者である Jonas Salk (1914–95) によって最初の研究施設が開設されたが，それ以降，Sydney Brenner を含む何人ものノーベル賞学者を生み出すなど，世界の生物学研究をリードする存在となっている。Sydney Brenner は，1996 年以降，ここを中心に研究活動を続けている。

[32]　**getting things started:**「物事を始めること」。このように get は目的語と過去分詞を伴ってその過去分詞のもとになっている他動詞とほぼ同じ意味を表すことがよくある (e.g. I'm afraid it'll take us forever to *get* this work *finished*. / I'm absolutely sure you can *get* the job *done* all by yourself.)。同じ表現型が「(主語以外の人に)…させる，してもらう」を意味する場合にも用いられることがあるので注意が必要 (e.g. I need to *get* my hair *cut*.)。

[32]　**that's gone through my whole life:**「私の人生はこれまでずっとそうだった」。

[33]　**that's what . . . :** "That's what . . ." のような That [This] is＋疑問詞…という表現型にも慣れておきたい (e.g. *That's what* I like about her.「彼女のそういうところが好きです」/ *That's not what* I mean.「私が言いたいのはそういうことではない」/ So *that's how* you do it.「なるほど，そういうやり方なんですね」)。本文後出 [46] の "that's how ideas emerge" は「アイディアはそうやって生まれるものだ」という感じ。

[33]　**the opening game:**「開幕戦」。getting things started の言い換え。

[35]　**a permanent post-doc:** post-doc (ポスドク) は postdoctoral「博士課程修了の (研究者)」の略。大学院で博士号を取得した後に年限付きで研究に専念できる身分。だから，a permanent post-doc という身分は制度上ありえない。

[38]　**Fred Sanger:** イギリスの生化学者 (1918–　　)。インスリンのアミノ酸配列を明らかにした功績により 1958 年にノーベル化学賞を受賞。1980 年には，核酸の塩基配列の決定により，2 度目のノーベル化学賞を Walter Gilbert とともに受賞。

[43]　**absolutely ridiculous:**「全くばかげている」。absolutely は文字どおりには「絶対的に」だが，後に来る形容詞などの意味を強める目的でしばしば用いられる (e.g. You're *absolutely* right.「全くあなたの言うとおりです」/ cf. A: It was a fabulous movie, wasn't it? B: *Absolutely*. / A: Do you think I should resign? B: *Absolutely* not.)。

[47]　**rubbish:**「ごみ」。このように(特にイギリス英語で) nonsense (「ナンセンス」「ばかげたこと」) の意味で使うことも多い (cf. I think what you've just said is complete *garbage*.)。いずれも不可算名詞であることにも注意。

[48]　**if I can coin a phrase:**「こういう言い方をしてよければ」。coin は「(単語や表現を)新しく作り出す」という意味の動詞。直前の stream of unconsciousness が自分で新しく作った表現であることを示す。ちなみにこの表現は，アメリカの心理学者・哲学者の William James (1842–1910) の「意識の流れ (stream of consciousness)」という有名な語句のもじり。

[48]　**there is the odd idea that . . . :** この場合の odd は occasional の意味で，全体としては every now and then there is an idea that . . . という意味。

[48]　**can be developed into . . . :** develop A into B は「A を発展させて B にする」。変化を表す動詞に into . . . が結びついて「(変化して)…になる」という意味を表すことにも慣れておきたい (e.g. These grapes will be *made into* wine. / What started out as an informal get-together has *evolved into* a full-fledged organization.)。

I'm not very good at getting things right the first time around. But I think that's a strength and not a weakness, because I think if one gets it straight the first time around it's probably boring. And getting it wrong half the time is the interesting thing.

Creativity is a subject that preoccupies a lot of people because everybody would like to be creative, and everybody wants to know where they can get it from. Of course if you could get a packet of creativity and buy it somewhere, that would be the ideal thing. One of the things about creativity is not to be afraid of saying the wrong thing. I think that's terribly important. Too many people are brought up, especially in our culture, to think that everything should be rational, should be worked out, and that daring ideas shouldn't be uttered, simply because they are likely to be wrong the first time around.

The way I do my thinking is to bounce a lot of balls in my head at the same time. Bounce, bounce, bounce. And if you go on bouncing you begin to notice that sometimes two balls are bouncing together. Those, I think, are the connections we have to make, and that means that you've just got to go on thinking about things and asking, 'If it were like this, what would be the outcome?' That's a very important thing to do in biology.

I've always felt that science makes contradictory demands on the people who work in it. It asks you to be highly imaginative, yet it asks you to put on blinders and drive through brick walls if necessary to get the answer. There are very few people who can contribute these opposites. Looking at my students, I've often found that all the characteristics of the one half were in one student, and all the characteristics of the other half were in another student. There are brilliant people who can never accomplish anything. And there are people that have no ideas, but can do things. Perhaps that's why science has to operate as a group, as a social unit.

*In 2002, Sydney Brenner was awarded the Nobel Prize in Physiology or Medicine. This next passage is taken from the press release put out by the Nobel Assembly announcing the award:*

### Press Release

The Nobel Assembly at Karolinska Institutet has today decided to award The Nobel Prize in Physiology or Medicine for 2002 jointly to Sydney Brenner, H. Robert Horvitz and John E. Sulston for their

- [50] **getting things right:** get ... right は「…を正しく[うまく]やる」(2章 [182])。すぐ後の get ... straight もほぼ同じ意味。反対はその後に出てくる get ... wrong。
- [50] **the first time around:**「一回目は」(cf. this time around)。
- [54] **a subject that preoccupies a lot of people:** preoccupy はしばしば be preoccupied with ... という形で用いて「(人が)…のことばかり考えている」「…で頭が一杯」という意味を表す (e.g. He's always *preoccupied with* office politics.)。ここでは能動文に生じている。
- [59] **I think that's terribly important:** terribly は，terrible「恐ろしい」の副詞形だが，このように単に後続する形容詞の意味を強めるために用いることが多い (e.g. I'm *terribly* sorry to have kept you waiting. / I wasn't *terribly* impressed with his speech yesterday.)。
- [59] **Too many people are brought up ... :** be brought up to ... で「…と教えられて育つ」「子供の頃に…するように教わる」(e.g. We *were brought up to* treat others with respect.)。
- [61] **should be worked out:** work out は「きちんと考える」「(よく考えて)解決する」。
- [61] **daring ideas:**「大胆な考え」。
- [64] **bounce a lot of balls in my head at the same time:**「頭の中でたくさんのボールを同時に弾ませる」。ここでは「頭の中でいろいろなアイディアを弾ませる」という感じ。
- [71] **makes contradictory demands on ... :** contradictory は「(互いに)矛盾する」「相反する」(cf. He often *contradicts* himself.)。make demands on ... は「…に努力や負担を強いる」。
- [73] **put on blinders and drive through brick walls:** blinders は競争馬の視野を限定する「馬の目隠し皮」。drive through brick walls は「煉瓦の壁を突き抜ける」という意味だが，ここでは「目標に向かって猪突猛進する」という感じ。
- [82] **the press release put out:** press release は「報道関係者に対する公式な発表」。put out は「発表する」。put out a press release はよく用いられる組み合せ。
- [85] **Karolinska Institutet:** カロリンスカ研究所。スウェーデン唯一の国立医科大学で，ノーベル生理学・医学賞の選考機関。

discoveries concerning "genetic regulation of organ development and programmed cell death".

## PROGRAMMED CELL DEATH
Normal life requires cell division to generate new cells but also the presence of cell death, so that a balance is maintained in our organs. In an adult human being, more than a thousand billion cells are created every day. At the same time, an equal number of cells die through a controlled "suicide process", referred to as programmed cell death.

Developmental biologists first described programmed cell death. They noted that cell death was necessary for embryonic development, for example when tadpoles undergo metamorphosis to become adult frogs. In the human foetus, the interdigital mesoderm initially formed between fingers and toes is removed by programmed cell death. The vast excess of neuronal cells present during the early stages of brain development is also eliminated by the same mechanism.

The seminal breakthrough in our understanding of programmed cell death was made by this year's Nobel Laureates. They discovered that specific genes control the cellular death program in the nematode *C. elegans*. Detailed studies in this simple model organism demonstrated that 131 of a total of 1090 cells die reproducibly during development, and that this natural cell death is controlled by a unique set of genes.

## THE MODEL ORGANISM *C. ELEGANS*
Sydney Brenner realized, in the early 1960s, that fundamental questions regarding cell differentiation and organ development were hard to tackle in higher animals. Therefore, a genetically amenable and multicellular model organism simpler than mammals was required. The ideal solution proved to be the nematode *Caenorhabditis elegans*. This worm, approximately 1 mm long, has a short generation time and is transparent, which made it possible to follow cell division directly under the microscope.

Brenner provided the basis in a publication from 1974, in which he broke new ground by demonstrating that specific gene mutations could be induced in the genome of *C. elegans* by the chemical compound EMS (ethyl methane sulphonate). Different mutations could be linked to specific genes and to specific effects on organ development. This combination of genetic analysis and visualiza-

- [91] **cell division:**「細胞分裂」。
- [95] **referred to as programmed cell death:** refer to A as B で「A を B と呼ぶ」。このように受け身の形でもよく使う。programmed cell death は，もうひとつの細胞死であるネクローシス necrosis（細胞破壊）と異なり，細胞の正常な機能である。
- [98] **embryonic:** embryo [émbriou]（「胎児」「胎芽」「胚」）の形容詞形。
- [99] **metamorphosis** [mètəmɔ́:rfəsɪs]:「著しい変化」という比喩的な意味でもよく使われるが，ここでは生物学の用語で「変態」。
- [100] **the human foetus** [fí:təs]:（妊娠 8 週以後の）「人間の胎児」。foetus はイギリス英語の綴りで，アメリカ英語では fetus。妊娠 8 週までは embryo という。
- [100] **the interdigital mesoderm:**「指間の中胚葉」。「アナログ」に対する「デジタル」という意味でよく使われる digital は本来「指の」という意味。digit は「指」という意味。
- [105] **The seminal breakthrough:** 本来「種子の」「精液の」という意味の seminal はこのように「将来性のある」「独創性に富む」「生産的な」という意味で使うことが多い。
- [106] **Nobel Laureates** [lɔ́:riəts]:「ノーベル賞受賞者」。
- [109] **die reproducibly:** reproducibly は「(誰がいつ実験を行っても)再現可能な方法で」の意。cf. This percentage ... could be obtained accurately and *reproducibly* in successive experiments. (OED) ここの文脈においては，apoptosis or programmed cell death と呼ばれるプロセスをとおして死ぬ，の意味となる。
- [115] **tackle in higher animals:** tackle は「(問題などに)取り組む」(4 章 [17])。higher animals は「高等動物」(cf. higher education)。
- [115] **genetically amenable:** amenable [əmí:nəbl] は普通は「(目的に)適した」「従順な」だが，genetically amenable で「遺伝子操作が可能な」という意味(この分野では頻出の組み合わせ)。
- [116] **multicellular:**「多細胞の」(cf. a *cell*「細胞」/ unicellular「単細胞の」)。
- [122] **broke new ground:** break new ground は「新分野を切り拓く」という意味の決まり文句 (cf. [3] *groundbreaking* research)。
- [122] **by demonstrating that specific gene mutations could be induced:**「特定の遺伝子変異が引き起こされうる[誘発されうる]ことを実証することによって」。
- [124] **ethyl methane sulphonate** [éθəl méθeɪn sʌ́lfəneɪt]:「メタンスルホン酸エチル」。

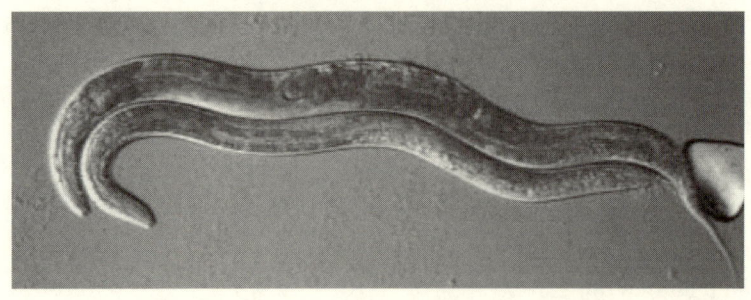

A pair of C. elegans

tion of cell divisions observed under the microscope initiated the discoveries that are awarded by this year's Nobel Prize.

*This last reading passage is taken from the transcript of an interview with Sydney Brenner conducted by a reporter from* European Molecular Biology Organization Reports (ER) *in 2003:*

**ER:** Have you ever thought about retiring now that you've been awarded the Nobel Prize?
**Sydney Brenner:** No, I've retired many times already. It's time to change again. What do you do if you retire? The interesting thing is to do research. It's better than anything else.
**ER:** In 1963, you wrote a letter to Max Perutz proposing to move beyond molecular biology. Why did you feel a need to switch your focus to developmental biology when molecular biology was still at such an early stage?
**SB:** It looked like the code was understood. We understood genes in principle, and how this information got turned into proteins. Of course, lots of detail remained to be solved, but we thought that could easily be done by other people.
**ER:** Weren't you interested in the details?
**SB:** No, not once I could see there was a solution to the problem. And the problem that still has no solution is how genes specify the complex structures in organisms like ourselves. So that's what I proposed to move into. Ultimately, we'd like to understand how brains are built and how brains work. Of course, it was a modest beginning. *Caenorhabditis elegans* was chosen because of its convenience and finite size, and the fact that we could work on it in a laboratory.

- [127] **the discoveries that are awarded by this year's Nobel Prize:** ノーベル賞公式サイト (http://nobelprize.org) に掲載された原文のままだが，不自然な英語であり，the discoveries that are awarded this year's Nobel Prize，あるいは the discoveries that are honoured/recognised by the award of this year's Nobel Prize などとすべきところ。
- [132] **thought about retiring:** think about [of] . . . ing は「…しようかと考える」(13章 [49]) (e.g. I'm *thinking of* taking early retirement. / Don't even *think of* smoking in here.)。
- [136] **do research:**「研究する」と言う場合の決まった言い方のひとつ (4章 [19], 7章 [12]) (cf. carry out [conduct] research)。
- [137] **Max Perutz:** マックス・ペルツ (1914–2002) は，オーストリア出身のイギリスの生化学者。球状タンパク質の構造研究により，1962年，John Kendrew とともに，ノーベル化学賞を受賞。
- [138] **switch your focus:** switch は「切り替える」(cf. It's sometimes difficult for me to *switch* from Japanese to English.)。
- [142] **in principle:**「原理的には」の意味だが，このように「細部は別として大枠は (了解している，合意している，等)」という場合によく用いられる。
- [146] **No, not once I could see:** not は "I wasn't interested in the details" を指す (cf. A: Does he mean what he says?  B: I hope *not*.)。once は「いったん…したら」の意味の接続詞。

**ER:** Are you surprised about the success of *C. elegans* now?

**SB:** I'm not surprised, no. I'm pleased. I think it was a very good choice, and people have taken it and expanded it. I've been told that there is a new *C. elegans* laboratory every week somewhere in the world. It's almost like McDonald's. Now 400 labs are doing all kinds of things with it — social behaviour and ageing are very popular now. The contact with the animal itself is very important for biologists because a lot of experimental research is remote. Francis Crick used to say "Sydney likes worms because they wriggle and you can watch them wriggling."

**ER:** It's quite an unusual step from working at the molecular level to take a step 'backwards' and work on whole organisms.

**SB:** But you see, my previous training was in medicine. In fact, I was a skilled anatomist and I knew a lot about neuroanatomy, embryology and histology. And I was a skilled microscopist as well, so in a sense, it was a step forwards because when we first tried to do embryology and study the brain, there just weren't the tools available. There wasn't the basic understanding that we now have through molecular biology. So it was time to go back. It's a very different culture from what you have now and all of us were amateurs. We never got a professional training. We could not, the subject did not exist. There was no academic way to study molecular biology. I think a lot of us who are self-taught in this field have carried that on. It's easy to teach yourself a new subject or a new technique. Everybody today believes they must go and do a course and study. It's a lot of nonsense. Motivation is more important in science than anything else, because if you are motivated you can learn anything.

- [158] **McDonald's:** 言わずと知れたハンバーガー・チェーンだが，発音が [məkdάnəldz] であることに注意。
- [161] **remote:**「動物そのものからは離れている」という意味。
- [161] **Francis Crick:** イギリスの分子生物学者（1916–2004）。核酸の分子構造および生体における情報伝達に対するその意義の発見により，1962 年，James Watson, Maurice Wilkins とともに，ノーベル生理学・医学賞を受賞。
- [162] **wriggle:** to twist and turn.
- [165] **take a step 'backwards':** take a step forward(s)「一歩前進する」という普通の表現との対比を明確にするために backwards に引用符がついている。歴史的に見て生物学研究が動物のからだのレベルからその分子レベルへと「進んだ」のに対して，ブレナーの研究が一見それとは逆の方向をたどったように思えることを指している。
- [167] **neuroanatomy, embryology and histology:**「神経解剖学，発生学，組織学」。
- [168] **microscopist:** one skilled in the use of the microscope.
- [170] **there just weren't the tools available:** just はこのように否定の意味を強める場合によく用いられる（e.g. I *just* can't figure her out.）。
- [179] **Motivation:** 要するに「やる気」のこと。If you are motivated, you can learn anything.（「やる気さえあれば何でも身につけられる」）はもちろん英語学習にも当てはまるはず。

# 2
# FOOD

## Introduction
### Shunichi Ikegami

A spirited young sushi chef escapes the narrow confines of Japan, trains himself in Peru and Argentina in South America, and finally moves on to the United States. A series of difficulties lead to failures, but every time he faces a setback his self-reliance enables him to start over again. Soon his original style of Japanese cuisine, complemented by uncanny marketing and social skills, draws the attention and firm support of Hollywood actors like Robert De Niro. His restaurant suddenly comes into the spotlight and receives many awards, while he becomes an instant celebrity, featured in numerous magazines and television programs. His restaurants can now be found in major world cities such as New York, London, Las Vegas, Los Angeles, Tokyo, Paris, and Milan. This is the success story of Nobu, or Nobuyuki Matsuhisa.

Of course I had been aware of the amazing popularity of Nobu. But I assumed his popularity could be attributed to the way the chef played into the exoticism of consumers in Europe and America by fusing the tradition of Japanese sushi with Latin American sensibilities and serving the food in such a beautiful manner that it looked as if it were an inlay on the plate. I also believed that the novelty of eating wonderfully fresh seafood must be a factor in his success as well. That is, I anticipated that Nobu's popularity would turn out to be rather fleeting because I simply thought he was liked by foreigners who knew nothing about Japanese cuisine and who were drawn not to the quality of the cooking or to the actual taste of the food but to the novelty of the experience.

An incident occurred several years ago that changed my way of thinking and made me want to taste Nobu's cooking. While I was in Italy researching the history of Italian food culture I visited

[1]　**A spirited young sushi chef** [ʃef]: spirited は「威勢のよい」「元気のよい」（cf. be in high/low spirits）。

[1]　**confines** [kánfaɪnz]:（このように常に複数形で用いて）「限界」「境界」で，しばしば beyond [within] the confines of ... という形で使われる（cf. It's cruel to *confine* [kənfáɪn] your cat in such a small room.）。

[4]　**a setback:**「物事の進行を妨げる出来事」「挫折」（e.g. suffer a *setback*）。

[5]　**start over:**「最初からやり直す」（cf. Don't tell me you've fallen in love with her *all over again*.）。

[5]　**Japanese cuisine** [kwɪzíːn]:「日本料理」。

[5]　**complemented by ... :**「…と相俟って」。complement は他動詞で「…を補う」。

[6]　**uncanny marketing and social skills:** uncanny は「不気味な」「薄気味悪い」という意味でよく用いられるが，ここでは（そこから派生した）「（能力などが）並外れて優れた」。social skills はよく使われる表現で「他人とうまくつき合う能力」（e.g. His lack of *social skills* makes him hard to work with.）。

[7]　**Robert De Niro:** アメリカの俳優，映画監督，プロデューサー。1974 年 *The Godfather Part II* でオスカーの助演男優賞。1980 年には *Raging Bull* で主演男優賞を受賞した。

[8]　**comes into the spotlight:**「スポットライトを浴びるようになる」「大いに注目されるようになる」。

[9]　**becomes an instant celebrity:**「突然有名人になる」という意味の決まった言い方（cf. *gain* instant *celebrity* / She became a billionaire overnight）。

[9]　**featured:** feature には名詞で「特集記事」「特別番組」などの意味があるが，ここはそれに対応する動詞としての用法で「…を特集する」「…の特集を組む」（e.g. Her latest film *features* an up-and-coming young actor.）。

[15]　**But I assumed ... :** assume は「（根拠もなく）決めてかかる」「思い込む」。be attributed to ... は「…が原因［理由］であると考える」。play into ... は「…におもねる」。exoticism (< exotic) は「外国趣味」。sensibilities は（このようにしばしば複数形で用いられて）「感性」。inlay [ínlèɪ] は「象眼細工」。

[22]　**fleeting:**「束の間の」「一過性の」（e.g. a *fleeting* thought）。

the Frescobaldi family for an interview. The Frescobaldis are a well-known noble family in Italy. They are also known for their production of high quality wine and olive oil, which they export all over the world. When I went with a camera crew to visit their gorgeous palace, located adjacent to Santo Spirito Church in Florence, the flowery city, the Marchesa Bona told me the following story.

On Saturday June 17, 2000, the family celebrated the re-opening of one of their castles located to the east of Florence. This castle, Nipozzano, has a history dating back more than a thousand years. To mark the occasion, a huge banquet was held and celebrities from all over the world were invited. The five hundred guests included then US President Bill Clinton and Italian President Carlo Ciampi as well as a host of leading figures from the worlds of politics, business, the movies, fashion, cooking and the food industry, and journalism. Four leading world chefs were selected for the occasion to demonstrate their culinary skills. The theme of the day was "the four seasons" and each chef offered creative and beautifully delicate "works" based on the season for which they were responsible. Nobu was assigned "spring." He offered an elaborate seafood and lobster salad with sugar tomato dressing as his expression of "spring," and it was very enthusiastically received.

Italians tend to prefer cooking that does not stray too far from tradition, relying solely on a chef's individual talent. Outlandish dishes, novel materials, or fancy sauces are not necessarily appreciated. Moreover, the Frescobaldi family is extremely proud of the part it has played since the medieval period in preserving the traditions of Italian culinary culture. The fact that this conservative representative of Italian food culture selected Nobu must mean that his cooking is not simply a matter of surface beauty and novelty but must also be cooking that pleases people to the very depths of their souls and bodies. His must be real cooking, I thought.

I finally was able to realize my dream of going to one of his restaurants. I visited the one in Roppongi and ordered a lunchbox that included small portions of many of the famous dishes created by Nobu. What did I think of the experience? Well, it was one surprise after another. In what sense? Well, that will remain my secret.

- [29] **the Frescobaldi family:** フレスコバルディ侯爵家。800年以上にもわたり，トスカーナ地方を中心にイタリアの政治，経済，文化に大きな影響を与えてきた名門一族。今日ではワインとオリーブ油の生産でも知られている。
- [29] **a well-known noble family:**「名の知れた貴族」。
- [33] **Santo Spirito Church in Florence, the flowery city:** サント・スピリト教会は，「花の都」として知られるフィレンツェを代表する建築のひとつで，15世紀にフィリッポ・ブルネレスキの設計で建造された。
- [34] **the Marchesa** [mɑːrkéɪzə] **Bona:**「ボナ・フレスコバルディ侯爵夫人」。
- [38] **mark the occasion:**「お祝いをする」という意味の決まった組み合わせ (cf. 10章 [1])。この場合の occasion は「特別な出来事」(cf. What's *the occasion?*)。
- [40] **Bill Clinton:** William J. Clinton (1946– ) はアメリカ合衆国第42代大統領 (1993–2001)。
- [40] **Carlo Ciampi:** カルロ・アゼリオ・チャンピ (Carlo Azeglio Ciampi, 1920– ) はイタリアの政治家。首相，国庫相を歴任後，1999–2006年に大統領。
- [41] **a host of leading figures:** a host of . . . は「多数の…」。leading figures は「(ある分野の)第一人者，旗手」(5章 [45])。
- [44] **culinary skills:**「料理の腕」。culinary [kʌ́lɪnèri; kjúːlɪnèri] は「料理の」。
- [46] **"works":**「作品」。喩えなので引用符がついている。
- [49] **was very enthusiastically received:** この場合の receive は「特定の評価をもって迎える[受け止める]」(e.g. How was the film *received* by the public? / cf. His first book met with a favorable *reception*.)。
- [50] **does not stray too far from tradition:**「伝統から離れ[外れ]すぎない」(cf. a *stray* cat)。
- [51] **Outlandish dishes:** outlandish は「ひどく風変わりな」。
- [52] **fancy sauces:** fancy はここでは「極上の」というより，「一風変わった」。
- [52] **appreciated:** この場合の appreciate は "I really want to talk to him, but I know he wouldn't *appreciate* it." のような場合に近い。

# The Nobu Matsuhisa Story

## Nobuyuki Matsuhisa

After graduating from high school, Matsuhisa trained as a sushi chef at Matsuei Sushi in Shinjuku. In 1972, a Japanese-Peruvian businessman invited him to move to Lima and open a traditional Japanese restaurant there.

The fish was good in Peru, straight out of the Pacific Ocean, and after his years spent training as a traditional Japanese sushi chef, Matsuhisa found the Peruvian style of cooking exciting. It was full of interesting flavours — like garlic and chillies — that were new to him. He discovered the South American way of preparing raw fish, in which the fish is marinated in citrus juice.

After three successful and exciting years in Peru, however, Matsuhisa's partners in the restaurant asked him to save money for the restaurant by economizing on his ingredients. In response, Matsuhisa quit the business and moved to Argentina. But meat, not fish, is at the heart of Argentinian cuisine. Feeling, he says, "like a fish out of water," Matsuhisa decided to move back to Japan. But he was still restless for new challenges, and soon enough decided to try working overseas one more time.

Matsuhisa took out a loan and moved with his young family to Anchorage, Alaska, where the fish was excellent. Money was tight so he did much of the building work for his new restaurant himself, as well as all the cooking. At the end of 1980, he took a day off to celebrate Thanksgiving.

Anchorage, in a whirl of light snow. In that increasingly snowbound town, silver with the settling flakes, flames shot up in an orange blaze. I stood rooted under the falling snow, silently watching the building burn down. Having rushed to the scene from a party at a friend's house, I was only wearing a T-shirt, yet I didn't feel the cold, nor anything else. The cinders from the burning building flew up into the sky, and some landed on my cheeks. They must have been hot, but I wasn't conscious of it at the time.

It was my restaurant that was burning; it had only been fifty days since it opened. In the six months before opening day, I had personally gone into the building with a hammer and saw to help with the construction. I had secured supply channels for ingredients, thought up a menu, and had even been coaching the staff. When the restau-

- [69] **straight out of the Pacific Ocean**:「太平洋直送の」（cf. fresh out of the oven「焼きたてほやほやの」）。
- [72] **garlic and chillies**:「ガーリックとチリトウガラシ」。
- [73] **marinated**:「マリナード（marinade: 酢，ワイン，油，香料等を混ぜ合わせた漬け汁）に漬けた」「マリネにした」。
- [74] **citrus juice**:「柑橘類の果汁」。
- [77] **economizing on his ingredients**:「食材を節約すること」。
- [79] **a fish out of water**: 日本語で昔よく使われたイディオム「陸（おか）にあがった河童」に相当する決まり文句だが，ここでは実際に魚が話題になっているために一種の洒落（a play on words, a pun）になっている。
- [80] **he was still restless for new challenges**:（be）restless for . . . は「…を求め（る気持ちが強く）てじっとしていられない」という感じ。challenge(s)は「自分の能力などを発揮できるようなやりがいのある目標（cf. a *challenging* job）」。
- [82] **took out a loan**: take out a loan は「融資を受ける」「借金をする」という意味の決まった言い方（cf. *take out* insurance「保険をかける」）。
- [82] **Anchorage** [ǽŋkərɪdʒ], **Alaska**: アメリカのアラスカ州アンカレッジ市。
- [83] **Money was tight**:「あまりお金がなかった」「資金不足だった」（cf. We are on a *tight* budget.）。日本語の「緊縮（財政）」などと似た発想の tight の用法。
- [85] **he took a day off**:「1日休みを取った」。
- [85] **Thanksgiving**:「感謝祭」。ニューイングランド地方に入植したイギリス人が1年間を無事に過ごしたことを記念して始めたと言い伝えられるアメリカの行事。11月の第4週の木曜日に祝われる。親族や友人が集まり，七面鳥を食べるのが慣習となっている。
- [86] **in a whirl of light snow**:「小雪が舞っていた」。
- [86] **In that increasingly snowbound town**:「どんどん雪に閉ざされていくその町で」（cf. We were stranded at the *fogbound* airport. / They were *snowed in* for a week.）。
- [87] **silver with the settling flakes**:「降り積もる雪で白銀の」。flakes: snowflakes.
- [88] **I stood rooted under the falling snow**: rooted は呆然としてその場で（身体から根が生えたように）身動きが取れない様子を表している。
- [88] **silently watching the building burn down**: watch がこのように目的語（A）と原形動詞（B）を伴うと「AがBするのをじっと見ている［見守る］」という意味を表す（e.g. I *watched* the plane take off and disappear from sight.）。burn down は「（建物が）焼け落ちる」「全焼する」。
- [91] **cinders**:「燃え殻」「灰」という意味の cinders はこのように複数形で用いるのが普通。
- [95] **personally**:「（他人に任せるのではなく）自分自身で」（e.g. I'll ask her *personally* for help.「私が自分で彼女に手伝ってくれるよう頼んでみます」）。
- [97] **I had secured supply channels for ingredients**:「食材を調達する経路を確保していた」。
- [97] **thought up a menu**: think up は「考えつく」「考案する」。
- [98] **had even been coaching the staff**:「（レストランで働く予定の）スタッフのトレーニングまでやっていた」。staff が集合名詞であることに注意（cf. I'm a member of the *staff*.）。

*Nobu: The Cookbook*

rant opened, it was very well received; day in and day out, it was always full.

I had worked for fifty days without taking any time off. I had accumulated debts in order to open the restaurant, but I felt encouraged by the way things were going. I figured I was making enough money for my wife and daughter, whom I'd left behind in Japan, to come and live with me. So I sent for them.

The fiftieth day was Thanksgiving. I had closed the restaurant with the intention of giving the staff and myself a break. We had all worked nonstop until then.

It was while I was having a good time at a party that night that I received a telephone call from my partner in the restaurant. "Nobu, the restaurant's on fire! Come as quickly as you can," he said in a panicky voice. I thought it was a sick joke and told him so, but he repeated, "There's a fire. Really, there is." As we talked on the phone, I began to hear sirens.

*Thanksgiving Day 1980 saw Matsuhisa's Alaska dreams burned to ashes. It took him another nine years of hard work to reach the point where he was ready to open his own restaurant again.*

I moved to Los Angeles and began working at a sushi bar. This time I wasn't starting from zero, but from below zero, saddled with debts. When I opened Matsuhisa in Los Angeles, it was nine years after what had happened in Alaska.

From the outset, I was determined to make Matsuhisa a place where I could create my ideal cuisine. I didn't skimp on buying good fish, so food costs always ran high. The restaurant was sure to get support, I was convinced, if only I used good ingredients and

- [99] **day in and day out, it was always full:**「来る日も来る日もレストランは常に客で一杯だった」。day in and day out は同じことが毎日続く様子を表す決まり文句で，ネガティブな意味合いを伴うことが多い (e.g. How can you expect me to enjoy doing the same thing *day in and day out*?) が，ここではレストランが連日満席であることを単に強調している。
- [101] **without taking any time off:**「全く休むことなく」。(cf. Today I'm taking *a day off* for the first time in a month.「今日は一ヶ月ぶりに休みを取っている」)。
- [103] **I figured . . . :**「日本に残して来た妻と娘がこちらに来て自分と一緒に暮らせるだけのお金は稼いでいると考えた」。figure (that) . . . は「(考えた末に)…と判断する」。
- [105] **I sent for them:** send for a person で「(人を)呼びにやる，呼び寄せる」(e.g. We'd better *send for* a doctor right away. / cf. Let's send for a sample of that material.)。
- [107] **giving the staff and myself a break:** give a person a break は「(人を)一休みさせる，リラックスさせる」の意味。他に「(人を)大目に見てやる」(e.g. I'll *give you a break* just this once.「今回だけは大目に見てあげよう」) という意味を表すこともある。また "Give me a break." は (不当な発言などに抗議して)「勘弁してよ」「いい加減にして下さい」という意味にもなる。
- [112] **I thought it was a sick joke:**「趣味の悪い冗談かと思った」。(cf. That guy really makes me *sick*.「あの男には本当にむかつく」)。
- [115] **saw:** 英語ではこのように see や witness が場所や時を主語，その場所や時に生じた出来事を目的語(+to のない不定詞句)でそれぞれ表現することがよくある(8章[138]) (e.g. This stadium has *seen* a lot of exciting games.)。
- [115] **burned to ashes:** burn to ashes は本文 [89] の burn down と同じ意味。「灰燼に帰す」。
- [119] **saddled with debts:**「借金を背負って」。be saddled with . . . は「…(問題など望ましくないもの)を負っている」。
- [122] **From the outset:**「最初から」。
- [122] **I was determined to make:** be determined to . . . は「きっと…しようと決心している」。
- [123] **skimp on . . . :**「…をけちる」(cf. [77] economize on his ingredients)。
- [124] **food costs always ran high:**「食材費は常に高くついた」の意 (cf. Supplies are *running* low.)。
- [124] **The restaurant was sure to get support:** be sure to . . . は「きっと…する」で，そう判断するのは(主語ではなく)話し手 ("England is [are] *sure to* win the match." の意味は「イングランドはきっと試合に勝つ」であって，「イングランドは試合に勝つことを確信している」ではない)。
- [125] **I was convinced:**「私は確信していた」で，(次の文の I thought と同様)挿入的に使われていて，確信の内容は文の残りの部分の内容全体。

put my heart into making good food. Making no profit was OK, I thought, as long as my customers were satisfied. I myself managed to get by and I could pay my staff and the people I worked with. With my Beverly Hills restaurant, I was determined to realize the dreams that had ended as mere good intentions at my place in Peru. [130]

*Matsuhisa was the first in a string of world-famous Nobu Matsuhisa restaurants. Today, "Nobu-style" cuisine is the key note at Matsuhisa's restaurants around the world. In his best-selling cookbook, Matsuhisa explains the essence of "Nobu style."*

Cooking is my life and this book is a straightforward and honest expression of that life — of me as a man and a chef. I give you my way of cooking freely and show you exactly how each dish is prepared and served in my restaurants. Some friends have questioned the wisdom of making these recipes accessible to the general public. They think, perhaps, that my business could be damaged in some way by revealing professional secrets. But cooking isn't like that. Food is imbued with the feelings and personality of the cook. Even if you were to follow my instructions faithfully, using precise amounts of identical ingredients, I am quite sure that you would never be able to perfectly recreate the same flavors and textures that I make. For I always put something special in my food — my heart, or *kokoro* as we say in Japanese — and, you, of course, must put your own heart into your cooking. [135] [140] [145]

When I stand in the kitchen, I'm driven by one basic desire: to delight and satisfy my customers and to hear them say they have enjoyed an excellent meal. I know there are many chefs who are either technically or artistically better than me. But I also know that my food has soul. For me, cooking is most about giving my customers little surprises that will lead them to make discoveries about their own latent tastes. It's about communicating my *kokoro* through every single dish I make. If this book inspires you to try out some of the recipes and gain new insights into your own way of cooking, I will be more than happy. Because that too would be another way of communicating *kokoro* through cooking. [150] [155]

People often ask me to define my food. I call it "Nobu-style" cuisine. It's firmly based on Japanese cooking — fundamentally sushi — but with North and South American influences. My intention has always been to draw on the very best of Japanese cooking in my own individual style. Such has been the aim of this book, too, and for this reason I have made no compromises with the ingredi- [160] [165]

- [126] **put my heart into making:** put one's heart into doing ... は「心を込めて…する」。
- [127] **as long as my customers were satisfied:**「お客さんが満足してくれさえすれば」。
- [127] **I myself managed to get by:**「私自身はどうにか暮らしていけた」。get by は「どうにかやっていく」。
- [129] **my Beverly** [bévərli] **Hills restaurant:** ベヴァリー・ヒルズはロサンゼルス市域内に位置する市で，ハリウッドに接する。映画俳優の邸宅が多い高級住宅地。このレストランとは前段落の Matsuhisa in Los Angeles のこと。
- [130] **good intentions:** 通例このように複数形で「善意」の意だが，それが実効性を伴わないという意味合いを帯びることが多い (cf. He is full of *good intentions*, but he hardly ever does anything about them. 「彼は善意に満ちた人だが，行動が伴うことはめったにない」)。
- [132] **the key note:**（音楽用語の「主音」から）「主眼」「基調」(cf. the keynote address「基調講演」for this year's conference)。
- [135] **straightforward:**「率直な」「腹蔵のない」。
- [138] **Some friends have questioned ...:** 動詞 question は単に「尋ねる」「質問する」ではなく，「(…の妥当性などを)疑問視する」「(…に)疑義を表明する，異論を唱える」という意味で用いることも多い(8章[11]) (e.g. Very few people *question* her judgment.「彼女の判断力を疑う人はほとんどいない」/ cf. There is no *question* that ...「…には疑問の余地がない」)。
- [139] **making these recipes accessible** [æksésəbl] **to the general public:** make A accessible to B で「B が A を利用できるようにする」(3章[21]) (cf. *allow* the general public *access* to these recipes)。
- [142] **Food is imbued with ...:** be imbued with ... は「…(感情や思想など)がこめられている」。
- [144] **identical:** exactly the same.
- [145] **recreate:** reproduce「再現する」。
- [145] **textures:**「(食べ物の)歯触り，舌触り」。
- [149] **I'm driven by one basic desire:** be driven by ... は「…に駆り立てられる，突き動かされる」(cf. She's been the *driving force* behind the project ever since it started. / He has an inner *drive* to succeed.)。
- [153] **For me, cooking is most about ...:**「私にとって料理で最も大切なのは…である」。A is about B はこのように「A の本質は B である」「A で大切なのは B である」という意味で用いられることがある(5章[95], 8章[15])。本文[167]の Nobu-style cuisine is all about ... のように強調のために all を伴うことも多い (e.g. This book will help you understand what philosophy *is all about*.)。
- [155] **their own latent tastes:** latent [léɪtnt] は「(才能などが)隠れた，気づかれていない」。
- [156] **every single dish I make:**「私の作るひとつひとつの料理すべて」。every single は every の意味をさらに強めた表現。
- [156] **If this book inspires you to ...:** inspire someone to ... は「人を…したい気持ちにさせる」(cf. 7章[101], 12章[173]) (cf. She is an *inspiring* teacher.)。gain an insight into ... は「…(の本質)がよくわかるようになる」という意味の決まった言い方(7章[65], 10章[31]) (cf. As usual, he made some *insightful* comments on my essay.)。
- [158] **I will be more than happy:** more than happy は very happy とほぼ同じ意味。
- [163] **draw on ...:**「…(経験，手持ちの情報や知識)を活用する」(5章[73]) (e.g. She has a wealth of teaching experience to *draw on*.)。

ents used to create the recipes — nothing but fresh, quality seafood and many ingredients that can only be found in Japan. Nobu-style cuisine is all about bringing out the best in the freshest seafood and drawing out the natural sweetness and textures of vegetables. Fish should always be fresh enough to eat raw. Shellfish, crustaceans and octopus should always, ideally, be bought when still alive. No seasoning — however subtle — can quite match real freshness. Taste the difference for yourself!

It goes without saying that the basics will only provide you with a foundation on which to build your cooking skills. The rest is really up to you. And what could be more fun than discovering your own distinct flavors? Nobu-style cuisine is based on sushi: I know how to cook rice well, how to choose the best fish and how to prepare and serve it. But it doesn't stop there. The important thing — and not just in cooking — is to adapt and apply the basics and to keep on experimenting with new ideas. In this way, Nobu-style cuisine is continually evolving. Don't worry if you don't get it right the first time. Try it over and over again and see for yourself whether you like your *toro* well-done or rare, and look for the exact degree of saltiness or spiciness to suit your palate. In time, any one of the recipes in this book could evolve into your own inimitable dish.

And don't forget to add plenty of *kokoro*!

[166] **quality seafood:** この場合の quality は限定用法の形容詞で「質の高い」「高級な」(e.g. a *quality* paper「高級(新聞)紙」)。

[168] **bringing out the best:** bring out ... は「(隠れていた)…を引き出す」(e.g. Too much stress tends to *bring out* the worst in most of us.「大抵の人はストレスが多すぎると性格の最悪の面が出てしまいがちだ」)。

[170] **fresh enough to eat raw:**「生で食べられるほど新鮮」。eat ... raw は「…を生で食べる」。

[170] **Shellfish, crustaceans and octopus:**「貝、エビやカニ、タコ」。crustacean [krʌstéɪʃən] は「甲殻類(の動物)」。

[171] **No seasoning — however subtle — can quite match real freshness:**「どんなに絶妙な調味料を使っても本当の新鮮さにはやはりかなわない」。A can match B はこの場合「A は B に対抗できる」(cf. When it comes to making puns, I'm certainly *no match for him*.)。

[172] **Taste the difference for yourself:**「ご自分で違いを味わってみて下さい」(e.g. This is a truly compelling novel. Read it and see *for yourself*.)。

[175] **The rest is really up to you:**「あとは本当にあなた次第です」(e.g. It's *up to* the CEO to make the final decision.)。

[176] **what could be more fun than ... :**「…より楽しいことがあるでしょうか」。…が最も楽しいことを強調するための修辞疑問文(rhetorical question)で、仮定法が用いられていることにも注意(cf. Nothing *could be* further from the truth.「そんなことは全くない」/ A: How are you doing? B: *Couldn't be* better.「絶好調です」/ What I *wouldn't give* for a house like that!「あんな家に住めたらいいのになあ」)。

[182] **Don't worry if you don't get it right the first time:**「最初はうまくいかなくても心配しないで下さい」。get ... right は「…をうまくやる」(1 章 [50]) (e.g. Very few people *got* this question *right*.「この問題を正解した人はほとんどいなかった」)。反対はもちろん get ... wrong。

[184] **look for the exact degree of ... :**「ご自分の味覚(palate [pǽlət])にぴったり合った塩やスパイスの量を探して下さい」(cf. palatable「口に合う」「趣味にかなう」)。

[185] **In time:**「そのうちに」。

[186] **could evolve into your own inimitable dish:**「誰にもまねのできないあなただけの料理へと進化することだってあるでしょう」。

# 3

# NATIONALITY

## Introduction
### Clive Collins

Mrs. Higden, one of the characters in Charles Dickens' novel *Our Mutual Friend* (1864–5), enjoys having reports of cases in the criminal courts read to her from newspapers by a young boy in her care called Sloppy. Sloppy, she says, is a "beautiful reader of a newspaper," because he "do the Police in different voices."

Mrs. Higden means that Sloppy, as he reads to her, dramatizes his reading, giving each of the police witnesses in the trials a different voice.

What Sloppy does is something most of us do when we read: we "hear" the voices of the characters when they speak in the text and we dramatize the voice according to our own understanding of the character. We do this silently, "hearing" the voice only in our own minds, unless, like Sloppy, we have to read the passage aloud for some reason.

It might be worthwhile to pause for a moment here in order to consider just how these processes of "speaking" and "listening" are achieved through language that is transmitted and received in silence. What are the conventions that we all of us, readers and writers, subscribe to?

The writer, by manipulating a body of linguistic devices to which the reader also has access, can shape the dialogue, the words spoken by a character, into an effective and recognizable voice. What are these linguistic devices? Vocabulary, the choice of words made by the writer for the character to speak, is an important tool, as is grammar, as is syntax, as is register. These may be used in order to give a particular manner of speech that is either idiosyncratic and thus identifies the uniqueness of the character through her or his voice, or else is stereotypical and thus associated with a particular

[1] **Charles Dickens:** ヴィクトリア朝イギリスの国民的文豪と称される小説家（1812–70）。*Our Mutual Friend*（「われらの共通の友人」といった意味）は，彼が完成させた最後の長編小説。

[2] **having reports of cases in the criminal courts read:** criminal court は「刑事裁判所」（cf. a civil court「民事裁判所」; a *criminal* case「刑事事件」）。have ... read は「...を読んでもらう」（read はもちろん過去分詞形）。

[5] **do the Police in different voices:** この意味はすぐあとに説明されるとおり。文法的にいえば，ここは do ではなく does であるべきだが，この言葉づかいは，Mrs. Higden が標準英語を話すような，教育のある人間ではないことを暗示している。

[6] **dramatizes his reading, giving ...:** dramatize には「（本などを）ドラマ化［芝居や映画に］する」の他に「劇的に表現する」という意味がある。ここでの「劇的に」の具体的な内容は giving 以下の分詞構文で具体的に述べられている。このような分詞構文の用法にも慣れておきたい。

[9] **we "hear" the voices:** 引用符は普通の意味で「聞こえる」わけではないことを示す。

[13] **read the passage aloud:** read ... aloud は「（人に聞こえるように）...を声に出して読む」「...を音読する」という意味の決まった言い方。aloud は loud(ly) と違って「大声」である必要はない。口語では read ... out loud とも言う。

[15] **It might be worthwhile to pause for a moment:** worthwhile は「（行為などが）それに必要な努力や時間などに値する」「やりがいのある」という意味だが，このように「何かをすることが重要または有益だ（からしてみるとよい）」と言いたい場合によく用いられる（cf. It may be a good idea to ...）。pause「小休止する」は，このように「考えるために（比喩的な意味で）ちょっと立ち止まる」と言う場合に使うのは典型的な用法のひとつ。for a moment との結びつきも一般的。

[20] **a body of linguistic devices:** a body of ... は「大量または多数の...（の集まり）」（cf. There is *a growing body of* evidence in favor of this theory.）。linguistic devices は「言語的な手段」。

[21] **has access** [ǽkses]**:** have access to ... は「...を使う［...を見る，...に入る］ことができる［立場にある］」という意味の決まった言い方（2 章 [139]）（cf. be allowed [denied] *access to* ...）。

[22] **recognizable voice:**「聞けば誰のかが分かる声」（cf. He had changed so much that I could hardly *recognize* him.）。

[23] **Vocabulary:**「語彙」。ひとつの言語の単語，熟語など（まとめて vocabulary items と呼ばれる）の総体（e.g. English has a larger *vocabulary* than French.），またはある人の知っている（あるいは使える）単語や熟語の総体（e.g. His limited *vocabulary* often makes it difficult for him to express himself properly.）という意味で用いるのが一般的だが，ここでの意味はすぐ後で言い換えられているとおり。

[25] **grammar ... syntax ... register:** syntax はいわゆる grammar「文法」の中でも，特に単語を組み合わせて文などの複合的な表現を作る際に従わなければならない規則の集合を指す（5 章 [61]）。register「言語使用域」とは状況に応じて使い分けられる，言語的手段の構成する（formal「形式ばった」, informal「くだけた」といった）レベルやスタイルのこと（e.g. in (a) formal *register*）。

[26] **idiosyncratic** [ìdiəsɪnkrǽtɪk]**:**「特異(的)な」（cf. idiosyncrasy [ìdiəsíŋkrəsi]）。

[28] **stereotypical:** < stereotype [stériətàip]:「固定観念」「ステレオタイプ」。ここでは「いかにも特定の職業などの人らしい」という意味。

[28] **associated with ...:**「...と結びついている」「...と連想関係にある」。

character type with which the reader is already familiar: the tough detective, the London cabbie.

While it may be easy to understand how the direct speech, that is the words actually spoken by a character, may be "heard" by the reader, the idea that there is an equally recognizable or "heard" voice emanating from the rest of the piece of writing is perhaps more difficult for us to accept. Yet the writer's style, so called, in any written text is as much a contrived "voice" as that given to any literary character and it is one that speaks to us from the words of the narrative itself. It is as audible and as characteristic a voice as that of any Sloppy, or Mrs. Higden, or police witness at a trial in the criminal courts of Victorian England and it is so for exactly the same reasons.

Writing is a self-dramatizing act. Some years ago, the distinguished American literary critic, Wayne C. Booth, suggested that the Charles Dickens who sat down to write each morning was not the same Charles Dickens who had eaten breakfast earlier with Mrs. Dickens and all of their children. This is perhaps a rather difficult point to grasp but it may be illustrated by referring to another work of fiction, a very funny novel called *The British Museum Is Falling Down* (David Lodge, 1965). In one chapter the reader encounters characters that speak in the literary "voice" of the American writer Ernest Hemingway. That is, they speak in very short sentences. Sentences in which things are good. Or bad. But it is difficult. It is very difficult. To imagine Ernest Hemingway spoke in the way Ernest Hemingway wrote. Writing is a self-dramatizing act. Any sort of writing is a self-dramatizing act.

If we are literate, then we are, at some time or another, writers. If we are writers we have not simply one voice but a number of voices that we may access or construct if given the occasion to do so. Why and how these considerations apply to each of us is something to ponder when reading the next passage, a father's description of the birth of his daughter. A sense of the author's personality and beliefs comes through successfully in this moving account of an actual event written by one of that event's main protagonists. However, even when writing a personal account of a real life event like this, a writer selects the voice that will be used to convey the story and the writer's feelings to the reader. This voice will be one of the many available to the writer: child, parent, student, teacher, participant, observer, authority. Such a voice can only be established by a choice of vocabulary, grammar and syntax that is consciously or unconsciously made. In this passage, Professor Sechiyama writes not

[34] **emanating from . . . :** emanate from . . . は(音，光，匂いなどが)「…から発する」(cf. His face *emanates* happiness.)。

[35] **the writer's style, so called:** so called はすぐ前の the writer's style「書き手のスタイル[文体]」を受けて「一般にそう呼ばれているのであるが」という感じを加えている。

[36] **is as much a contrived "voice" as . . . :**「…と同じように(自然に生じたのではなくて)人為的に作られた『声』である」。contrived (< contrive「考案する」「工夫して作る」) は「いかにも人為的な」「わざとらしい」という否定的な意味で普通は用いられるが，ここではそうでないことに注意。

[42] **a self-dramatizing act:**「自己演出の行為」。

[42] **distinguished:**「傑出した」「高名な」という意味の形容詞 (cf. She quickly *distinguished* herself from her peers.)。

[43] **Wayne C. Booth:** アメリカの文学批評家，修辞学者 (1921–2005)。代表作は *The Rhetoric of Fiction* (1961)，邦訳『フィクションの修辞学』。

[47] **may be illustrated by referring to . . . :**「…に言及することによって例証されるかもしれない」とは，「別の小説という具体例を参照することによってここで問題になっている考え方が理解し易くなるのではないか」というような意味。

[49] **David Lodge:** イギリスの小説家，文芸批評家，批評理論家 (1935–   )。

[50] **Ernest Hemingway:** アメリカの小説家 (1899–1965)。「ハードボイルド」と形容される，抽象化を避けた簡潔な文体が特徴。この後に続く文章はヘミングウェイの文体をもじっている。

[58] **access:** ここでは gain access to . . . または make . . . accessible という意味の他動詞として用いられている (cf. [21])。

[63] **protagonists** [proʊtǽgənɪsts]:「主役」「主人公」。

as a distanced academic but as a father who was an intensely involved participant in the story he has to tell.

# Miyon

## Kaku Sechiyama

At the time when I was due to leave for the United States on sabbatical, my partner and I were expecting our first child. We had initially thought that I would go first, while she stayed in Japan to have the baby. We were worried about the language problem and other aspects of life in the United States. But in the end we decided to go together and have the baby in the United States. This would give the baby triple citizenship, as my partner is Korean (*zainichi*) and all babies born in the United States automatically become US citizens. No doubt this would make various procedures complicated. But as a sociologist, I thought this would be sort of interesting.

Before the concept of citizenship became widely accepted, people must have seen the world differently from the way they see the world today, separated by national boundaries. I thought having triple citizenship might well give our baby a perspective that was a little liberated from the restrictive notion of people being "Japanese," "Korean," or "American."

We arrived in the United States in the middle of August. In order to make the trip easier for my partner, we had decided to stay overnight on the west coast, rather than fly direct to the east coast. We arrived in Boston the following day, relieved that the baby had not decided it was time to be born in the middle of our journey. The first thing we did was to go to see a gynecologist in the university's medical center. The receptionist, a middle-aged woman, looked at us and smiled, "You came from Japan in your thirty-fourth week of pregnancy? You are brave!" I realized that neither of us had ever spoken to a medical doctor in English before. My partner was calmer than I was. I was glad to hear her say, "It's no problem! After all, childbirth is not an illness."

We were asked to provide various kinds of information, such as

[73] **I was due to . . . :** be due to . . .（不定詞句）は「…することになっている」「…する予定である」（e.g. Our next meeting *is due to* be held a week from tomorrow.）。be due は「（列車，バスなどが）到着予定である」「（赤ちゃんが）生まれる予定である」「（本などが）出版予定である」など「…が生じる[現れる]予定である」という場合には to 不定詞句なしで用いられるのが普通（e.g. Their first baby *is due* early next week. / The next train *is due* in ten minutes. / cf. the *due* date「（支払い，出産などの）予定日」「（図書館などから借りた本の）返却日」）。

[73] **on sabbatical** [səbǽtɪkl]: 「（大学教員に対して与えられる）研究休暇で」。

[74] **my partner and I were expecting our first child:** cf. She *is expecting* (a baby [child]). 「妊娠している」「出産予定である」。

[76] **to have the baby:** have a baby は「出産する」という場合の決まった言い方のひとつ（e.g. She's going to *have a baby* soon. / cf. give birth to a baby）。

[77] **in the end:** 「結局は」。in the end はこのように「いろいろ考えた末にやはり」という場合によく用いられる表現（e.g. I wonder what he's decided to do *in the end*.）。

[82] **I thought this would be sort of interesting:** 「これはなかなか面白いことになるぞと思った」。sort of と kind of は口語ではこのように「なかなか」「ちょっと」「かなり」という副詞的な意味で用いられることがよくある（e.g. "Do you like her?" "Yeah, *kind of*." 「うん，まあね」）。

[84] **people must have seen the world differently:** see . . . differently は「…の見方が違う」に相当する決まった組み合わせ（e.g. You and I seem to *see* things *differently*. 「あなたと私ではものの見方が違うようですね」）。

[87] **might well give our baby a perspective:** might (may) well はこのように「多分…」という意味を表すことが多い（e.g. She *may well* not want to join us. 「彼女は多分仲間に入りたがっていないだろう」）。

[88] **a little liberated from the restrictive notion of . . . :** 「…という窮屈な考え方から少し解放された」。

[92] **rather than fly direct to the east coast:** 「東海岸へ飛行機で直行するのではなくて」。A rather than B はこのように「B ではなくて A」という B を否定する意味になるのが普通であることに注意。fly direct to . . . は「…に飛行機の直通便で行く」。direct はこのように directly の代わりに副詞的に用いられることも多い（cf. a *direct* flight to Chicago）。

[95] **go to see a gynecologist:** 「婦人科医（gynecologist [gàɪnəkúlədʒɪst]）の診察を受けに行く」。see a doctor は「医者に診察してもらう」という場合の決まった言い方のひとつ。

the mother's place of birth and her first language. Because my partner was less confident in speaking English than I was, I answered on her behalf. "My wife is Korean but she was born in Japan. Her first language is Japanese." And then I continued, "I am Japanese, she is Korean, but I suppose the baby is going to be American!" The receptionist laughed and said something quite surprising. "Well, that's a typical American. My grandmother is Irish, my grandfather is...." I was so happy that I could not really understand the rest of what she said. Our baby will have a Japanese father and a Korean mother who was born and brought up in Japan. The baby will not be "a typical Japanese" in Japan. But in the United States people call a baby of Asian parents, who have just arrived and who hardly speak English, "typical." I was impressed by this nation of immigrants.

But I could not be impressed for long. We had to answer some medical questions — "asthma, anemia, seizure" — for someone who only knows words like "stomachache" and "cold," technical terms of this kind are quite difficult. Fortunately my partner was in good shape and there was nothing to worry about. Nonetheless, I started to worry about what I would do if something unexpected happened during the birth. After that, I began studying medical terms by watching the medical drama *ER* on television with a dictionary in my hand.

The actual childbirth was not going to take place in the university's medical center but at a big hospital nearby. This hospital's facilities were said to be ranked within the top ten in the United States. I practiced driving to the hospital in preparation for the moment when I would have to take my partner in for the delivery. But because I had only come to the United States recently, I would swerve to the other side of the road every time I took a left turn. I felt really bad that my partner had to co-drive from the passenger seat, telling me again and again "move to the right, right!" Two weeks before the due date, we went to take a look at the hospital. It certainly was an impressive facility. She would be giving birth in a private room and would be moved to another private room afterwards. It looked like a hotel.

We looked at each other and smiled, "This is going to be great!" Perhaps the baby felt our excitement. From that night, intermittent pains started and the interval between contractions started to get shorter and shorter. I wrote up a memo using a dictionary, and at four in the morning I called the university's medical center, got in touch with the doctor, and explained the situation. The doctor told

[115]　**I was impressed by this nation of immigrants:**「この移民の国に感銘を受けた」。be impressed by [with] ... は「…に感心する」「…が素晴らしいと思う」という場合によく用いられる表現。次の I could not *be impressed* for long は「感心してばかりもいられなかった」という感じ。

[118]　**asthma** [ǽzmə], **anemia** [əníːmiə], **seizure** [síːʒər]:「喘息，貧血，発作」。

[120]　**my partner was in good shape:** be in good shape は「体調がよい」という場合の決まった言い方で，人間以外のものの「状態がよい」ことを表すのにも使える (e.g. Her company *is in pretty good shape*.)。反対に「体調[状態]が悪い」は be in bad shape (e.g. The economy *is in really bad shape*.)。

[121]　**there was nothing to worry about:** There is nothing to worry about. は「何も心配することはない」「全く心配はいらない」という場合に用いる決まり文句。

[124]　**the medical drama *ER*:** *ER* は日本でも放送されたアメリカの人気テレビドラマ。ER は Emergency Room (「緊急治療室」「救急室」) の略。

[130]　**take my partner in for the delivery:** take ... in はここでは「…を病院に連れて行く」。この場合の delivery は「分娩」「出産」(cf. The baby *was delivered* by caesarean section.「帝王切開で」)。分娩室は a *delivery* room。

[141]　**the interval between contractions:**「陣痛の間隔」。

us to go straight to the hospital. We sped through the dark streets and arrived at the hospital in almost half the time it took us to get there during the day.

Soon after we got to the hospital we went to the delivery room. Lots of staff came in and out. Of course I was right next to my partner the whole time, translating for her, and making cups of tea. I am so happy I was able to be right there at the time of the baby's birth. I have heard some men say they would not know what to do if they were put in a position like that. In my case, I had to be there as a translator, and actually there were plenty of things for me to do. In Japan, being with your wife at the time of the birth is regarded as something that requires a sense of determination and is considered a big deal. But the hospital we went to assumed that I would be there. When you think about it, it is quite strange that one of the parents has to stand outside the room when their baby is about to be born. I think it is really important to share the exact moment of the birth of a family member, in all its pain and excitement. Moreover, I think if partners were usually together at the moment of childbirth it would help establish the practice of men getting more involved in the subsequent care of the child. The convention of a wife going home to her parents to give birth should become a thing of the past. In order to make this change practically possible, there should be a system that allows husbands to take time off from work at the time their children are born. I had always thought this was necessary but after the birth of our child I began to believe in this even more strongly.

The paperwork involved in getting US citizenship for a newborn is relatively easy. On the day of our baby's birth, the person at the hospital who was in charge of birth certificates called our room. I was asked to provide information about the father and mother and also whether the baby needed a social security number. The following day, I just filled out a form with her name. In the United States, it is necessary to decide on the name immediately so one has to prepare in advance. I signed the form at the hospital. The form then was sent to the city government office which would issue the birth certificate. The social security card, which is required if you want to be legally employed in the United States, was sent to us about two weeks later. Our own social security cards say "not valid for employment," but because our daughter is an American citizen there is no such restriction on her card. She is just a "typical" American. In order to get her US passport, all I needed to do was to go to the post

- [149] **Lots of staff:** staff が集合名詞であることに注意 (cf. a member of (the) *staff*)。
- [156] **is considered a big deal:**「大変なことだと考えられている」。a big deal は(「大きな取り引き」という原義から派生した)「重要なこと」「たいしたもの」という意味であるが,"Big deal." は(日本語の「たいしたものだ」と同様)皮肉の意味になることにも注意 (e.g. A: His 50th book has just come out. B: *Big deal*.)。「A は B であると考えられている」「A は B と見なされている」と言いたい場合に consider を使うと，このように A is considered B (または A is considered to be B) となって B の前に as を用いないのが普通。
- [157] **assumed:** assume は「…を当然のことと思う」「…を前提とする」(e.g. on the *assumption* that ...「…という想定に立って」)。
- [158] **When you think about it:**「考えてみれば」という意味の決まった言い方 (cf. A: Did he mention my name? B: Come to *think of it*, he did.)。you は一般の人を表す。
- [163] **it would help ... :**「男性がその後の (subsequent) 子育てに，より積極的に関わる習慣を確立するのに役立つことになる」。help はこのように直後に不定詞句 (to はあってもなくてもよい) を伴って「…するのに役立つ」という意味を表すことが多い (e.g. The government needs to come up with a measure to *help* (*to*) *boost* the economy. / cf. This book has certainly *helped me* (*to*) *understand* what cultural geography is all about.)。
- [167] **to take time off from work:**「仕事を休む」。
- [169] **believe in this even more strongly:** believe in ... は「(主義，思想など)が正しいと思う」。even は「さらに」「いっそう」の意味で比較級の意味を強める場合によく用いられる。
- [171] **paperwork:**（書式 (forms) への記入などの）「事務手続き」。
- [175] **a social security number:** アメリカ在住者が持つ，納税，社会保障などに使われる番号。その番号が記されているものを social security card と言う。
- [179] **issue the birth certificate:**「出生証明書を発行する」。issue は「発行する」という意味の動詞 (cf. the latest *issue* of ...「…の最新号」)。

office and send in an application form, along with her birth certificate. And once she grows up, she will be eligible to vote in both Japan and the United States, unlike her mother, who is equally unable to vote in both Japan and Korea.

Interestingly, in registering the birth, I had to fill out the name of the father first on both the Korean and Japanese documents. But in the US paperwork, the name of the mother comes first. In fact, the congratulations message we received from the hospital did not even include the name of the father. Perhaps this is a better system, especially for single mothers. Furthermore, in Japan, the baby is registered in his or her parent's registry regardless of the place of birth. But in the United States, it's the local government of the town where the hospital is located that is in charge of providing the baby's birth certificate. We actually lived in Cambridge, but because the hospital was located across the river in Boston the birth certificate was registered in the city of Boston. This shows that the US emphasis on where a person is born is very much in operation at the local level as well.

We gave our baby three names, even though the three different registration systems did not require us to do so. Her Japanese name is 瀬地山美瑛. It comes from 美瑛, pronounced "Biei," a hilly town in central Hokkaido. Her mother and I liked visiting there when I was teaching at Hokkaido University. I hope that our daughter will one day come to love the sky, the hills, and the farms that seem to change their beauty every season as much as she comes to love her own name. I hope the landscape of the area will remain the same until our daughter grows up enough to understand why we named her for it.

Her Korean name, 金美瑛, sounds quite natural in Korean. The way her personal name is pronounced is "Miyon" in both Japanese and Korean. I stuck to the Korean pronunciation because I hope she grows up strong enough to acknowledge her identity as a minority in Japanese society, just as her mother does. I struggled to come up with the English spelling of her name. I thought that if I spelled it "Miyong," English speakers would be likely to read it "My Yong." So I decided on "Meayong." Her middle name would be my partner's family name, Kim. So our daughter's American name is "Meayong Kim Sechiyama." Perhaps she will only use "Kim" when she grows up, because "Meayong" is a difficult name to pronounce. This official American name differs from the romanized way of spelling her name in Japan (Miyon) and also the Korean way of spelling the name (Miyoung or Miyung). The Korean government changed the

- [192] **the name of the mother comes first:** come first は「最初に来る」で日本語と同じ発想の表現だが,「…が最優先される」という比喩的な意味でもよく用いられる (e.g. Bill won't come to the meeting if we have it on Sunday. His family always *comes first* on weekends.)。
- [199] **Cambridge:** もちろん,ここではイギリスの大学町ケンブリッジではなく,アメリカのマサチューセッツ州ケンブリッジ。Harvard University と Massachusetts Institute of Technology (MIT) の所在地。
- [202] **is very much in operation at the local level as well:** be in operation は「(原理などが)作用している」「(機械などが)作動している」。at the local level as well は「(アメリカ合衆国という国家全体のレベルと同様ケンブリッジやボストンといった)地域のレベルでも」。
- [206] **a hilly town in central Hokkaido:**「北海道の中央部にある丘の多い町」。
- [212] **until our daughter grows up enough . . . :**「なぜその町にちなんだ名前を私たちがつけたのかを娘が理解できるほどに成長するまで」。name A for [after] B は「B にちなんで A に名前をつける」(12 章 [11]) (e.g. This pond *is named after* a famous novel by Soseki Natsume.)。
- [216] **I stuck to the Korean pronunciation:**「韓国語の発音をそのまま使うことにした」。stick to . . . は「…(考え方や主義)を貫く」「…(それまでしてきたことなど)をそのまま続ける」(e.g. A: Would you like to have some wine this time? B: I think I'll *stick to* beer.)。
- [218] **I struggled to come up with . . . :**「娘の名前の英語の綴りを何とかして考え出そうとした」。come up with . . . はこの場合「…を考え出す」(e.g. We need to *come up with* some new ideas to get the project off the ground.)。

traditional Korean spelling when it issued her passport to go along with the spelling as it was put down in the U.S. birth certificate, but in the Japanese passport her name is spelled as Miyon. This will make things confusing for her if one day, for example, she needs to get certificates of grades from Japanese and Korean institutions, because her name would be spelled differently in the two sets of documents. But she will always be "Miyon" regardless of the language. I hope this will become her identity.

This is what I want to say to Miyon:

The reason why your name is pronounced Miyon is because that way we hope you will be sensitive to issues facing Korean Japanese people in Japan. And it is because we hope you will properly understand these issues as social contradictions. The reason we formalized all three of your potential citizenships is that we want you to confront the silliness of this modern system called citizenship in your own life and because we want you to free yourself from the narrow framework of citizenship. In a sense, your birth means that the number of people in this world has increased by three. In my life I am going to support three Miyons — of Japan, Korea, and the United States — three Miyons who will work together to confront the world.

[245] **has increased by three:** increase by three は「(世界の人口が) 3 人増える」。by ... はこのように数量の増減の幅を示すのに用いることがよくある (e.g. The price of fuel has been reduced *by* 10% [*by* half].)。

# 4
# BABIES

## Introduction
## Kazuo Hiraki

The things that we do every day, without too much thought, are [1]
often rather difficult to explain when we think about how we actually do them. For example, without paying much attention to what
we're doing, we crawl out of bed in the morning and somehow
manage to get dressed in front of a mirror. We enjoy talking with [5]
friends over a cup of tea. We watch a favorite television drama after
dinner. We take routine activities such as these so much for granted
that we hardly pay any attention to them. But when you think about
it, how do you know that the person in the mirror is actually you?
Why is it so much fun to chat with good friends? And how do we [10]
distinguish between what we see on the television screen and incidents that happen in our real lives?

In order to answer even really simple questions like these, it is
necessary to untangle the workings of the mind, or brain — that is,
we need to understand the mechanism of the cognitive function. [15]
But this is a far from easy task. Researchers all over the world are
tackling the problem from different angles, trying to figure out the
brain mechanism that sustains our cognitive function. But the human brain is so complex that despite all this research much remains
shrouded in mystery. [20]

One promising method for understanding the mechanism of the
cognitive function is to explore its origins, because the things we do
rather casually are not things we learned to do suddenly, in one day.
They all became possible for us through a process of development
that started when we were infants. So in order to understand the [25]
"basis" of our adult minds, we need to study babies at the threshold
of this process of development.

The text of today's session is taken from a book called *The Infant's*

- [10] **Why is it so much fun:** fun が名詞，それも不可算名詞であることに注意（e.g. It's been great *fun* talking to you. / We had a lot of *fun* at the party last Sunday, didn't we?）。
- [13] **it is necessary to untangle the workings of the mind, or brain:** untangle は「(もつれたものを)ほどく」という原義から「(複雑な仕組みなどを)解明する」。動詞の前に来る接頭辞 un- は，動詞の意味を反転させる（cf. unfold「(たたんだものを)広げる」，untie「(結んだものを)ほどく」）。the workings of ... は「…の仕組み」という意味でよく用いられる表現（e.g. *the workings of* the human mind / cf. how the mind *works*）。通例 workings と複数で用いられる。
- [15] **the cognitive function:**「認知機能」。
- [17] **tackling the problem:** tackle は「(問題などに)取り組む」という意味でよく用いられる他動詞（1 章 [115]）（cf. address [oneself to] a problem）。
- [17] **trying to figure out ... :** figure out は「…(物事の仕組み，人の行動原理など)を(いろいろ考えて)理解する」「…(問題)を(努力して)解決する」という意味を表す重要な句動詞(本文 [48])（e.g. I can't *figure out* how this gadget works. / I have always found him hard to *figure out*.）。分詞構文が主節の内容を別の角度から(またはより具体的に)言い直すのに用いられていることに注意(3 章 [6]，8 章 [57] [170]，10 章 [44])。
- [19] **despite all this research much remains shrouded in mystery:** research はこのように不可算名詞として用いることが多い(1 章 [136]，7 章 [12])（cf. do [conduct] *research* on [into] the workings of the mind）。shrouded in mystery は「謎に包まれて」という意味のよくある組み合わせ。
- [26] **at the threshold of this process of development:** threshold は本来「敷居」だが，このように「何かの始まる時点」「出発点」という意味で比喩的に用いられることが多い（cf. I have a rather low pain *threshold*.）。

*World* that was written by Philippe Rochat, a professor at Emory University in Atlanta, Georgia. He is well known for his research that attempts to understand the ways in which notions such as "self" and "socialization" work in the mind from the perspective of behavioral development. His research is having an impact not only on the field of developmental psychology but also on such areas as brain science, neurology, artificial intelligence, and robotics. Why don't you also try to observe babies a little scientifically? You probably see some babies every day. Take a close look at the way they interact with the world around them. Babies are not merely cute and adorable; they also provide us with key insights into the mechanism of our mind.

# Deciphering the Infant World

## Philippe Rochat

Our understanding of the infant world is rapidly emerging from prolonged darkness. After centuries of oversight and neglect in the study of modern psychology, infants are finally being considered a major source of scientific enlightenment regarding the origins of the human mind. Infants are now systematically scrutinized for the way they develop, perceive, act, think, feel, and know.

Figuring out what is meaningful for infants entails supposing what might be the formative elements of their mental life. It requires considering what might be the building blocks of their psychology and what is relevant to their development. Not unlike in other areas of science, such ideas guide research and ultimately determine how infants are theoretically accounted for. If, for example, researchers assume that the social aspect of infant behavior is all important, then a social infant is accounted for. In contrast, if they assume that infants are primarily oriented toward the exploration of physical objects, then a more rational infant physicist will be brought forth. Infancy research, not unlike any other scientific enterprise, is always guided by fundamental assumptions and ideological choices, a "theoretical carving."

[34] **developmental psychology:**「発達心理学」。
[35] **artificial intelligence:**「人工知能」。
[35] **robotics:**「ロボット工学」。日本語でも「ロボティックス」ということが多くなっている。

[42] **oversight** [óuvərsàit]: ここでは「見落とし」「見過ごし」(cf. You've *overlooked* one important fact.)。他に「監督」「管理」の意味もある (cf. We need someone to *oversee* the project.)。
[44] **a major source of scientific enlightenment regarding the origins of the human mind:**「人間の心の起源を科学的に理解するのに役立つ知識を豊富に与えてくれる研究対象」。a source of ... は「…(知識, 情報, 着想など)の供給源」という意味でよく用いられる表現 (e.g. a reliable *source of* information「信頼できる情報源」)。enlightenment < enlighten: help ... to understand something better (cf. I found the notes very *enlightening*)。
[45] **Infants are ... scrutinized:** scrutinize は「詳しく調べる」(cf. The police are *examining* the scene of the crime *for* clues.)。
[48] **entails:** A entails B は, 「A は B を含意する」「A ならば B である」という原義から発して, 「A には B が必然的に伴う」「A は B を内容として含む」「A をするには B をすることが必要だ」といった意味を表すことが多い (e.g. What does your job *entail*?「どういうことをするお仕事なのですか?」)。この文脈では, 次の文の requires と実質的に同じ意味と考えてよい。
[49] **the formative elements of their mental life:**「乳児の心理発達に関わる要因」(cf. during one's *formative* years「人格形成期に」)。
[50] **the building blocks of their psychology:**「乳児の心理(機構)の基本的な構成要素」。building blocks は「建築用のブロック」だが, このように比喩的に「基本的構成要素[単位]」という意味で用いられることが多い。本文の最後の段落で用いられている constitutive elements と同じ意味。この場合の psychology は「心理学」ではなく「心理」。このように学問分野の名称がその学問分野の研究対象を表すのはかなり一般的な転用のパターン (e.g. human anatomy「人体の解剖学的構造」, the geography of Tokyo「東京の地理」)。
[51] **what is relevant to their development:**「乳児の発達にはどのような要因が関与するのか」。relevant to ... は「…と関わり[関連性]がある」(cf. What you've just said doesn't have any direct *relevance to* today's topic.)。反意表現は irrelevant to ...。
[51] **Not unlike in other areas of science:** not unlike は「似ていなくはない」だが, 実質的には「似ている」という意味 (cf. It is *not uncommon* for university students to live in dormitories.)。乳児の心理発達に関わる要因として何が重要であると研究者が考えるかによって, 研究の進め方や乳児をどのような存在として捉えるかが決まってくる, ということ。
[53] **If, for example, researchers assume ... :**「例えば乳児の行動の社会的な側面が何よりも重要 (all important) であると研究者が想定すれば, 社会的存在としての乳児という説明がなされることになる」。
[55] **In contrast, if they assume ... :** in [by] contrast は「それに対して」「それとは対照的に」。be primarily oriented toward ... は「主な関心が…にある」(cf. Not many students are politically *oriented*.)。a more rational infant physicist は「より理性的な物理学者としての乳児」(前文の a social infant と対比させられている)。
[60] **a "theoretical carving":**「理論による(研究対象の)特定の切り分け方」。直前の2つの名詞句 (fundamental assumptions and ideological choices) の内容を言い換えた表現で, 比喩的な言い方であることを示すために引用符に入れられている。

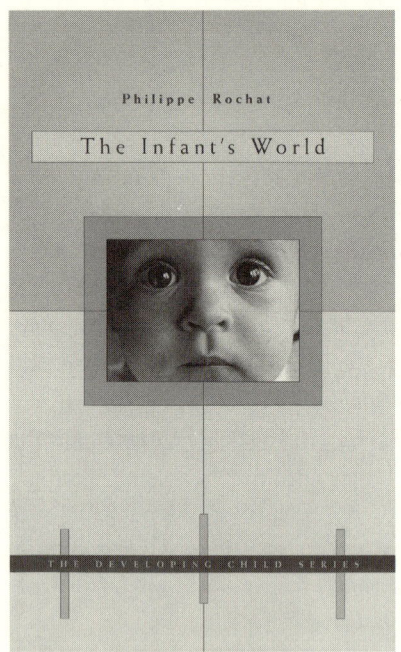

*The Infant's World*

It is intriguing to think about the reasons for particular theoretical carving and why researchers are inclined to focus on one particular aspect of infant psychology rather than another. In other words, what determines researchers' own take on the infant world? There is only limited serendipity underlying scientists' choice of issues and priorities in research. Instead it reflects a Zeitgeist, an intellectual and political climate: the particular aesthetic of an era, what is fashionable and mainstream. This is particularly evident when considering the historical reasons for studying infants.

Current infancy research is part of a tradition that is deeply rooted in Western philosophy, in particular the tradition of dividing mental life into separate arenas such as cognition, perception, motivation, attention, social behavior, emotions, or personality. The resulting representation of mental life is a sort of juxtaposition of separate "psychologies" that function as distinct units. Such parsing does not foster what is particularly apparent in infancy: the great interdependence of all those arenas.

Since antiquity, deciphering the mind has been a major exercise among philosophers who thought about the nature and origins of mental life. Aristotle (384–322 BC) distinguished discrete categories of emotions, sense perceptions, and intellects. René Descartes (1596–1650) introduced the distinction between primary and secondary

[61] **intriguing:** very interesting, unusual or mysterious.

[62] **researchers are inclined to . . . :** be inclined to . . . は tend or want to . . . (cf. His natural *inclination* is always to say no.)。

[64] **researchers' own take on the infant world:**「乳児の世界に対する研究者自身の見方」。one's take on . . . は「…についての意見[見方]」(e.g. What's *your take on* his latest proposal?)。

[64] **There is only limited serendipity** [sèrəndípəti] **underlying . . . :**「科学者が研究においてどのような問題を選択し，どういう優先順位をつけるかが偶然運よく決まることはめったにない」。偶然で決まることはないというのは「むしろ時代の精神を反映している」という意味。serendipity は「思いがけなく何かよいことが起こること」(cf. *serendipitous* discoveries)。underlying < underlie: be the basic cause of.

[66] **a Zeitgeist, an intellectual and political climate:**「時代精神，すなわち知的・政治的風潮」。その内容はコロン以下で具体的に示されている。Zeitgeist [tsáɪtgàɪst] はドイツ語から入った語で，「時代精神」の意味。英語に直訳すると time spirit。climate は「(特定の地域・時代の)風潮」。

[68] **mainstream:** ここでは「主流の」という意味の形容詞 (cf. the *mainstream* of literary theory)。

[70] **a tradition that is deeply rooted in Western philosophy:**「西洋哲学に深く根差した伝統」。be rooted in . . . は「…に根差している」という意味の決まった言い方。

[71] **the tradition of dividing mental life into separate arenas such as . . . :**「心の働き[仕組み]を…といった別々の領域に分割する伝統」。arena は「競技場」だが，このように比喩的に用いることも多い。cognition は「認知」，perception は「知覚」。前者の方が，より高次の処理を意味する。

[73] **The resulting representation of mental life is . . . :**「その結果，心の働きは…としてイメージされるようになっている」。resulting をこのように限定形容詞的に用いると，「(あることから)結果的に生じる」という意味になる (e.g. The city was hit by a huge earthquake and the *resulting* damage was catastrophic.)。representation は通例「表象」「表示」などと訳されるが，要するに他の何かを表しているもののこと。

[74] **juxtaposition of separate "psychologies" that function as distinct units:** juxtaposition < juxtapose:「並置する」(put things next to each other)。distinct units「別々の単位」の distinct は separate の言い換え。

[75] **Such parsing does not foster:** parsing は「(文法的な)分析，解析」だが，ここでは前出の theoretical carving を言い換えたもの。foster: help or encourage . . . to develop.

[76] **the great interdependence of all those arenas:**「別個であると一般に考えられているそれら複数の心の領域すべてが大きく依存し合っている[密接に関連し合っている]こと」。

[78] **Since antiquity** [æntíkwəti]:「古代以来」。

[78] **deciphering the mind:**「人間の心を解読する(decipher)こと」。

[80] **discrete categories of . . . :**「…という截然と分かれた複数のカテゴリー[範疇]」。discrete は「離散的な」「不連続の」(反意語 continuous「連続的な」)だが，ここでは前出の separate や distinct [74] と同じ意味と考えてよい。

[82] **the distinction between primary and secondary qualities of sensation:**「感覚によって捉えられる第一性質と第二性質との区別」。感覚に現れた性質のうち，物自体に対応物を持つものを第一性質，持たないものを第二性質と呼ぶ(詳しくは章末注を参照)。

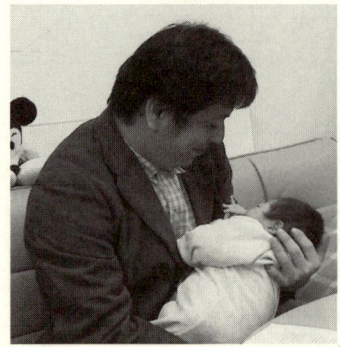

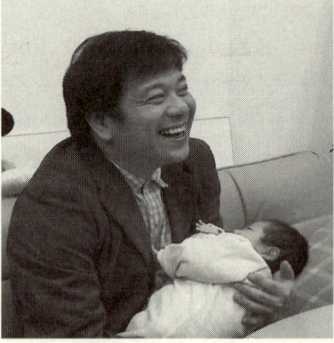

Professor Kazuo Hiraki in his office

qualities of sensation to account for the origins of perception within a mechanist framework. The German philosopher Immanuel Kant (1724–1804) considered that knowledge and the functioning of the mind can be reduced to thinking in relation to a limited number of basic a priori categories such as time, space, and causality. Such categorizing of mental phenomena has had lasting influences.

The philosophical tradition of parsing mental phenomena influenced the modern scientific approach to the mental life of infants. For example, the pioneer work of Jean Piaget on infant cognition is based on the Kantian parsing of a priori categories (space, time, causality, and objects). Following Kant's framework, Piaget assumed that these categories reflect the world as it is known by the infant, a world essentially dominated by midsize physical objects. Following Kantian parsing, Piaget approached children as little physicists experimenting primarily with objects and theorizing about them.

To a large extent, the Kantian categories adopted by Piaget in his study of infant cognitive development pertain to the nature of knowledge in an abstract, formal sense. Piaget's approach to infant cognition is more epistemological (pertaining to formal knowledge) than psychological. Take the category of space, for example. As reasoned

- [83] **within a mechanist framework:**「機械論的な枠組みの中で」。within a . . . framework または within the framework of . . . は「…(理論など)の枠組みの中で」「…の立場[観点]から」といった意味。mechanist < mechanism「(哲学における)機械論」。機械論は自然現象や人間の活動などを，物理・化学法則に従う機械的運動として決定論的，かつ還元論的に説明しようとする立場。モデルとなる機械は，時代を下るにつれ，時計(17世紀から18世紀)から蒸気機関(19世紀)，そしてコンピュータ(20世紀)へと移り変わっていく。デカルトは，精神と肉体は独立した実体であるという心身二元論を導入しつつ，肉体について人間機械論の立場に立っていた。
- [86] **can be reduced to . . . :** reduce A to B「A を B に還元する」とは，複雑な対象 A をより基本的な原理等 B に分解することによって理解・説明すること。
- [87] **basic a priori categories:**「基本的でアプリオリなカテゴリー」。a priori [à: prió:ri, èi praió:raɪ] は a posteriori と対を成す語で，概念，判断，あるいは，知識を区別するために用いる。アプリオリな知識とは，経験に先立ち，あるいは，経験に依拠せずに獲得される知識(たとえば，論理学の知識や数学の知識など)を意味し，アポステリオリな知識とは，経験を待ってはじめて成立するような知識(物理学や生物学の知識など)を意味している。認識論の文脈を離れて，心理学の文脈では，「アプリオリ」を「生得的」ないし「先天的」と呼ぶ場合もある(詳しくは章末の注を参照)。
- [87] **causality** [kɔ:zǽləti]:「因果性」「因果関係」。
- [88] **has had lasting influences:**「長く影響を与え続けてきた」。動詞 last の現在分詞形に由来する形容詞 lasting (＝long-lasting) は「(効果，価値，印象などが)持続する，長続きする」という意味 (e.g. One of my high school teachers made a *lasting* impression on me.)。
- [91] **Jean Piaget:** ピアジェはスイスの発達心理学者 (1896–1980) (5章 [122])。ジュネーヴ大学教授。子どもの知能の起源を乳児期にまで遡って探究した。
- [94] **the world as it is known by the infant:**「乳児によって認識される世界」。人間と(例えば)トカゲとでは世界の見え方が(多分)相当違うように，世界の認識のされ方は認識主体によって異なりうるが，ここでは乳児の認識する世界が問題になっている。as は，このようにあるものにさまざまな様相がある場合に，(他の様相もあることを含意しつつ)そのひとつの様相を表現する際によく使われる(6章 [7]) (e.g. Japan *as* we know it「私たちが知っている日本」)。
- [97] **theorizing about them:**「身の回りにある物体についての理論を考案する」。theorize (about . . .)「…について理論を考案する」とは「…(の特性など)を(何らかの原理に基づいて)説明しようとする」ということ (e.g. Since ancient times, there has been a great deal of *theorizing about* how the mind works.)。
- [100] **pertain to . . . :**「…に関係するものである」。
- [102] **is more epistemological (pertaining to formal knowledge) than psychological:**「…は心理学的であると言うよりは(形式的な知識に関係する)認識論的なものである」。
- [103] **Take the category of space, for example:** "Take . . . , for example." は，議論の過程で「…を例として取り上げてみよう」という場合の決まり文句。
- [103] **As reasoned by Piaget:**「ピアジェが推論したように」。動詞の reason は「理性，論理的思考能力 (reason) を駆使して判断する」。

by Piaget, it might be a specific domain of cognition for which particular principles apply: that objects are permanent even if they perceptually come and go, that objects cannot be in two places at the same time, and that they move continuously through space (they do not pop out of nowhere when entering the perceptual field). But such a view of spatial cognition does not account for other, more psychological ways that infants apprehend space. For infants, space is more than an object of formal reasoning. It is primarily the environmental context in which they develop perception and action. Space is where infants take their first steps, learn to explore, and locomote in new ways. Space is a place for boldness and independence in avoiding obstacles and dangers. It is where one gets lost and eventually reunited. Space might be an abstraction of basic principles, but for infants it is primarily a very real, concrete location for perception and action.

One way to account for infant psychology is to start with the possible range of basic experiences that infants have in their environment. Such an approach begins with a description of the infants' environment, not with speculations about what might be in their heads. It is an approach that tries to avoid any kind of separation or dualism between infants and the environment they experience. Within this approach, infant psychology is fundamentally inseparable from a description of the environment and what infants might be capable of experiencing when interacting with it. The idea is to consider first the ecological niche of infants, and from there to figure out how their minds work in relation to it.

We share the same world with infants, but not their environment. We breathe the same air and witness the same objects and events that are controlled by the same physical laws. We share with babies the same body structure and are equipped with the same sensory systems. But we do not engage in the same kind of activities, nor do we have the same needs and motivations.

The ecological niche of infants is specific and comes with particular kinds of experience. Imagine an infant in her crib, just fed and diapered, awake and happily looking around. She might bring one of her hands to her mouth and suck one of her fingers. Or she might explore the colorful lining of the crib. She might also make eye contact with a talking face leaning over her with a smile. Each instance captures one of three primary categories of experience that are the foundations of the infant world; the experience of the self, objects, and people. These three very basic categories of experience are contrasted and invariant from the moment infants are born, and

- [105] **even if they perceptually come and go:**「(物体は)知覚的には現れたり消えたりしても」。例えば，ものは見えなくなっても，(普通は)実際に消滅したわけではなく，どこかで存在し続けている，ということ。この場合の come and go は「見えたり隠れたりする」「ある[いる]と思ったらいつのまにかなく[いなく]なる」といった意味 (e.g. It's one of those fads that *come and go*.)。
- [107] **move continuously through space:**「空間を連続的に移動する」。continuous の反意語は前出 [80] の discrete「離散的な」「不連続の」。
- [108] **do not pop out of nowhere:**「どこからともなく突然現れたりはしない」(cf. appear out of nowhere)。
- [110] **more psychological ways that infants apprehend space:** apprehend は「把握する」「認識する」。ここでも psychological は epistemological との対比で用いられている。
- [113] **infants take their first steps:**「乳児が歩き始める」。
- [114] **locomote:** locomotion (「移動」)という名詞から派生した動詞。このような普通とは逆方向の派生を逆成 (back formation) と呼ぶ (e.g. enthuse < enthusiasm)。
- [116] **gets lost and eventually reunited:** (get) reunited は「はぐれた (get lost) 相手(例えば母親)と再会する」。
- [116] **Space might be an abstraction of basic principles . . . :** an abstraction of basic principles である epistemological な空間に対して，幼児の psychological な空間は a very real, concrete location for perception and action である，ということ。
- [124] **dualism:**「二元論」(cf. monism「一元論」, pluralism「多元論」)。
- [128] **the ecological niche of infants:**「乳児の生態的地位」。「生態的地位」とは，元来，個々の種または個体群が自然界において占める地位を示す生態学的概念(6 章 [34])。生物的環境(＝食物連鎖)の中の位置もしくは生息場所の究極単位を意味する。ここでは乳児を取り巻く「乳児に固有な環境」を意味する。
- [133] **are equipped with the same sensory systems:**「同じ感覚機構を身につけている」。be equipped with . . . は「(人が)…(必要なもの)を身につけている」「(場所などに)…が装備されている」という意味の決まった表現 (e.g. Every classroom in this building is *equipped with* a state-of-the-art DVD player. / cf. Many people consider her to be well *equipped to* lead the new team.)。
- [136] **comes with particular kinds of experience:**「特定の種類の経験を伴う」。それぞれの ecological niche にはそこに特有の経験があることが含意されている。A comes with B は「A には B が伴う」。よく使われる come with the territory (e.g. I teach for a living. Having to mark thousands of papers *comes with* the territory.「何千枚もの答案を採点しなくてはならないのも仕事のうちだ」) というイディオムもこのパターンの応用例。
- [137] **crib:**「ベビーベッド」。
- [138] **diapered:** diaper [dáɪəpər]「おむつ」がそのままの形で「おむつをつける」という意味の動詞として使われている。
- [140] **lining:** 普通は「裏張り」「裏地」だが，ここではベビーベッドの内側に取り付ける保護パッド。
- [140] **make eye contact with a talking face leaning over her:** make eye contact with . . . は「…と視線を合わせる」。lean over . . . は「…に向かってかがみ込む」(cf. *lean against* the wall / *lean on* someone's shoulder / *lean out of* the window)。
- [145] **invariant:** never changing.

each corresponds to specific perceptual and action phenomena that babies are equipped to experience and learn from.

When infants bring their hands to their mouths, touch any other parts of their own bodies, move a limb across their fields of view, or cry, these actions are accompanied by perceptions that uniquely specify the infant's own body (that is, the *self*). When an object touches the baby or the baby hears someone else's voice, the perception is of things in the environment that are different from the self (that is, *objects*). Aside from self and physical things, *people* are a distinct feature of the infant environment. Babies experience them differently than either their own bodies or other physical objects. We will see that infants from birth are particularly attuned to people, preferring for instance to look at facelike displays over any other non-facelike visual stimuli. Aside from possible prewired attunement, people have the special feature of reciprocating and engaging in prolonged face-to-face interactions: games with high-pitched vocal interventions, particular facial expressions, and of course, the predominantly human sustained eye-to-eye contact. These three fundamentally distinct and contrasted classes of experience — the self, objects, and people — are differentiated from birth and even possibly in the womb. They are, I propose, the constitutive elements of the infant world and the basic contexts of the development of infants' mental life.

[150] **perceptions that uniquely specify the infant's own body** (that is, the *self*)：「乳児の身体(すなわち自己)を一義的に特定する知覚」。つまり「この見え方，感じ等は自分の身体にしかないという知覚」。

[154] **a distinct feature of the infant environment:**「乳児の環境の，他とははっきり異なる特徴」。

[155] **Babies experience them differently than . . . :**「赤ちゃんは(自分以外の)人間を…(を経験するの)とは異なった仕方で経験する」。differently (および different) は (「…とは違って」，「…とは異なる」の「…とは」を表す場合に)，from . . . の代わりにこのように than . . . を伴うことがある (cf. The movie was quite *different from* what I'd expected [*than* (what) I'd expected].)。

[157] **are particularly attuned to . . . :** be attuned to . . . は「…によく適用している」「…に対して適切に反応できる」。

[158] **preferring . . . over . . . :** 主節の内容を例示するために分詞構文が用いられていることに注意。over は prefer と結びついて「…よりも」という意味を表している (cf. She has control *over* me. / His height gives him an advantage [edge] *over* other players.)。

[159] **prewired attunement:** prewired は文字通りには「あらかじめ配線されている」だが，もとになっている wired が「遺伝的に組み込まれている」という意味を表すことがあるのと類似の用法 (e.g. Many linguists believe that a large proportion of the capacity for language is *wired* genetically into the human brain.)。attunement は「適応すること」「慣れること」。つまり prewired attunement は「(赤ちゃんが)誕生前から(人に)慣れるように仕組まれていること」。

[160] **reciprocating and . . . :** reciprocate [rɪsíprəkèɪt] は「やりとりする」。

[161] **prolonged:** この場合「長い時間持続する」。

[161] **high-pitched:**「高い声の」。pitch は「声の高さ」。

[163] **the predominantly human sustained eye-to-eye contact:**「持続的に視線を交わし合うという，主として人間に見られる行動」。

[166] **even possibly in the womb:**「ことによると子宮の中でさえ」。

**「第一性質と第二性質」**
　視覚によって捉えられた形と色は，どちらも物に備わる性質のように思われるが，デカルトらの近代哲学者によると，形は知覚者とは独立に物自体にその対応物を持っている性質であるのに対して，色の場合は，それに対応する性質を物自体のなかに見出すことはできず，たんに，色という感覚を生み出す力を見出すことができるだけである。一般に，知覚者とは独立に物自体に備わる性質を「第一性質」と呼び，他方，知覚者のなかに感覚を生み出す力として物に備わる性質を「第二性質」と呼ぶ。前者は知覚者のあり方とは独立に規定しうる性質であるため客観的性質と呼ばれ，後者は，知覚者のあり方に依存して初めて規定しうる性質であるため主観的性質と呼ばれている。論者によって若干の違いはあるが，一般に，前者には，大きさ，形，運動と静止，数などが属し，後者には，色，音，味，におい，あるいは，暖かさ，冷たさなどが属すると見なされている。この区別は，自然には形や大きさなど数学的に規定される性質のみが属しており，色や音などの感覚的性質は属さないと見なす近代的自然観の中核をなしており，ガリレオやデカルトが提起した後，とくにジョン・ロック (John Locke, 1632–1704) が『人間知性論』(1690) のなかで詳細な定式化を行うことになった。

**「アプリオリなカテゴリー」**
　カントの認識論においては，経験的認識は，直観と思考，あるいは，感性(直観の能力)と悟性(思考の能力)の共同によって成立すると見なされる。そして直観の形式として時間と空間の概念，思考の形式として，因果性などの概念(カテゴリー)が考えられている。これらの形式は，どんな経験的認識が成立する場合にも，必ず成立していなければならない前提と見なされており，その意味で，それらは認識を可能にする条件と見なされている。時間，空間，因果性などは，この「認識を可能にする条件」という意味で a priori な概念と見なされる。本文の著者は，時間と空間もカテゴリーと呼んでいるが，カントに即する限り，カテゴリーは「純粋悟性概念」であり，思惟のアプリオリな形式を示すものなので，この点は正しくない。

# 5
# LANGUAGE

## Introduction
### Yoshiki Nishimura

One of the reasons why language has attracted the interest of so many great scholars in such a wide variety of disciplines over the years is probably their shared belief that there is something about language that reveals the unique way the human mind works. Some have gone so far as to suggest that it is our capacity for language that most clearly sets us human beings apart from other animal species, including chimpanzees and bonobos, who are thought to share approximately 98% of their DNA with us. In other words, to these scholars, language is exactly what makes us human. The great majority of those specializing in the scientific study of language believe that, despite the immense diversity they exhibit, the world's languages, estimated to number in the thousands, have quite a few characteristics in common. What's more, they believe that some of these characteristics, generally referred to as linguistic universals, serve to distinguish human language from the communication systems of all other species. It should not come as a surprise, then, that many researchers view their investigation of language as part of an attempt to figure out what makes the human mind the unique thing that it is.

There are a number of different theories, which, while sharing the perspective outlined above, contrast significantly when it comes to how (knowledge of) language is organized and where these organizing principles come from. One of the most important and divisive issues is how our capacity for language, i.e., the tacit knowledge that allows us to use our language the way we do (e.g. to communicate with one another), is related to other facets of human cognition (e.g. categorization, memory, reasoning). There are basically two competing approaches. One is generally known as the

[4] **the unique way the human mind works:** この場合の unique は本来の「他に類のない」「独特の」という意味 (cf. I don't think this is a *uniquely* Japanese phenomenon.)。本文 [18] [57] [114] の unique も同じ。the way/how...works は「…の仕組み」という感じ。

[4] **Some have gone so far as to . . . :** go so [as] far as to... は「…(極端とも思われること)までする」「…しさえする」という意味の決まった言い方。

[6] **sets us human beings apart . . . :** set A apart (from B) または set apart A (from B) は「(特徴などが) A を (B から) 区別する [際立たせる]」(cf. What *differentiates* humans *from* other species?)。

[11] **the immense diversity they exhibit:** they がすぐ後の the world's languages を指すことに注意。

[12] **have quite a few characteristics in common:**「共通点がかなり多くある」。have...in common は「共通点が [ある, ない, 多い, 少ない]」などと言う場合によく用いられる表現型 (6 章 [196], 11 章 [168]) (e.g. I wonder *what* these two cases *have in common*.「この 2 つの事件の共通点は何だろう」)。本文 [42] の what the world's languages have in common も同じパターン。

[13] **What's more:**「その上」(cf. furthermore, moreover)。

[16] **It should not come as a surprise:**「驚くには当たるまい」。"It should come as no surprise" とも言う (cf. *Not surprisingly,* he didn't show up. / Will her new book sell as well as her previous one? — *I wouldn't be surprised.*)。

[21] **when it comes to . . . :** (…には名詞句または -ing 句が来て)「…(する) ということになると」(e.g. You're the expert *when it comes to* the fast-growing otaku market.)。非常によく使われる言い回し。

[24] **divisive:**「(問題などが) 争いの原因になる」「人々を分裂させる」(< divide)。

[27] **cognition** [kɑɡníʃən]:「認知」「心の仕組み」(how the mind works)。

[27] **categorization:**「カテゴリー化」。[150] の注を参照。

[28] **competing approaches:**「競合するアプローチ (考え方)」。動詞 compete から派生した competing は「競合する」という意味で限定形容詞的によく用いられる (e.g. *competing* theories about the origins of human cognition)。

[28] **the modular** [mɑ́dʒələr] **view of language:**「モジュール (module [mɑ́dʒuːl]) 的な言語観」。心というシステムは関連はしているけれども自律した複数の下位システム (subsystems) から構成されており, その自律した下位システム (=モジュール) のひとつが言語の知識である, という考え方。本文 [36]–[37] も参照。

Noam Chomsky, *The Generative Enterprise Revisited*

modular view of language and the other, for lack of a better term, we will call the holistic (or integrated) view of language.

Representing the modular approach is generative grammar, which was founded by Noam Chomsky in the 1950s and has since drastically changed the way we look at language. Take a look at Notecard 1 and you will get an immediate sense of the way Chomsky thinks about language. The modular view is so called because it simply means seeing knowledge of language as a module, a cognitive subsystem "distinct from other subsystems of the mind/brain." There are two more points worth noting about the quotation on Notecard 1. First, contrary to conventional wisdom, Chomsky says that the essence of language does not reside in the fact that it serves as a means of communication. Second, in Chomsky's approach greater emphasis is placed on what the world's languages have in common than on how they vary from each other.

To get an idea of why the opposing view is characterized as holistic or integrated, let's see what Michael Tomasello, a leading advocate of this view, has to say about the issue. Take a look at Notecard 2, which quotes part of his review article of Steven Pinker's best-selling *The Language Instinct*. In this book, which is an excellent introduction to the generative enterprise, Pinker tries to convince the reader that language acquisition is possible because human beings are innately endowed with a system of universal principles specific to language. But as its provocative title "Language is not an instinct" suggests, Tomasello's review article challenges this modular view, outlining an alternative that deserves to be called holistic or integrated. It is also to be noted that Tomasello stresses the importance of variation among different languages and considers the essence of language to be directly linked to the unique way human beings communicate with each other.

Another important and polarizing issue concerns the internal

[29] **for lack of a better term:** ある表現を導入する際に「他に適切な言い方がないので」と言う場合の決まり文句。

[30] **holistic** [hoʊlístɪk]:「全体論的な」(cf. holism)。すぐ後で見るように，the holistic view of language とは「言語の知識は人間の認知（＝心の仕組み）全体との関連を考えてはじめてその本質を解明することが可能になる」という考え方。

[31] **Representing the modular approach is . . . :**「モジュール的な研究方法を代表するのが…である」。…以下を新たに導入するための倒置の構文。(意味は変わってしまうが)普通の語順にすると，" . . . *represents* the modular approach" となる。

[31] **generative** [dʒénərətɪv] **grammar:**「生成文法」。Noam Chomsky（1928– ）の創始したこの言語理論については，2002 年に行われたチョムスキーへのインタビューも収録されている『生成文法の企て』（岩波書店）（英語版は *The Generative Enterprise*），特に「訳者による序説」を参照。

[39] **contrary to conventional wisdom:**「通念[常識的な考え方]に反して」。conventional [received] wisdom は「通念」に相当する決まった言い方。

[44] **the opposing view:**「対立する考え方」。定冠詞がついているのは「2 つの競合する考え方」([28] two competing approaches) のうちの残ったひとつだから。

[45] **what Michael Tomasello, a leading advocate of this view, has to say . . . :** what は has の目的語であることに注意(7 章 [77])（cf. have *something* to say）。leading は限定形容詞的に用いて「最も重要な」(2 章 [41])（e.g. *leading* figures in contemporary philosophy「現代哲学の旗手たち」/ cf. the *leading* hitter「首位打者」）。advocate [ǽdvəkət] は「特定の主義や考え方を支持[擁護]する人」。対応する動詞は advocate [ǽdvəkèɪt]。Tomasello の考え方の全体像については『心とことばの起源を探る』（勁草書房）（原著は *The Cultural Origins of Human Cognition*）を参照。

[48] *The Language Instinct*: 邦訳は『言語を生みだす本能』（NHK ブックス）。酒井邦嘉『言語の脳科学』（中公新書）も参照。

[51] **are innately endowed** [ɪndáʊd] **with . . . :**「生まれつき…が備わっている」(10 章 [47])（cf. genetic [biological] *endowment*）。innate は「生得的な」で genetically determined「遺伝的に決定された」，bioprogrammed などと言い換えられることもある。Pinker の用いた instinct「本能」も同じ趣旨。

[52] **specific to . . . :**「…に特有の」(cf. *specifically* linguistic)。

[52] **provocative** [prəvɑ́kətɪv]:「挑発的な」「論争を挑むような」(cf. sexually *provocative* / The book has *provoked* controversy.)。

[53] **challenges this modular view:**「このモジュール的な考え方に異を唱える」。動詞 challenge のこのような用法にも慣れておきたい (e.g. His authority has rarely been *challenged*.)。

[55] **It is also to be noted that . . . :** it is to be noted that . . .（または it should be noted that . . .）は，本文 [83] の it's important to note that . . . と同じく，…の重要性に注目させる場合によく用いられるパターンのひとつ (cf. It is *worth noting* that . . .)。

[59] **polarizing:** polarize (< pole「極」「対極」。e.g. the North/South *Pole*) は「(問題などが人々を) 2 つの対極的な立場に分かれさせる」(14 章 [28])（e.g. a *polarizing* figure in the Japanese political arena)。

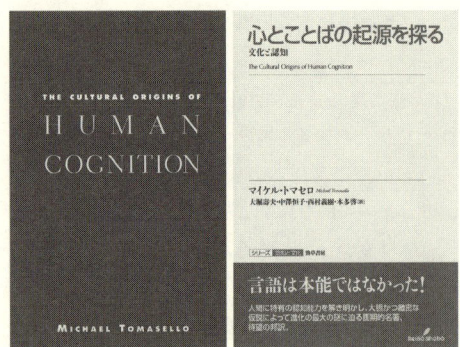

Michael Tomasello, *The Cultural Origins of Human Cognition*

structure of our knowledge of language. Although there is a general consensus among researchers that syntax, or grammar in the narrow sense of the term, is one of the defining features of language, the question of how grammar is related to meaning has long been, and remains, a highly controversial issue. There is no question that native speakers of any language have at their disposal a set of rules, of which they are hardly ever conscious, that make it possible for them to produce and understand an infinite number of novel phrases and sentences. In other words, we tacitly know how to put together prepackaged expressions (e.g. words, idioms, formulaic phrases) to form new and more complex ones in ways that would be acceptable to other native speakers. Furthermore, there is no denying that the vast majority of the messages we want to get across can only be conveyed by (mostly subconsciously) drawing on conventionalized patterns for constructing composite expressions and that, therefore, grammar and meaning are closely connected. The subject of dispute is exactly what these connections are. Again, there are basically two contrasting views. One of them, lying at the core of generative grammar, is known as the autonomy thesis (or the autonomous-syntax hypothesis). The other, characteristic of a prominent theory in the holistic/integrated camp, is called the symbolic view of grammar.

At this point, take a look at Notecard 3, which is one formulation of the autonomy thesis.

It's important to note that the view Huddleston is putting forward here should not be taken to imply that there are no principled relations between syntax and semantics (or phonology, for that matter), an obviously ludicrous view that he explicitly warns us not to attribute to this thesis. No sensible linguist would deny that syntax and semantics have significant points of connection. What the autonomy thesis means is simply that it is possible to isolate a syntac-

[61] **syntax** [síntæks]:「統語論」(3章 [25])。複数の語を組み合わせて句や文を作る際に従わなければならない規則の総体(に関する理論)。

[62] **one of the defining features of language:** a defining feature of ... は「…を…たらしめている特徴」「…の本質を決定する特徴」(cf. a *distinctive feature of* Japanese society)。

[64] **There is no question that ...:**「…には疑問の余地がない」という意味の決まった言い方 (cf. without *question* / call [bring] ... into *question* / Some people have *questioned* whether it was really an honest mistake on his part.)。

[65] **have at their disposal ...:** have ... at one's disposal は「…を自由に[好きなように]使える」という意味のよく使われる表現 (cf. She *has* a huge vocabulary *at her command*.)。

[69] **prepackaged expressions:** この場合 prepackaged「あらかじめパッケージに入っている」とは,複数の単語で構成されていても(その場でいちいち組み立てるのではなく)ひとつの単語と同じように丸ごと記憶されている,ということ。

[69] **formulaic** [fɔ̀ːrmjəléɪɪk] **phrases:**「定型表現」「決まり文句」(cf. fixed expressions, set phrases)。

[71] **there is no denying:** there is no ... ing は「…することはできない」という意味を表す決まったパターンだが,何かが事実であることを強調する there is no denying ...「…は否定できない」は特によく用いられる (cf. *There is no* accounting for taste.「蓼(たで)食う虫も好き好き」)。

[72] **get across:** get A across (または get across A) (to B)「A (考えなど)を(B (人)に)伝える[理解させる]」(e.g. I sometimes find it hard to *get* my ideas *across* to him.)。

[73] **drawing on ...:** draw on ... は「…(知識や経験)を利用する[に頼る]」(2章 [163])。

[74] **composite** [kəmpázɪt; kómpəzɪt]:「合成の」。ここでは complex の言い換えで,いくつかの prepackaged expressions が組み合わされているという意味。

[78] **the autonomy** [ɔːtánəmi] **thesis** [θíːsɪs]:「(統語論)自律性テーゼ」。

[79] **a prominent theory in the holistic / integrated camp:** R. W. Langacker [lǽnəkər] (1942– )の創始した cognitive grammar「認知文法」のこと。

[80] **the symbolic view of grammar:** symbol (> symbolic) にはいくつかの異なる意味があるが,ここでは(音声)形式とそれが表す意味の組み合わせからなる「記号」のこと。Notecard 7 などで見るように,文法の知識を構成する単位が(大多数の単語と同じく)すべて何らかの意味を担っている,という考え方。

[83] **putting forward:** put forward ... (または put ... forward) は「…(理論や計画)を提案[提出]する」(cf. advance a new theory)。

[85] **semantics (or phonology, for that matter):** semantics [səmǽntɪks]「意味論」とは,言語表現の意味を扱う言語学の部門または言語表現の意味についての(暗黙の)知識を指す。phonology [fənáləʤi]「音韻論」とは,言語音の分布や変化についての規則またはその知識を研究する分野,またはそれに関する理論。for that matter「もっと言えば」「それを言うなら」は直前の発言にさらに何かを付け加える合図となる表現。

[86] **ludicrous** [lúːdɪkrəs]:「ばかげた」「理不尽な」。

[87] **No sensible linguist would deny that ...:**「まともな言語学者なら…ということを否定したりなどしないであろう」。主語に仮定の意味内容が含まれた仮定法過去の文 (cf. I *wouldn't* worry about it.)。sensible は「分別[まともな判断力]のある」(cf. a *sensible* idea)。

[89] **isolate:** ここでは(「孤立させる」ではなく)「分離する」「それだけを取り出す」。

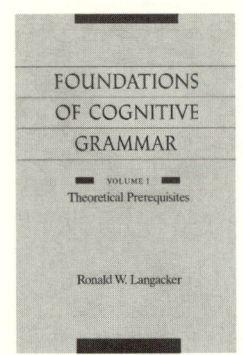

Ronald W. Langacker, *Foundations of Cognitive Grammar*

tic component, a purely formal level of representation organized independently of semantic factors.

What might have been behind the postulation of this thesis is the attitude toward meaning taken by Chomsky before he launched his theory of generative grammar. You'll see why this might be the case if you look at Notecard 4. Before going on to find out what the symbolic view of grammar is all about, let's pause to take a look at Notecards 5 and 6 and see how Chomsky himself formulates the autonomy thesis.

Finally, let's move on to the symbolic view of grammar, turning to Notecard 7 to see how Ronald W. Langacker, one of its keenest proponents, formulates it. Not surprisingly, as a radical alternative to the autonomy thesis, the symbolic view emerges naturally from an attitude toward meaning diametrically opposed to Chomsky's quoted above. As you can see in Notecards 8 and 9, Langacker is quite explicit about the role meaning is to play in linguistics and the way it is to be reflected in how one conceives of grammar.

The dispute over the nature of linguistic knowledge has been going on for decades and very few scholars expect it to be settled any time soon. But since language is an essential part of what makes our species what it is, this seemingly unfortunate state of affairs could be taken to mean that there remains a challenging research agenda awaiting YOU, one that will be of utmost importance if you want to figure out what it means to be human.

|  | 生成文法 | 認知言語学 |
|---|---|---|
| 言語の知識全体の<br>位置づけをめぐって | モジュール的<br>言語観<br><br>ノートカード1 | 統合的<br>言語観<br><br>ノートカード2 |
| 言語の知識の内部構造<br>(文法と意味の関係)を<br>めぐって | 統語論(≒文法)の<br>(意味からの)自律性<br><br>ノートカード3, 5, 6 | 記号(=音声と意味の組み<br>合わせ)現象としての文法<br><br>ノートカード7, 8, 9 |

生成文法と認知言語学の基本的差異

- [92] **behind the postulation:** この場合の behind...「…の背後にある」とは「…の根底にある」「…の(隠れた)理由となる」といった意味 (e.g. What's the idea *behind* this new program?)。postulation < postulate [pástʃəlèit] は「(理論などの前提として)措定する」「公準(postulate [pástʃəlɪt])として立てる」。
- [93] **launched:** launch は(「(船を)進水させる」「(ロケットなどを)発射する」の他に)このように「(理論などを)世に問う,創始する」という意味で用いられることもある。
- [95] **what . . . is all about:** what . . . is (all) about は「…の本質(はどこにあるのか)」といった意味(all は強調)でよく用いられる表現(2章 [153], 8章 [15]) (cf. Teaching *is about* helping students broaden their horizons.)。
- [97] **formulates:**「定式化する」だが,ここでは「自分のことばで表現する」という感じ。
- [103] **diametrically opposed to . . . :**「…と正反対」と言う場合の決まった組み合わせ。
- [108] **very few . . . any time soon:** any time soon は否定的な意味の表現(この場合は very few)と組み合わせて「当分は…することはない」という意味を表すのによく用いられる (e.g. I'm afraid the problem won't go away *any time soon*.)。
- [111] **a challenging research agenda:**「取り組む価値のある研究分野」。challenging は「困難であるがそれゆえに(能力を試されるという意味で)やりがいのある」。agenda は本来「議事」(e.g. the first item on the *agenda*「第一議題」)だが,ここでは「これから取り組もうと考えている問題やテーマ」といった感じ。
- [112] **of utmost importance:**「この上なく重要な」と言う場合によく用いられる決まった組み合わせのひとつ (cf. *of* primary *importance*)。

# Language, Mind, and Grammar

## Notecards

---

**NOTECARD 1**  Chomsky (1991: 50–51)

The properties of the language faculty seem to be unique to humans in interesting respects and distinct from other subsystems of the mind/brain. The mind, then, is not a system of general intelligence, as has been assumed over a broad spectrum, including classical rationalism and empiricism and modern variants of empiricist thought including dominant tendencies in contemporary philosophy and cognitive science, in particular most of the AI literature, and in modern psychology, including a spectrum that ranges from Skinner to Piaget. Rather, the mind has distinct subsystems, such as the language faculty, a cognitive system, a system of knowledge.

This faculty, furthermore, is internally highly modularized, with separate subsystems of principles governing sound, meaning, structure and interpretation of linguistic expressions. These can be used, to a sufficient degree, in thought and its expression, and in specific language functions such as communication; language is not intrinsically a system of communication, nor is it the only system used for communication. The language faculty is based on fixed principles with limited options of parametric variation as the system is "tuned" to a specific environment.

[115]

[120]

[125]

[130]

---

**NOTECARD 2**  Tomasello (1995: 152)

It would seem reasonable to think of language as a mosaic of different skills — a new function made out of old parts, in Bates' (1979) terms — some of which may be specific to language (e.g. speech) but some of which may be the same skills as those children use in other domains of their cognitive and social cognitive development. As these skills are used repeatedly in concert for purposes of linguistic communication, they cohere into a more modularized functional domain.

Languages are cultural artifacts that differ radically among

[135]

[140]

- [114] **the language faculty:**「言語機能」。faculty はもともと心理学の用語。心（the mind）がいくつかの別個の（生得的な）「機能」または「能力」から構成されているという考え方における「機能」または「能力」を指す（cf. 4章 [71]）(e.g. the *faculty* of sight)。ここでの Chomsky の用語法における module や autonomous/distinct/separate subsystem と概念内容は同じと考えてよい。the language faculty は，linguistic competence, knowledge of language とも言い，人類に共通であると考えられているその初期状態（the initial state）に関する理論は「普遍文法（universal grammar, UG）」と呼ばれる。

- [118] **rationalism and empiricism:**「合理論[合理主義]」と「経験主義」。両者の決定的な違いは生得観念（innate ideas）の存在を認めるか否かにある。

- [121] **the AI literature:** AI は artificial intelligence「人工知能」の略。この場合の literature は「文献」。

- [122] **Skinner:** B(urrhus) F(rederic) Skinner (1904–90) はアメリカの行動主義（behaviorism）心理学者。行動主義は，Chomsky の生成文法登場以前にアメリカ言語学界の中心であった言語学派（American structuralism「アメリカ構造主義」）がその基盤としていた心理学の理論。Chomsky は，Skinner の著書 *Verbal Behavior*（1957年刊）に対する書評論文（1959年刊）で，行動主義に基づく言語研究を厳しく批判した。

- [122] **Piaget:** Jean Piaget (1896–1980) は発生的認識論（genetic epistemology）の提唱者として知られるスイスの発達心理学者（4章 [91]）。Piaget と Chomsky は 1975年にパリ近郊のロワイヨーモン（Royaumont）修道院での会議で直接論争を行った。その会議の模様は *Language and Learning: The Debate between Jean Piaget and Noam Chomsky*（邦訳『ことばの理論　学習の理論』）に記録されている。

- [125] **is internally highly modularized:**「内的にも高度にモジュール化されている」。内容はすぐ後の with 以下で説明されているが，ひとつのモジュールである言語機能がまたいくつかのモジュールから構成されているということ。

- [132] **fixed principles with limited options of parametric variation:** fixed principles はすべての自然言語に共通の原理を，parametric variation は言語間の差異を，それぞれ指すと考えればよい。parametric のもとになっている parameter [pərǽmətər]「パラメータ」は，この場合にはいくつかの値（選択肢）を取りうる可変部分のこと。

- [133] **a specific environment:**「（英語，日本語などの）特定の言語が使われている環境」。特定の環境に置かれるとパラメータの値が設定されて特定の言語の知識が生じると考えられている。

- [136] **a mosaic** [mouzéɪk] **of different skills:**「さまざまなスキルの寄せ集め」。すぐ後の a new function made out of old parts「古い（＝言語以外で用いられている）部分[部品]からなる新しい機能」はその言い換え。

- [142] **in concert** [kánsərt]:「一緒[一斉]に[協調して]（働く）」(cf. a *concerted* [kənsə́ːrtɪd] attack「一斉攻撃」)。

- [142] **they cohere into ...:** cohere into ... は「結合[凝集]して…になる」。a more modularized functional domain「よりモジュール化した機能領域」。全体で a new function made out of old parts と同じ内容を表している。

- [144] **cultural artifacts:**「（人間）文化の産物」。artifact（イギリス英語では artefact と綴るのが普通）は「（自然に生じたのではなく）人間が作ったもの」。言語をこのように捉える場合，言語に生物学的な基盤がある（人間という種だからこそ言語を生みだせた）ことが前提になっている（人類に共通であると同時に人類にのみ見られる文化にも当然生物学的な基盤があると考えられている）ことにも注意。

different cultures, and languages change in important ways as the communicative needs of their speakers evolve over time. In addition, many of the subcompetencies of language acquisition would seem to be shared with other domains of cognition: competence with words depends on general processes of symbol formation and categorization; competence with syntax depends on general processes of symbol formation, categorization, and hierarchical organization; and competence with pragmatics depends on general skills of social interaction and communication. And, of course, the whole point of language — its semantic dimension — is for individuals to convey to one another something of the experiences they have nonlinguistically.

---

NOTECARD 3                          Huddleston (1976: 33)

Syntax is independent from semantics and phonology, in the sense that syntactic units, categories, functions are not identifiable in semantic or phonological terms.

---

NOTECARD 4                           Chomsky (1955: 141)

Meaning is a notoriously difficult notion to pin down. If it can be shown that meaning and related notions do play a central role in linguistic analysis, then its results and conclusions become subject to all of the doubts and obscurities that plague the study of meaning, and a serious blow is struck at the foundations of linguistic theory.

---

NOTECARD 5                            Chomsky (1977: 57)

It seems to me fair to conclude that although there are, no doubt, systematic form-meaning connections, nevertheless the theory of formal grammar has an internal integrity and has its distinct structures and properties. It seems to me reasonable to adopt the working hypothesis that the structures of formal grammar are generated independently, and that these structures are associated with semantic interpretations by principles and rules of a broader semiotic theory.

- [149] **symbol formation:**「記号の形成」。symbol については [80] の注を参照。
- [150] **categorization:**「カテゴリー化」。categorize「カテゴリー化する」とは「(事物を)分類する」こと (category は分類項目)。単語の多くは (もの，行為，属性などの) カテゴリーの名前であると考えられる。
- [152] **hierarchical** [hàɪərɑ́ːrkɪkəl] **organization:**「階層的な構造化」。多くの文は階層構造をもつ (hierarchically organized)——構成要素(例えば語)がただ並列されているのではなく，いくつかの構成要素がまとまりをなし，そのようなまとまり同士が次々に結合してより大きなまとまりが生じる，という形で組み立てられている——と考えられる。ここでの主張は，syntax「統語論」に特徴的なそのような構造化 (e.g. ((AB) (C (DE)))) は文の組み立て方 (syntax「統語論」に相当) などの言語の知識以外の認知領域にも見られる一般的なプロセスである，ということ。
- [153] **pragmatics** [præɡmǽtɪks]:「語用論」。特定のコンテクストで用いられた言語表現はその本来の意味を越えたメッセージを伝達する(例えば，電話で「田中さんいらっしゃいますか?」と言えば，「田中さんがいれば電話口に呼び出してほしい」という意味に解釈される)のが普通である。「語用論」はそのようなメッセージが生成される仕組みを解明する言語学の部門またはそうした仕組みについての(暗黙の)知識を指す用語。
- [154] **And, of course, the whole point of language . . . :** 本文 [130] の Chomsky の発言と対照的な主張であることに注意。
- [160] **syntactic units, categories, functions:** 統語論の(暗黙の)知識を構成する単位や原理。例えば，名詞，動詞などの文法カテゴリー(品詞)，主語などの文法関係。こうした単位や原理を意味や音声に基づいて定義することは不可能である(統語論は意味と音声から自律した知識の領域を構成している)というのがこの引用の趣旨。
- [163] **pin down:**「明確にする」「正確に把握する」(e.g. The police are trying to *pin down* the cause of the multiple pileup.)。
- [166] **become subject to . . . :**「…にさらされることになる」(cf. The program content *is subject to* change without notice.)。
- [166] **plague** [pleɪɡ]:「つきまとう」。
- [171] **the theory of formal grammar has . . . :** formal grammar (ここでは syntax に相当) の formal (< form) は semantic (< semantics = meaning) と対比させられていると考えればよい。has 以下が syntax の semantics からの自律性の内容を具体的に述べていることに注意。has an internal integrity「内的な統合性をもつ」と has its distinct structures and properties「独自の構造と特性をもつ」は同じことの別の観点からの表現。
- [174] **the working hypothesis:**「作業仮説」。実際に正しいかどうかは別にして，一応妥当であると考えることにより，研究を効率的に進めるための仮説。
- [177] **a broader semiotic** [semiátɪk] **theory:** broader は言語以外の記号現象(あるものが別の何かを表すという現象)にも適用されるという意味合い。semiotic theory は「記号理論」(cf. semiotics「記号論」/ semiosis「記号現象」)。言語表現に意味を与えるのは formal grammar の原理や規則とは別個の，より一般的な(言語の知識に特有ではない)原理や規則である，ということ。

> **NOTECARD 6**                   Chomsky (1979: 138–9)
>
> I was skeptical about the general belief that syntax was based on semantic generalizations. Many structural linguists and many philosophers — Quine, for example — claimed that grammatical concepts must be defined on the basis of semantic notions. They also identified the concept of grammaticality with the notion of meaningfulness. But it seemed to me that a grammatical sentence may not have any literal meaning. Furthermore, I tried to show that every clear formulation of a hypothesis concerning the alleged necessity to define syntactic notions in semantic terms led to incorrect results. Thinking about these questions led to what was later termed the hypothesis of autonomy of syntax. The viewpoint of this work was that, given a linguistic theory, the concepts of grammar are constructed (so it seems) on the basis of primitive notions that are not semantic (where the grammar contains the phonology and syntax), but that the linguistic theory itself must be chosen so as to provide the best possible explanation of semantic phenomena, as well as others.

> **NOTECARD 7**                   Langacker (1991: 516)
>
> Grammar is inherently symbolic; only units with both semantic and phonological import are required for its proper characterization.

> **NOTECARD 8**                   Langacker (1987: 12)
>
> Meaning is what language is all about; the analyst who ignores it to concentrate solely on matters of form severely impoverishes the natural and necessary subject matter of the discipline and ultimately distorts the character of the phenomena described. But it is not enough to agree that meaning is important if this results, say, merely in positing a separate semantic "component," treating grammar separately as an autonomous entity. I contend that grammar itself, i.e. patterns for grouping morphemes into progressively larger configurations, is inherently symbolic and hence meaningful. Thus it makes no more sense to posit separate grammatical and semantic components than it does to divide a dictionary into

- [180] **structural linguists:**「構造主義の言語学者」。言語学における構造主義 (structuralism) はスイスの言語学者 Ferdinand de Saussure (1857–1913) によって創始されたとされる理論で，その後いくつかの学派に分かれてそれぞれ独自の展開を見せた。そのひとつが注 [122] のアメリカ構造主義(言語学)。

- [181] **Quine:** Willard Van Orman Quine (1908–2000)。論理学，分析哲学，言語哲学，科学哲学など広い分野にわたって優れた業績（*Word and Object*『ことばと対象』，*From a Logical Point of View*『論理的観点から』等々)を残し，長年ハーヴァード大学教授を務めた 20 世紀アメリカを代表する哲学者。

- [183] **They also identified ... :** identify A with B は「A イコール B である[A は B と等しい]と考える」。

- [183] **the concept of grammaticality:** この場合の grammaticality「文法性」，grammatical「文法的」とは grammatical well-formedness「文法的適格性」，grammatically well-formed「文法的に適格」のことで，文法規則に従っている(違反していない)という特性。

- [184] **the notion of meaningfulness:** meaningfulness「有意味性」とは semantic well-formedness「意味的適格性」のことで，要するに言語表現が意味をなす (make sense) という特性。

- [185] **a grammatical sentence may not have any literal meaning:**「文法的には適格な文であっても字義どおりには意味をなさない場合がある」。そのような文の例として Chomsky が挙げた "Colorless green ideas sleep furiously." (Chomsky によると Revolutionary new ideas appear infrequently. と文法構造は同一)は言語学の世界で最も有名な例文のひとつ。literal meaning と言っているのは figurative「比喩的」な意味を除外して考えたいため。

- [192] **primitive notions:**「原始概念」。他の概念を定義するために用いられることはあってもそれ自体は定義の対象にならない(それ以上基本的な概念に還元できない)概念。

- [198] **Grammar is inherently symbolic:** 次の文で説明されているように，一種の記号である(意味と音韻の両面をもつ)ことが文法(の知識)を構成する単位すべての本質であるということ。inherently は「本来[内在]的に」(cf. accidentally)。本文 [211] [222] [227] 等の symbolic も同じ意味(「象徴的」という意味ではないことに注意)。

- [199] **semantic and phonological import:** 本文 [226] の semantic and phonological content と同じと考えてよい。

- [199] **its proper characterization:** its は grammar を指す。

- [204] **impoverishes:** impoverish [ɪmpávərɪʃ] は「貧しいものにする」「質を損なう」(cf. poverty)。

- [204] **the natural and necessary subject matter of the discipline:** 言語のこと。subject matter は「主題」「素材」。the discipline はここでは linguistics を指す (cf. interdisciplinary)。

- [206] **But it is not enough ... :**（意味から）自律した文法はそのままにしておいて（言語理論に）単に意味「部門」を付け加えたのでは，言語の本質が意味（の表出）にあることを十分に認識したことにならない，ということ。なお，この場合の say は「例えば」。

- [210] **morphemes:** morpheme [mɔ́ːrfiːm]「形態素」は意味をもつ最小の単位(いわゆる単語の多くは複数の形態素からなる)。

- [210] **larger configurations:**「より大きな形態[構成体]」。複数の有意味な要素によって構成された表現（複合語，句，文など)。

- [211] **Thus it makes no more sense ... :** to divide 以下のことをするのが意味をなさないのは当然であるが，to posit 以下のことをするのも意味をなさない点ではそれと同断である，ということ (cf. She is *no less* intelligent *than* her brother.)。

two components, one listing lexical forms and the other listing lexical meanings. Grammar is simply the structuring and symbolization of semantic content; for a linguistic theory to be regarded as natural and illuminating, it must handle meaning organically rather than prosthetically.

### NOTECARD 9 — Langacker (1988: 46–7)

Languages provide for the symbolization of ideas by observable sequences of sounds. We must therefore acknowledge in some fashion the reality of meanings, sounds, and the symbolic associations between them. The status of a distinct and autonomous domain of "grammar" is on the face of it less secure, for it is hard to envisage a realm of "grammatical content" analogous to semantic and phonological content. Undeniably, there are conventional patterns for the assembly of complex symbolic expressions out of simpler ones, and "grammar" is the obvious term for referring to them. But the reality of "grammar," so defined, does not itself establish the character of the elements that specify these patterns. In particular, it leaves open the possibility that these elements are themselves symbolic in nature, schematic units which embody the commonality of well-formed symbolic expressions and serve as templates for the computation of novel instantiations. What could be more natural and straightforward? If workable, this approach affords a coherent and integrated view of the various facets of linguistic organization. I consider it a curious anomaly in the history of our discipline that this natural conception must be explained and defended while the autonomy thesis — with all its unnaturalness and conceptual obfuscation — commands widespread and often unquestioning allegiance.

[214] **lexical forms . . . lexical meanings:** lexical form, lexical meaning はそれぞれ「語形」，「語義」にほぼ相当する。lexical < lexicon [léksɪkàn]「語彙」「辞書」（＝dictionary, vocabulary）。lexicon は [69] の prepackaged expressions（専門用語では lexemes「語彙素」または lexical items「語彙項目」）の集合体。lexicon の構成要素はいわゆる「語」だけではないため，word form と word meaning を避けて lexical form と lexical meaning を用いている。

[215] **the structuring and symbolization of semantic content:** structuring of semantic content「意味内容の構造化」とは，言語表現の対象となるものや事態に特定の捉え方を適用すること。認知文法では，同じものや事態を表すのに用いることのできる複数の語彙項目（e.g.「上り坂」「下り坂」）や文法形式（e.g. The Chinese invented gunpowder. / Gunpowder was invented by the Chinese.）はそうしたものや事態に対する異なる捉え方を表していると考えられている。

[217] **illuminating:**「ものごとの本質を照らし出す」「本質の解明に役立つ」（cf. a *revealing* account of what it was like to live in Tokyo during the 1950s）。

[218] **organically rather than prosthetically:** organically「有機体的に」とは「（言語の）本質の一面として」とか as an integral part (of language) という感じ。prosthetically (cf. prosthesis「人工的補充物」) はその反対に「取ってつけたように」。

[220] **Languages provide for . . . :** Languages make it possible for ideas to be symbolized by observable sequences of sounds. この場合の provide for . . . は「…を可能にする」。

[224] **on the face of it:**「一見したところでは」。「事実かどうかは別にして」という含みがある。

[225] **it is hard to envisage** [ɪnvízɪdʒ] **. . . :** envisage は「思い描く」（cf. envision）。全体として，言語の知識の中に「意味の領域」と「音韻の領域」は明らかに実在するが，それらから独立した「文法の領域」の実在性は自明とは言えない，ということ。

[227] **patterns for the assembly of . . . out of simpler ones:** Notecard 8 の "patterns for grouping morphemes into progressively larger configurations" と同じ内容。

[231] **In particular . . . :** 単語などを組み合わせて句や文を作るパターンとしての文法は間違いなく実在するけれども，それらのパターン（およびその構成要素）自体が（抽象的な）記号である（音韻と意味の両面を持っている）という可能性がある（ので音韻と意味の領域から自律した文法の領域が実在すると考えなければならないわけではない），という趣旨。

[233] **schematic units . . . :** schematic [skɪmǽtɪk] は specific の反意語として用いられている。well-formed symbolic expressions「形式と意味の両面からなる適格な表現」とは普通の具体的な文などのこと。schematic units とは複数のそうした表現から抽出された共通のパターン（例えば二重目的語構文）のこと。serve as 以下は，（そのようなパターンが）それらに語句を当てはめることにより新しい具体的な文など（novel instantiations）を作り出すこと（computation）を可能にする「鋳型」「枠組み」（templates [témpləts]）として機能する，ということ。

[236] **workable:**「実行可能な」（cf. if this approach can be made to *work*）。

[238] **a curious anomaly:**「奇妙な［興味をそそる］変則性」（8章本文 [45]）（cf. I'm *curious* to know what makes that guy tick.）。

[241] **obfuscation:** < obfuscate [ábfəskèɪt]:「（意図的に）明確にしない，理解し難くする」。

[241] **commands . . . unquestioning allegiance:** この場合の command は「（支持や尊敬を当然のこととして）集める，受ける」（e.g. She *commands* a great deal of professional respect.）。unquestioning は「疑問をいだかない」「確固たる」（cf. 2章 [138], 8章 [11]）。allegiance [əlíːdʒəns] は「忠誠」（e.g. pledge *allegiance* to . . .「…に忠誠を誓う」）。

# 6
# LIFE

## Introduction
### Takashi Ikegami

Almost 20 years have passed since Christopher G. Langton launched the new science paradigm called Artificial Life. The aim of "Alife" research is to propose a new way of understanding living states. "What is life?" has been, and still is, a great mystery among scientists. It still isn't clear what distinguishes living from non-living states. As Langton explains in the first of the readings below, artificial life tries to attack the question in a new way, by engaging with life not as we see it but "as it could be." The study of artificial life is looking for the answer not in the real physical world but in a virtual world, a world based on dynamics and computation.

Before moving on to the main texts for this session, I'd like to introduce two fascinating examples of artificial life studies. The first study, created by Thomas S. Ray and called Tierra, involves the simulated evolution, inside a computer, of self-reproducing programs. Each program is a set of instructions like a DNA string. The basic function of the program is to copy the entire instruction set into another location after seeking out an empty space. Two other important operations are the death of the program and random mutation. As a metaphor for a death state, any program has a slight chance of being removed from the space. And programs can also change their instruction code or vary the execution order of their operations as a metaphor for mutation. After setting up the environment, all we have to do is simply observe the evolution of the programs! Interestingly, parasite programs are always emerging and occupying space. Those programs use the instruction sets of other programs to reproduce themselves. As evolution proceeds, those parasites are removed by more sophisticated parasites. Finally, a set of mutually cooperative parasite programs emerges, made up

[1] **Christopher G. Langton:** アメリカのコンピュータ・サイエンティスト。「人工生命」という研究分野の創始者であり、「人工生命」という言葉の考案者。

[1] **launched the new science paradigm:** launch は「(船を)進水させる」、「(ロケットなどを)発射する」という意味が基本だが、このように「事業や活動を開始[創始]する」と言う場合にもよく用いられる (e.g. The Metropolitan Police have *launched* a thorough investigation into this incident.)。この場合の paradigm [pǽrədàim] は「特定の理論的枠組み(によるものの見方)」といった意味 (cf. a *paradigm* shift)。

[7] **by engaging with . . . :** engage with . . . は「…に取り組む」(e.g. This article *engages* with the hotly debated issue of making English a second official language in Japan.)。

[7] **life not as we see it but "as it could be":** as は Japan as we know it「われわれの知っている日本」や Earth as (it is) seen from Mars「火星から見た地球」のような場合の as と同じ用法(4章 [94])。"as it could be" は Langton の文章からの引用。

[10] **dynamics:** 日本語でもダイナミクスというが、一般に時間発展するプロセスのことをいう。

[13] **Tierra:** アメリカの進化生物学者 Thomas S. Ray (オクラホマ大学動物学教授・コンピュータ・サイエンス特任教授)が開発した仮想コンピュータシステムであり、コンピュータ上に創造されたデジタル生態系の名。Tierra とはスペイン語で「地球」を意味する。

[18] **random mutation:** 突然変異。遺伝子に生じる主に偶発的な要因による塩基の置換や欠損など。ここでは人工生命の遺伝子であるビット列(0 と 1 の配列)に拡張して用いている。

[21] **instruction code:** 人工生命がどのように振る舞うかを決定するプログラム。それは生命の遺伝子に対応する。

[21] **vary the execution order of . . . :**「…を実行する順序を変える」(cf. This project might be difficult to *execute*.)。

[24] **parasite programs:** 寄生するプログラム。別の親プログラムに寄生して増殖するプログラムを指す。

of what Ray calls "social parasites." All these processes occur in an autonomous way without any help from us. Isn't this like a life system? Ray has now extended his Tierra world so that the programs can immigrate into other memory spaces using the internet. This net-wired Tierra may eventually develop new species (programs) that we can't observe in a single niche (memory space).

The second example is Karl Sims' Evolving Virtual Creatures. Sims simulated the structure of motion of virtual creatures in a 3-dimensional virtual physical world. This is different to Tierra in that the creatures don't reproduce but can physically move around. Each creature is constructed as a collection of rigid body parts, e.g. solid 3-dimensional cubes of various shapes. Using the internal logical gate network as a neural circuit, creatures can hit, kick, turn round or jump using their body parts. The logical gate network and the body shape together determine how a creature can move around. Sims evolved the gate network and the shape using the genetic algorithm (GA) explained in the extract from Jeff Elman's article that is included in the main text for this session. As the evolution proceeds, the creatures acquire more elegant and sophisticated motion styles. Surprisingly, the motion styles found in the virtual water are quite similar to what we actually see in real water! Sims went on further to see how creatures develop to reach a "food" place in some wise ways. When two virtual creatures are competing for food, one creature can get the food by blocking the other creature's reaching action. This was the Alife version of the robot-contest ("robocon"), which has become a gateway to success in robotics studies. These are only two out of many interesting experiments. Please look into other artificial creatures if you are interested in this topic, and if possible try to breed one of them! Understanding life is not to analyze it but to synthesize it! This is the message from artificial life studies.

[34] **a single niche:** niche はここでは生態学的なニッチ (ecological niche) を指す (4 章 [128])。生態学的な関係(例えば，食う食われるの関係)が多層に絡み合っているとき，その関係の場所を指す。

[35] **Karl Sims' Evolving Virtual Creatures:** Karl Sims は，アメリカの CG プログラマー，CG アーティスト。大学時代に生物学を専攻していた彼の作品は，生物進化のコンピュータ上での実験のような趣をもっている。"Evolving Virtual Creatures" は *Computer Graphics* (Siggraph '94 Proceedings), July 1994, pp. 15–22 に掲載された論文である。実際の作品 Evolved Virtual Creatures (1994) は，口絵を参照。

[40] **the internal logical gate network:** 論理ゲートとは，AND や OR などのビット値に対する演算規則のことである。これを組み合わせて論理ゲートのネットワークを内部的につくりあげること。

[41] **a neural circuit:** 神経回路。ここでは実際の神経回路を模してつくった形式的なネットワークのこと。

[44] **the genetic algorithm（GA）:**「遺伝的アルゴリズム」。生物進化を模してコンピュータ上で人工的に機能や形質を進化させるためのアルゴリズム。人工生命の研究において形態進化などでよく用いられる。

[45] **Jeff Elman:** アメリカ，カリフォルニア大学サンディエゴ校教授。専攻は認知科学。特に神経ネットワークを使った自然言語の文法学習の研究が著名。

[54] **a gateway to success:** a gateway to ... は本来「…への入口[通路]」だが，このように比喩的に用いられることも多い。

# The Artificial Life Workshop

## Christopher G. Langton

In September 1987, the first workshop on Artificial Life was held at the Los Alamos National Laboratory. Jointly sponsored by the Center for Nonlinear Studies, the Santa Fe Institute, and Apple Computer, Inc., the workshop brought together 160 computer scientists, biologists, physicists, anthropologists, and other assorted "-ists," all of whom shared a common interest in the simulation and synthesis of living systems.

During five intense days, we saw a wide variety of models of living systems, including mathematical models for the origin of life, self-reproducing automata, computer programs using the mechanisms of Darwinian evolution to produce co-adapted ecosystems, simulations of flocking birds and schooling fish, the growth and development of artificial plants, and much, much more.

The workshop itself grew out of my frustration with the fragmented nature of the literature on biological modeling and simulation. For years I had prowled around libraries, sifted through computer-search results, and haunted bookstores, trying to get an overview of a field which I sensed existed but which did not seem to have any coherence or unity. Instead, I kept literally stumbling over interesting work almost by accident, often published in obscure journals if published at all.

Thus, the primary goal of the first workshop on Artificial Life was to see what was out there, and to present as many different methodological approaches as possible within a receptive and unbiased atmosphere. Although many of the participants were already familiar with some of the models, I think it is safe to say that many of the models and systems presented were new to most of us, and that some of the models were genuinely quite surprising to everybody.

Throughout the workshop, there was a growing sense of excitement and camaraderie — even profound relief — as previously isolated research efforts were opened up to one another for the first time. It quickly became apparent that despite the isolation we had all experienced a remarkably similar set of problems, frustrations, successes, doubts, and visions. Even more exciting was that, as the

[60] **the first workshop:** この場合の workshop は「研究(集)会」(e.g. a *workshop on* cultural diversity)。

[61] **the Los Alamos National Laboratory:** アメリカのニューメキシコ州ロスアラモスにあるロスアラモス国立研究所は，1943年に設立され，原子爆弾が製造された場所として名高い。その後も科学技術開発の国際的な地位を保っている。

[62] **the Center for Nonlinear Studies:** 非線形研究センターは，ロスアラモス国立研究所に属する研究機関(1980年設立)。ラングトンは，1986年，この研究所に招かれ，人工生命の研究を開始した。Nonlinear Studies (非線形の研究)とは，一般に解析的に解くことのできない方程式やモデルを研究すること。

[62] **the Santa Fe Institute:** サンタフェ研究所は，1984年，アメリカのニューメキシコ州サンタフェに設立された複雑系研究のメッカ。世界的な複雑系研究者の交流する場としての機能をもっている。

[67] **a wide variety of ...:**「多種多様な…」と言う場合によく用いられる表現のひとつ。本文[114]の a wide range of ... も頻出の組み合わせ。

[69] **self-reproducing automata:** 生命の基本のひとつである自己複製を可能とするオートマトン(離散的な状態をもち，離散的な時間と空間の発展規則にしたがうシステム)のことをいう。あるパターンが外からの助けを借りずに自律的にコピーされる。

[70] **co-adapted ecosystems:** お互いに適応しあって進む生態系のこと。

[71] **flocking birds and schooling fish:**「群れをなす鳥や魚」(cf. *a flock of birds*, *a school of fish*)。

[73] **the fragmented nature of the literature:** この場合の literature は「文献」。全体として「文献がいろいろなところに分散していて見つけにくいこと」という意味。

[75] **I had prowled around ...:** prowl around ... は「(何かを求めて)…をさまよい歩く」。

[75] **sifted through ...:** sift through ... は「…(大量のデータなど)の中を探しまわる」(cf. I *rummaged through* the drawers.)。

[77] **a field which I sensed existed:**「存在すると感じていた分野」。which は existed の主語に相当することに注意 (cf. Over the years I have come across languages (*which*) I hadn't even known existed.)。「感じ取る」「察知する」という意味の動詞 sense は，[95]のように目的語として名詞句を取る他に，このように that 節を伴って用いられることも多い (e.g. I immediately *sensed that* something was wrong.)。

[78] **stumbling over ...:** stumble over ... は，文字通りには「…につまずく」だが，ここでは「…を偶然(思いがけないところで)見つける」(cf. I finally *tumbled to* what they were up to.)。

[80] **obscure journals:** obscure は「無名の」。journal は「定期的に刊行される学術誌」。

[80] **if published at all:**「(公表されないことが多いが)公表されていたとしても」。

[82] **to see what was out there:** out there はよく用いられる組み合わせで，いくつかの区別できる意味を表すが，ここでは「世の中(のどこか)に」といった感じ (cf. There are still many hard problems *out there* we don't know how to solve.)。

[83] **a receptive and unbiased atmosphere:** receptive は「新しい考えなどを受け入れる姿勢のある」(e.g. a *receptive* audience)。unbiased は「偏見のない」。

[85] **it is safe to say ...:**「…と言っても差し支えない」と言う場合の決まり文句 (cf. This warning can be *safely* ignored.)。

[89] **there was a growing sense of ...:**「…の気分が高まっていった」。英語らしい表現法 (cf. *There is growing concern* about avian flu.)。

[90] **camaraderie** [kæ̀məráːdəri]:「仲間意識」(cf. He has developed *rapport* with his students.)。

workshop progressed, one could sense an emerging consensus among the participants — a slowly dawning collective realization — of the "essence" of Artificial Life. Although I think that none of us could have put it into words at the time, I think that many of us went away from that tumultuous interchange of ideas with a very similar vision.

Perhaps, however, the most fundamental idea to emerge at the workshop was the following: Artificial systems which exhibit life-like behaviors are worthy of investigation on their own rights, whether or not we think that the processes that they mimic have played a role in the development or mechanics of life as we know it to be. Such systems can help us expand our understanding of life as it could be. By allowing us to view the life that has evolved here on Earth in the larger context of *possible* life, we may begin to derive a truly general theoretical biology capable of making universal statements about life wherever it may be found and whatever it may be made of.

# Artificial Life

## Jeff Elman

### THE HARDEST KIND OF INTELLIGENCE: STAYING ALIVE!

In 1987, a workshop (the first of what would become a series) was held at Los Alamos National Laboratory. Researchers from a wide range of disciplines met to exchange views on what was becoming a theme of growing interest in a number of different scientific communities: Artificial Life, or Alife, as it is more popularly known. Although the methods and specific goals of the different subcommunities varied, there were also a number of perspectives which were shared. One idea was captured in Alife researcher Rik Belew's comment that "the smartest dumb thing anything can do is to stay alive." This accorded with ideas that had been developed by MIT roboticist Rodney Brooks. Brooks pointed out that the bulk of evolution had been spent getting organisms to the stage where they had useful sensory and motor systems; phenomena such as tool use, agriculture, literature, and calculus represent only the most

[95] **sense an emerging consensus among the participants:**「参加者の間で意見の一致が形成されつつあるのを感じ取る」。

[96] **dawning:** この場合 emerging の言い換え (cf. It suddenly *dawned* on me that she had known the truth all along.)。

[98] **many of us went away . . . :**「興奮しながら意見を交換し合った結果，参加者の多くが別れる時にはとても似通った考えをもつに至っていた」ということ。tumultuous [t(j)u(:)mʌ́ltʃuəs] は「騒々しい」(cf. tumult [t(j)úːmʌlt]「大騒ぎ」「喧噪」)。

[103] **are worthy of investigation on their own rights:**「(既知の生命と関係があってもなくても) それ自体研究に値する」。ここでは on their own rights となっているが，in their own rights の方が普通 (e.g. This is a phenomenon that may merit examination *in its own right*.)。

[120] **Rik Belew:** アメリカのカリフォルニア大学サンディエゴ校教授。専攻は認知科学。

[121] **the smartest dumb thing:** smart はアメリカ英語ではこのように「賢い」「利口な」という意味で用いられるのが最も一般的。the smartest dumb thing とは「もっとも賢い愚鈍なこと」。存在しつづけるということは，どんな生き物にも可能な単純な行為ではあるが，人工生命に関してはその生きつづけることがとても大変だということ。

[122] **This accorded with . . . :**「これは…と一致[合致]した」(cf. be in accord with . . . )。

[123] **Rodney Brooks:** アメリカのマサチューセッツ工科大学にあるコンピュータ・サイエンスおよび人工知能研究所の所長。専攻はロボット工学。

[123] **the bulk of evolution:** the bulk of . . . は「…の大部分[大半]」。

[124] **had been spent . . . :** spend + 時間を表す語句 + -ing は非常によく用いられるパターンなので，自分でも使えるようにしておきたい (e.g. You mean you *spend most of your waking hours doing something you don't really want to do?*)。

[124] **organisms:** organism(s) は「生物」という意味でよく用いられる語 (cf. a form of life / a life form / Is there life on Mars?)。

[125] **sensory and motor systems:**「感覚と運動のシステム」(cf. sensorimotor systems)。

[126] **calculus** [kǽlkjələs]:「微積分学」。

[126] **represent only the most recent few "seconds" . . . :**「進化という時計の一番最近のほんの数「秒」の間に起こったことにすぎない」。"seconds" となっているのは，進化を時計に喩えた場合の「秒」であることを示すため。

recent few "seconds" in the evolutionary clock. Brooks inferred from this that one should therefore concentrate on the hard job of building systems which have sound basic sensorimotor capacities; the rest, he suggested, would come quickly after that.

## EMERGENTISM

A central insight which underlies much of the work in Alife is the notion of emergentism: many systems have behaviors — "emergent properties" — which result from the collective behavior of the system's components rather than from the action of any single component. Furthermore, these behaviors are often unanticipated (and in the case of artificial systems, unplanned or unprogrammed). Examples of emergentism abound in nature. Indeed, our very bodies are a compelling example. Our 100 trillion or so cells interact in complex ways to produce coherent activity; no single cell — or even single group of cells — predicts or accounts for the highest level behavior. Social organizations are another example. No matter how autocratic the social structure involved, complex interpersonal dynamics usually give rise to group behaviors which could not have been predicted in advance. Many Alife researchers have come to the conclusion that emergentism is a hallmark of life. Artificial systems which exhibit emergentism (particularly behaviors which in some way resemble those of biological lifeforms) are especially interesting.

One example of what seems like a very simple system that displays interesting emergentism comes from what are called cellular automata. These are systems which are built out of (usually) two-dimensional grids. At any given point in time, each cell in the grid can assume one of a small number of states; most simply, ON ("alive") or OFF ("dead"). At each tick of the clock, cells may change their state, according to a simple set of rules which usually depend on the states of a cell's eight immediate neighbors. A simple rule set which is the basis for a popular computer game (the "game of life") is the rule of "23/3": If a cell which is already alive has exactly 2 or 3 neighbors which are also alive, it survives to the next cycle; if a cell is not alive but has exactly 3 living neighbors, then it is "born"; in all other cases, a cell dies (or remains dead). If one seeds the initial population of cells with the pattern shown in Figure 1, something very striking happens. Over time, the pattern changes in a way which looks as if it is tumbling and deforming, and in the process glides down and to the right. This is called a "glider."

In addition to providing additional examples of what seem like

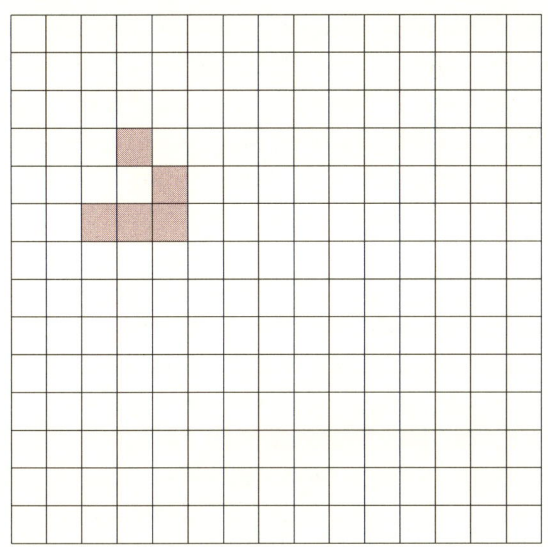

Figure 1: A grid for a cellular automaton. The cells in red are in an "on" state.

[127] **Brooks inferred from this:** infer [infɚ́:r] は「推論する」で，このように from ... で推論の材料になる事実を表すことが多い．

[129] **sound:**「しっかりした」「確固とした」(e.g. She's always capable of *sound* judgment.)．

[131] **Emergentism:** 創発主義．予測できない構造が生成することを人工生命の研究の目的にすること．

[132] **underlies much of the work:** underlie ... は「...の基盤[根底]にある」という意味の他動詞 (cf. one of the *underlying* assumptions of this study)．

[138] **abound in nature:** A abounds in B は「A が B に多い」(cf. This book *abounds with* thought-provoking ideas.)．

[139] **a compelling example:** compelling は「説得力のある」(cf. A *convincing* case has yet to be made for his theory.)．

[142] **No matter how autocratic ... :** autocratic [ɔ̀:təkrǽtik] は「専制[独裁]的な」(cf. autocracy [ɔ:tákrəsi]「専制[独裁](の行われている社会[国家])」)．このように no matter で始まる節では may be などの述語が省略されることが多い（cf. 14 章 [112]）(e.g. *No matter how* difficult the current situation (may be), we will eventually prevail.)．

[146] **a hallmark of life:** a hallmark of ... は「...の顕著な[際立った]特徴」(cf. This movie *has* [*bears*] *all the hallmarks of* the director's style.)．

[151] **cellular automata:**「セルラーオートマトン」とは，離散的な状態をもち，離散的な時間と空間の発展規則にしたがうモデルのこと．ここでいう cellular (細胞的) は空間が碁盤のマス目のようであることに対応している．

[152] **two-dimensional grids:** 碁盤のマス目のこと．

[153] **At any given point in time:**「任意の時点で」．「時点」に相当する英語の表現は point in time だが，「現時点で」の意味でよく用いられる at this point in time は間違った表現 (at this point, at the present time などと言うべき) であると考える人も多い．

[159] **the rule of "23/3":** コロン (:) 以下で説明してあるライフゲームの規則のこと．

[162] **one seeds ... :** seed はもともと「...(種など)をまく」の意味．ここでは「図 1 のようなパターンを持った細胞の最初の集団 (the initial population of cells) をセットする」ということ．遺伝学的用語としての population は「個体群」「集団」を意味する．

biological behavior (e.g., some patterns reproduce copies of themselves), cellular automata can be viewed as complex mathematical objects, and their properties have been extensively studied. More recent work by Melanie Mitchell and Randy Beer has also investigated ways in which these systems can solve computational problems.

## Evolution

Most artificial systems are built by some external being. Biological systems, however, evolve. Furthermore, biological change has both a random element, in the form of random genetic variations; and also a quasi-directed element, insofar as variants which are better adapted to their environment often produce more offspring, thus altering the genetic makeup of succeeding generations. This insight prompted computer scientist John Holland, in a 1975 monograph called *Adaptation in Natural and Artificial Systems*, to propose what he called the Genetic Algorithm, or GA. The GA was intended to capture some of the characteristics of natural evolution but in artificial systems.

Imagine, for example, that one has a problem which can be described in terms of a set of yes/no questions, and the goal is to find the right set of answers. The solution may be hard if there are interactions between the answers to particular questions; indeed, there may be multiple solutions, depending on how different questions are answered. The GA would model this by constructing an artificial "chromosome"; this is really just a vector of 1's and 0's, each bit position standing for the answer (1=yes, 0=no) to a different question. We begin with a population of randomly constructed chromosomes.

The GA has much in common with natural evolution. It is especially powerful when there are high-order interactions between the many different sub-parts to a problem. Although the original GA makes simplifying assumptions which are questionable (e.g., there is not the genotype/phenotype distinction found in nature), it is widely used in Alife, sometimes in conjunction with neural networks.

## Alife in the Future

The Alife approach is still fairly young, and much of the work has a preliminary character. As a corrective to previous modeling approaches, there is no question that the Alife perspective is valuable. The emphasis on emergentism, the role of the environment, the

- [171] **Melanie Mitchell:** アメリカのポートランド州立大学教授。専攻はコンピュータ・サイエンス。
- [171] **Randy Beer:** アメリカのケース・ウェスタン・リザーヴ大学教授。専攻はコンピュータ・サイエンス，認知科学，生物学。
- [178] **a quasi-directed element:** quasi- [kwéizai, -sai, kwάːzi, -si] は「…に準じる」，「（完全ではないが）ある程度は」といった意味を加える連結形。quasi-directed は「ランダムではなくある程度の方向性をもった」。
- [178] **insofar as . . . :** to the degree that . . . と同意。
- [178] **are better adapted to . . . :**「…によりよく適応している」。
- [179] **offspring:**「子孫」。単複同形であることに注意。
- [180] **the genetic makeup of succeeding generations:**「後続世代の遺伝子の構成」。この場合の makeup は「構成」「組み立て」(e.g. What is the ethnic *makeup* of this organization? / cf. This organization *is made up of* people from all walks of life.)。genetic makeup はよく用いられる組み合わせ。
- [181] **John Holland:** アメリカのミシガン大学教授。電子工学，コンピュータ・サイエンス，心理学を専攻。遺伝的アルゴリズムの父と称される。
- [183] **The GA was intended to capture:** be intended to . . . は「…することを目的としている」「…するためのものである」という意味でよく用いられる表現パターン (cf. This book *is designed to* help you improve your reading skills.)。
- [192] **chromosome:**「染色体」。
- [196] **The GA has much in common with . . . :**「GA には自然界の進化と共通点が多くある」。「…と共通点がある［ない，多い，少ない，ほとんどない］」などと言いたい場合に英語では have something [nothing/much/little] in common with . . . などを用いることが多い (5 章 [12]，11 章 [168]) (cf. I wonder *what* the two approaches *have in common*.)。
- [199] **simplifying assumptions which are questionable:** simplifying assumptions は「物事を実際よりも単純化した想定［前提］」（例えば，自然界には存在する genotype と phenotype の区別を無視すること）。questionable は「（真実性や妥当性に）疑問の余地がある，疑わしい」(cf. *There is no question that* . . .「…には疑問の余地はない」本文 [206] / No one has ever *questioned* her sincerity.)。
- [200] **the genotype/phenotype distinction:** 実際の生命では「遺伝型」と「表現型」は分かれている。しかし人工生命ではそうとは限らない。
- [201] **neural networks:**「神経ネットワーク」「神経回路網」。もちろんコンピュータ上に模擬的につくられた形式的なもの。
- [205] **As a corrective to . . . :**「…を矯正する考え方として」。

importance of an organism's body, the social nature of intelligence, and the perspective offered by evolution are notions which go well beyond Alife. Further, by trying to understand (as Chris Langton [210] has put it) life, not necessarily as it is, but as it could be, we broaden our notion of what counts as intelligent behavior. This expanded definition may in turn give us fresh ways of thinking about the behavior of more traditional (biological) lifeforms. But it is also clear that Alife has a long way to go. As is true of many modeling [215] frameworks, the bridge between the initial "toy" models and more complete and realistic models is a difficult one to cross.

- [209] **notions which go well beyond Alife:**「Alife をはるかに超えた領域にまで適用可能な概念」。
- [212] **what counts as intelligent behavior:** count as . . . は「…と見なされる」(cf. I doubt that my vote will *count for* much.)。
- [215] **Alife has a long way to go:** have a long way to go は「目標を達成するにはまだまだ時間や努力が必要である」という意味を表す決まった言い方 (cf. The Internet *has come a long way* in the last decade.)。

# 7
# LISTENING

## Introduction
### Toshikazu Hasegawa

Elephants have a mysterious appeal. They are the largest land mammals on earth — male Asian elephants, for example, weigh about five tons on average — and for many people their sheer size is a source of fascination. Some people find their slow and leisurely movements soothing. And elephants have also long played an important part in human history. I am not sure if you could categorize them as "domestic animals," but certainly they have been used to assist human labor and have played an essential role in various rituals in many societies. In ancient Carthage and also in successive Indian dynasties, they were even used in warfare like today's armored cars.

Since 2002, I have been conducting research on Asian elephants. There is a comparatively large body of research focusing on African elephants, but very little research has been focused on Asian elephants, which are smaller in size and live in forests rather than on open grasslands. I have already made a number of trips to Sri Lanka and with a group of researchers have begun a study on elephant behavior.

Investigation into the behavior of Asian elephants in Sri Lanka is urgently needed, not least because it is becoming essential to find ways to protect them from human development and population increase. Because of the steady destruction of their natural habitat, more and more elephants are being forced to encroach upon farmland, thereby becoming a threat to local communities. Some elephants are even descending upon villages these days, and occasionally attacking residents. In Sri Lanka, it is reported that about fifty people die every year in such attacks. In turn, more than a hundred elephants are killed by poachers each year.

Elephants in Sri Lanka.
Photo by Naoko Irie.

[3] **their sheer size:** sheer は the sheer amount [number / size] (of ...) という形で(...の)数量や大きさを強調するのによく用いられる (e.g. I was overwhelmed by *the sheer number* of unfamiliar technical terms in the book.)。

[4] **leisurely:**「ゆったりとした」(< leisure [líːʒər, léʒər])。

[9] **ancient Carthage** [káːrθɪdʒ]:「古代カルタゴ」。アフリカ北岸，現在のチュニジア一帯を支配した古代フェニキア人の都市国家。地中海世界の覇権をめぐりローマと3回にわたるポエニ戦争を戦った後，紀元前146年，ローマ遠征軍に破壊された。第二次ポエニ戦争の際(前218–前201年)，カルタゴの将軍ハンニバルは，ゾウを含む大軍を率いてイベリア半島からアルプスを越え，ローマ近くまで進軍し，ローマ軍を撃破した。

[9] **successive Indian dynasties:** 歴代のインドの王朝は，カルタゴよりさらに大がかりにゾウを軍事目的に使用していたと言われる。

[12] **I have been conducting research on ...:** conduct research on ... は「...に関する研究を行う」と言う場合の決まった表現のひとつ(1章[136]，4章[19])(cf. *do research on* ...)。この場合の research が不可算名詞であることに注意 (e.g. *a large amount of research*)。

[16] **Sri Lanka:**「スリランカ」英語の発音は(英語の単語には元来 /sr/ という子音連続がないため，および現地[シンハラ語]での発音に準じて)[ʃriláːŋkə] となることが多い。

[22] **natural habitat** [hǽbətæt]:「自然の生息地」。

[23] **encroach upon farmland:** encroach upon ... は「...(領域など)を侵犯する」(cf. trespass on ...)。

[28] **poachers:**「密猟者」(cf. Elephant *poaching* is a major problem both in Africa and in Asia.)。

My research team has been utilizing various technologies such as GPS and DNA analysis to enhance our understanding of Asian elephant behavior. We are also investigating elephant cognition and communication, using a variety of techniques borrowed from previous studies of human infants and primates. As the English saying "elephants never forget" suggests, elephants seem to possess very good memories. Much needs to be done, however, before we can assess their brain mechanism.

Another fascinating aspect of elephants is their ability to communicate through infrasonic sounds that are inaudible to human ears. These very low frequency sounds are believed to be effective for communicating across long distances, since on theoretical grounds one would predict that low frequencies would be less rapidly attenuated by obstacles such as leaves and branches, by air turbulence, and by the viscosity of the air itself. Scholars believe that elephants are able to communicate with each other across great distances in this way. But our understanding of this mode of elephant communication is also lacking and further research is necessary.

The reading for this session introduces us to another intriguing line of research into elephant communication behavior. We humans tend to assume that sounds are always heard through ears, and indeed elephants have fairly sizable ears, but research shows that elephants are also able to detect sound in quite a different way. Apparently, when an elephant produces a vocal call it actually produces two separate sounds, one which travels through the air and another which travels through the ground. Listening elephants receive the sound wave through their ears and the seismic wave through their feet.

In evolutionary terms, elephants flourished during the Tertiary period, when the earth was covered by vast grasslands. In the Quaternary period, their numbers decreased dramatically because of drastic climate change and the appearance of *Homo sapiens*, their most threatening predators. The elephants we see today are the last descendants of these animals that once ruled the earth. Elephants provide us with important lessons in understanding the evolution of life on earth and also for gaining insight into the complexity of the relationship between human development and environmental protection. In that respect, the educational value of the elephant is even more impressive than its physical size.

- [30] **GPS:**「全地球位置把握システム（Global Positioning System）」。
- [38] **infrasonic sounds:**「超低周波［可聴下周波］音」（cf. ultrasonic「超音波の」）。
- [42] **attenuated:** attenuate は「減衰する」。
- [42] **air turbulence:**「気流の乱れ」（cf. There's no cause for alarm. It's just a little *turbulence*.（旅客機の機内放送））。
- [43] **the viscosity** [vɪskásəti] **of the air:**「空気の粘性」（cf. viscous [vískəs]）。
- [56] **the seismic wave:** seismic [sáɪzmɪk] は通例「地震の」（e.g. the *seismic* center「震源」）だが，ここでは「地面の震動による」。
- [58] **the Tertiary** [tə́ːrʃəri] **period:**「第三紀」。地質年代は，先カンブリア時代，古生代，中生代，新生代と大別されるが，最後の新生代の大部分を占めるのが第三紀で，約6500万年前から200万年前まで。哺乳動物や双子葉植物が栄え，活発な火山活動・造山活動により，ヒマラヤなどの大山脈ができた。
- [59] **the Quaternary** [kwátərnèri, kwətə́ːrnəri] **period:**「第四紀」。新生代の第三紀の後に続く紀で，約200万年前から現在まで。ヒト属が新しく出現した。
- [65] **gaining insight into ... :** insight を含む非常によく用いられる表現のひとつで「…の本質がわかる」といった感じ（2章[156]，10章[31]）（cf. This book will *give you insight into* how the mind works.）。

# Four Ears to the Ground

## Allan Burdick

From time to time, leaving the American Museum of Natural History after hours, I pass the elephants in the Akeley Hall of African Mammals. They occupy the center of the room: a cluster of them, on a wide dais, milling eternally in the state of taxidermy. Aside from them and me and a savanna of glass-eye ungulates, the hall is empty. My footsteps produce the only sound, which seems somehow amplified by the elephants' great mass.

We share a regular, wordless dialogue, the elephants and I, but only lately have I come to understand what they have to say. For years now, scientists have understood that elephants communicate at a frequency typically too low for the human ear to perceive — about twenty hertz. Propagating through the air, these vocal calls can reach an elephant five miles away. For better reception, the listening elephant spreads its earflaps forward, effectively transforming its head into a satellite dish.

As it turns out, this is only half the story. Recently a Stanford University researcher, Caitlin O'Connell-Rodwell, discovered that an elephant's vocal call actually generates two separate sounds: the airborne one and another that travels through the ground as a seismic wave. Moreover, the seismic version travels at least twice as far, and seismic waves generated by an elephant stomping its feet in alarm travel farther still, up to twenty miles. What's most remarkable, however, is how elephants presumably perceive these signals: they listen, it seems, with their feet.

Seismic communication is widespread. Creatures from scorpions to crocodiles rely on ground vibrations to locate potential mates and to detect (and avoid becoming) prey. The male fiddler crab bangs territorial warnings into the sand with its oversized claw. A blind mole rat pounds its head against the walls of its underground tunnels, thus declaring its dominance over the blind mole rat two tunnels over, which may or may not be listening with its own head pressed to the wall.

O'Connell-Rodwell was first inspired by the seismic songs of planthoppers, tiny insects she studied early in her career. The planthopper sings by vibrating its abdomen; this causes the under-

- [69] **the American Museum of Natural History:** アメリカ自然史博物館は，1869 年に設立された アメリカ有数の博物館。ニューヨークのセントラルパーク沿いにある。
- [70] **after hours:** 「閉館後に」(「勤務時間後」や「閉店後」と言う場合にも用いられる)。
- [70] **the Akeley Hall of African Mammals:** Akeley [éɪkli] Hall はアメリカの博物学者・探検家 Carl Akeley (1864–1926) の名前を記念した展示室。
- [72] **on a wide dais:** dais [deɪs] は「(広間などの)台座」。
- [72] **milling eternally in the state of taxidermy:** mill は「多数の人や動物がうろうろと動き回る」。taxidermy [tǽksədə̀ːrmi] は「剥製(術)」。
- [74] **ungulates** [ʌ́ŋgjələts]:「有蹄動物」。
- [77] **only lately have I come to understand:**「最近になってはじめてわかるようになった」。only lately という否定の意味を含んだ句が強調のために文頭に来たことに伴って倒置が生じていることに注意 (cf. *No sooner had I reached* for the phone than it started ringing.)。
- [77] **what they have to say:** what は they have something to say の something に対応している (5 章 [45]) (cf. This brochure gives you a glimpse of *what* our school *has to offer*.)。
- [80] **Propagating through the air:** propagate [prɑ́pəgèɪt] は「(音などが)伝わる，拡散する」。
- [84] **As it turns out:** 予想や期待に反する内容を導入する際に用いられることの多い表現で，「実は」という感じ (cf. *It turns out that* this task is harder than it appears.)。
- [84] **this is only half the story:** story を用いた決まった言い方のひとつで「これだけではありません」といった意味を表す (cf. That's *not the whole story*.)。
- [87] **airborne** [éərbɔːrn]:「空気で運ばれる」(cf. The plane was *airborne* before I knew it.)。
- [87] **travels:** このように travel は(「旅行する」ではなく)「(光，音，情報などが)伝わる」(e.g. Light *travels* faster than sound.) という意味でも普通に用いられることに注意。
- [89] **stomping its feet:** stomp one's feet は「足を踏み鳴らす」(cf. I saw several people *stomping on* a flag.)。
- [89] **in alarm:**「怖がって」「警戒して」(cf. an *alarming* increase in crime rate)。
- [94] **to locate potential mates:** locate は「…のいる[ある]場所を突き止める」(e.g. Looks like he's doing everything in his power to make himself hard to *locate*.)。
- [95] **prey:**「餌食」「被食者」であるが，このように不可算名詞扱いされることが多い (cf. birds of *prey* / fall *prey* to . . . )。
- [95] **The male fiddler crab bangs . . . into . . . :** fiddler crab は「シオマネキ」。bang は本来「大きな音を立てて激しく叩く」(e.g. Stop *banging* on the door.) という擬音動詞(9 章 [49]) (cf. I heard *a bang* which seemed to come from next door.) であるが，ここでは bang A into B で「A を B に叩き込む」。このような用法の拡張は英語では非常に一般的 (cf. *scratch* the soil / *scratch* a drawing in the soil // *kick* the door / *kick* the door down / *kick* a hole in the door)。
- [96] **A blind mole rat:** (blind) mole rat は「メクラネズミ」で，穴居性の齧歯動物。
- [101] **inspired by the seismic songs of planthoppers:** inspire はここでは「インスピレーション[着想]を与える」(12 章 [173], cf. 2 章 [156]) (be inspired by …で「…に着想を得る」)という感じ (cf. She's an amazingly *inspiring* teacher.)。planthopper は「ウンカなど，植物の汁を吸う昆虫」。
- [103] **abdomen** [ǽbdəmən]:「腹部」(cf. *abdominal* muscles)。

lying leaf, and ideally all nearby planthoppers, to tremble. She observed that planthoppers in the peanut gallery would lift a foot or two, presumably for better hearing: the other feet, bearing more weight, thus became more sensitive to vibration. Years later, O'Connell-Rodwell saw similar behavior among elephants at a water hole in Namibia. Minutes before a second herd of elephants arrived, members of the first group would lean forward on their toes and raise a hind leg, as if in anticipation. "It was the same thing the planthoppers were doing," she says.

Was it? Several elegant experiments by O'Connell-Rodwell demonstrate that elephants do indeed generate long-range seismic signals. But can other elephants hear them? Early evidence from northern California's Oakland Zoo, where an elephant named Donna is being trained to respond exclusively to seismic cues, strongly suggests that the answer is yes. "We haven't sealed the deal," says O'Connell-Rodwell, " but it looks promising."

As a communication medium, she notes, seismic waves would offer the elephant several advantages. They dissipate less quickly than airborne waves, they aren't disrupted by changes in weather or temperature and they aren't swallowed by dense jungle foliage. Complex vocal harmonics don't translate well into seismic waves. But even the simplest long-range message — "I'm here" or "Danger!" — beats a fancy one that can't be heard at all.

Air is the faster medium: an airborne elephant call will reach a distant listener before the seismic version does. The delay between signals may confer its own advantage, however, O'Connell-Rodwell proposes. The delay increases with distance; an astute listener would soon learn to gauge distance from the delay. Combined with its airborne counterpart, a seismic signal would enable the animal to coordinate its movements with faraway colleagues, to forage more effectively, and to detect unseen danger. It is compass, yardstick, and e-mail in one — an elephantine Palm Pilot.

And the elephant's palm is the key, O'Connell-Rodwell believes. It may be that the seismic vibrations propagate from the elephant's feet to its inner ear — a process known as bone conduction. That would explain some of the odder features of elephant anatomy, including the fatty deposits in its cheeks, which may serve to amplify incoming vibrations. In marine mammals, similar deposits are called "acoustic fat."

But O'Connell-Rodwell thinks the elephant ear may be tuned even more accurately to the ground. "They do have nerves connected to their toenails, and they do lean on them. It could be a

- [105] **the peanut gallery:** 本来は「劇場の最上階最後部席」「天井桟敷」。
- [108] **a water hole:** 「(動物の水飲み場になっている)水たまり」。
- [109] **Namibia:** ナミビアはアフリカ南西部の共和国。南アフリカ共和国の占領時代を経て，1990年に独立した。
- [109] **a second herd of elephants:** 象の群れは herd という (cf. *a flock of* sheep / *a gaggle of* geese / *a colony of* penguins / *a school of* fish / *a bed of* oysters / *a pride of* lions)。
- [118] **We haven't sealed the deal:** seal the deal は「(調印，捺印などをして)契約を成立させる」という意味から，ここでは「確固たるものにする」「確証する」。
- [121] **dissipate:**「消散する」。
- [122] **they aren't disrupted:** disrupt は「(交通や通信を)途絶させる」(cf. An unexpected heavy snowfall *disrupted* traffic in this area throughout the day.)。
- [123] **foliage** [fóuliɪdʒ]**:** 集合不可算名詞で「草木の葉」(cf. a room decorated with *greenery*)。
- [124] **Complex vocal harmonics:** harmonics はもともと「倍音」の意味。倍音とは，振動体の発する音のうち，基音の振動数の整数倍の振動数をもつ部分音のこと。しかしここでは，全体として「複雑な音声」くらいの意味。
- [124] **translate well into ... :** この場合の A translates into B は「A がその特性ゆえに B に変換が可能[容易]である」という感じ (cf. This sentence doesn't *translate* easily *into* English.)。
- [126] **beats a fancy one:** この場合の A beats B は「A は B に優る」「A の方が B よりはまし」といった意味を表す。fancy は「手のこんだ」「高級な」「しゃれた」で，simple(st) の対義語として用いられている。
- [130] **an astute listener ... :** astute [əstjúːt] は「理解力などが鋭い」。
- [131] **gauge** [geɪdʒ]**:**「測定する」「判断する」。
- [133] **coordinate its movements with ... :** coordinate A with B は「A を B と調和させる」「A を B とうまく協調させる」(cf. *coordinated* efforts to get the project off the ground)。
- [133] **forage** [fɔ́ːrɪdʒ]**:**「食糧などを探しまわる」。
- [134] **compass, yardstick, and e-mail in one:**「羅針盤(方向を定める)，ヤード尺(距離を計る)，e メール(通信する)がひとつになったもの」(cf. all rolled *into one* / (all) wrapped *in one*)。
- [135] **an elephantine** [èləfǽntiːn] **Palm Pilot:**「ゾウのパーム・パイロット」。パーム・パイロットは，米国パーム・コンピューティング社製の手のひらサイズ (palm-sized) の小型情報端末。
- [138] **bone conduction:**「(聴力の)骨伝導」。
- [140] **the fatty deposits:**「脂肪の蓄積物」。
- [141] **marine mammals:**「海棲哺乳動物」。
- [142] **acoustic** [əkúːstɪk] **fat:**「音響脂肪」。

direct line to their head." A colleague is now exploring whether the fleshy pad of an elephant's foot contains Pacinian and Meissner corpuscles, specialized nerve endings that detect faint motion and vibration. The tip of an elephant's trunk has more of these structures per square inch than does any other animal organ, and it is supremely touch-sensitive. (In addition to lifting a foot to improve its hearing, an elephant sometimes holds its trunk to the ground, as if it were an amplifier, says the Stanford biologist).

All of which raises the question, Which is doing the hearing here — the elephant foot or the elephant ear? The truth is, "hearing" is a construct of human language. To us, a "sound" is what happens when airborne acoustic waves vibrate tiny hairs inside our head. An "ear" is an acoustic organ that looks like ours.

Properly defined, however, sound is a series of compression waves in any medium: air, liquid, solid matter. Animals have evolved all manner of translating these mechanical waves into neural signals. A fish senses motion with a line of specialized receptors on both sides of its body. Walk toward a fish tank, and your footsteps startle the fish. Did it hear you or feel you? To the fish, there's no difference.

Perhaps, in our ear-o-centric view of the world, we have constrained our senses. "The animals have been paying attention to something that we haven't been noticing," O'Connell-Rodwell says. Lately she has begun exploring the possibility that other large mammals — bison, rhinoceroses, hippopotamuses, lions, giraffes — rely on seismic cues in their daily lives.

Paradoxically, the discovery that elephants and perhaps other large mammals may communicate seismically comes at a time when it is increasingly difficult for us to hear them. Just as the night sky is slowly becoming obscured by "light pollution" from countless streetlights and other artificial sources of illumination, so the sounding board of earth has become muddled with "bioseismic noise": rumbling trucks, electric generators, jet vibrations, the hum and trundle of civilization and commerce. Does this human static disrupt elephant conversations in the wild? Does it drive them nuts in captivity? The zoo environment is stressful enough without having to hear from every pothole within a twenty-mile radius. Then again, I manage to sleep through the most fearsome Manhattan traffic. "My guess is, elephants in urban environments have become desensitized to seismic signals, as people have," suggests O'Connell-Rodwell.

In the end, the primary casualty of bioseismic noise is us. The human foot happens to be a remarkably sensitive listening device.

- [146] **the fleshy pad of an elephant's foot:**「ゾウの肉づきのよい足の裏」。
- [147] **Pacinian and Meissner corpuscles** [kɔ́ːrpəslz]**:** Pacinian corpuscle は,「パチニ小体」。皮膚や腱の深層に存在する,神経末端を囲む結合組織の層からなる微小なタマネギ様の小体で,圧覚や振動覚の感覚レセプターとしての機能をもつ。イタリアの解剖学者 Pacini (1812–83) に由来する。Meissner corpuscle は,「触小体」。平たい細胞とカプセルで覆われた神経末端からなる卵型の感覚器官。ドイツの解剖学者 Meissner (1829–1905) に由来する。
- [151] **touch-sensitive:**「ものに触れると敏感に反応する」(cf. a *heat-sensitive* device)。
- [154] **All of which raises the question . . . :**「以上のすべては…という問題を提起する」。which は,この節の直前まで O'Connell-Rodwell の述べていたこと全体を指している。
- [156] **a construct** [kʌ́nstrʌ̀kt] **of human language:**「人間の言語の構築物」「人間の言語がつくりあげたもの」。「現実に存在するもの」に対応していない(実在のカテゴリーを適切に切り出していない)という含みがある (cf. 14 章 [92]) (e.g. a theoretical *construct* of utmost importance)。
- [159] **Properly defined:**「適切に定義すると」。
- [159] **compression waves:**「疎密波」「圧縮波」。縦波の一種で,空気中の音波や地震の P 波などがその例。縦波の場合,媒質の振動方向が波の進行方向と同じであり,媒質に疎密が生じてその変化が伝わっていくので,「疎密波」と呼ばれる。
- [160] **all manner of . . . :**「あらゆる種類の…」という意味の決まった言い方。manner が単数形であることに注意(10 章 [24])。
- [162] **receptors:**「感覚器官」「受容器」。
- [165] **our ear-o-centric view of the world:**「われわれ(人間)の耳中心の世界観」。
- [169] **bison** [báɪsən]**:**「ヤギュウ」「バイソン」(単複同形)。
- [172] **comes at a time when . . . :** A comes at a time when B は非常によく用いられる表現型で,A の起こるタイミングが B と一致していることの重要性や意外性を強調する。
- [175] **the sounding board of earth has become muddled with . . . :** sounding board は「共鳴板」「反響板」。become muddled with . . . は「…が入り交じってごっちゃになる」。
- [177] **the hum and trundle of . . . :**「…のガヤガヤ,ゴロゴロという音」。
- [178] **this human static:** static は「雑音」。
- [179] **in the wild:**「野生の状態で(の)」(cf. in captivity)。
- [179] **drive them nuts:** drive . . . nuts は「…の気を狂わせる」で,drive . . . crazy / mad や drive . . . up the wall (e.g. That noise is *driving* me *up the wall*.) などと同じような意味 (cf. Am I going *nuts*?)。
- [181] **pothole** [pʌ́thòʊl]**:**「舗装した路面のくぼみ」。
- [181] **Then again, I manage to sleep through . . . :** then again は「(直前に言ったことを受けて)そうは言ったものの」。sleep through . . . は「…(騒音など)にもかかわらず眠り続ける」(cf. I *slept past* noon.)。
- [183] **My guess is . . . :** I guess . . . とほぼ同じ意味。
- [183] **become desensitized** [diːsénsətàɪzd] **to . . . :**「…に対して敏感でなくなる[鈍感になる]」。
- [186] **casualty** [kǽʒuəlti]**:**「(事故や災害の)死傷者,被害者」。

It is nearly as dense with pressure receptors as is the elephant's trunk. O'Connell-Rodwell suspects that once upon a quieter time, we paid closer attention to seismic signals than we do today. Vibrations from instruments such as the talking drum or the didgeridoo, or even from foot-stomping dances, may have spoken volumes to distant, unshod listeners. Then came telephones, automobiles, asphalt — and footwear. We hardened our soles to the world of sound.

The echo of my footsteps haunts me now. When last I strolled through the darkened Akeley Hall, it struck me that this is what it would be like to be entombed in a shoe. The silent elephants, the hushed lions, the stilled giraffes — a continent of primordial instincts urged me toward the exit. Loosen, unlace, enter the world barefoot.

- [189] **O'Connell-Rodwell suspects that . . . :** suspect は「…ではないかと思う」と that 節の内容を肯定する意味を持つことに注意（10 章 [160]）（cf. I *doubt* that he's ever read this book.）。
- [189] **once upon a quieter time:** once upon a time「昔々」をもじった表現で，昔はもっと静かだったという含み。
- [191] **talking drum:** 言語のイントネーションを連想させる音を出す，西アフリカ起源の太鼓。
- [191] **didgeridoo** [dìdʒərədúː]:「ディジェリドゥー」。木の内部をくりぬいて作ったオーストラリア先住民（アボリジニ）の楽器。
- [192] **may have spoken volumes to distant, unshod listeners:** speak volumes は「（表情や出来事が）大いに物語る」という意味の決まった言い回し（e.g. The tone of her voice *spoke volumes* about how she really felt.）。unshod は「靴を履かない」「裸足の」。
- [194] **We hardened our soles to . . . :** harden one's heart to . . .「…に心を動かされなくなる」「…に対して冷淡[鈍感]になる」をもじった言い方。sole「足の裏」（「靴底」の意味も）の発音が heart の類意語 soul と同じであることもこの表現の面白さに貢献している。
- [195] **haunts me:**「私の脳裏を離れない」。haunt は「つきまとって悩ませる」場合に用いることも多い（e.g. What you say today may come back to *haunt* you years later.）。
- [196] **it struck me that . . . :** この場合の strike は「（突然）…という考えが浮かぶ」（cf. Didn't it *strike* you *as* strange that he made no comment?）。
- [197] **be entombed in a shoe:** entomb [entúːm] は「埋葬する」「閉じ込める」。
- [198] **primordial** [praɪmɔ́ːdiəl]:「原始（時代から）の」。

# 8

# BASEBALL

## Introduction
### Takashi Shimizu

Some things look right and are actually true. For example, it looks like the sun is much hotter than the earth, and, actually, it is. But there are also quite a lot of things that look obvious but are not really true at all. For example, it really does look as if the sun goes around the earth and the earth is flat. But history has shown that this idea, which seemed right for so long, was in fact wrong.

So a convincing explanation cannot simply be accepted as proof that the right conclusion has been reached. You need to be able to distinguish between an explanation that "looks right and is right" and one which "looks right but is wrong." In order to do this, you have to question what seems obvious and think through the problem on your own. What is right can only be understood by collecting all the data and other relevant materials and reorganizing them logically, like the master detective in a mystery novel.

This is basically what "doing research" is all about, whether it is in the field of the natural sciences, social sciences, or human sciences. And it is such a pleasure to uncover a surprising new truth, thereby replacing a previously very convincing explanation, just by analyzing your data and materials and coming to your conclusion logically.

The explanation that "this baseball ground produces a lot of home runs because it's located at a high altitude, and that makes the balls fly farther" is convincing enough, and so people tend to simply take this kind of reasoning for granted. But in order to ascertain whether the explanation is really true or not, someone has to collect all the relevant data, analyze it, and think the problem through on their own.

The authors of this paper did precisely that. As a result, they

[7] **convincing:**「説得力のある」「納得のいく」という意味で，説明，根拠，主張などについてよく用いられる形容詞（cf. Her arguments *convinced* the rest of us that she was right. / I'm fully *convinced* that we're doing the right thing.「確信している」/ a compelling argument [reason]）。

[11] **question:**（単に「質問する」ではなく）「疑問視する」「疑義を唱える」という意味で用いることが多い（2章 [138]）（cf. In our discipline, certain fundamental principles are widely accepted virtually *without question.* / I find his conclusion highly *questionable.*）。

[11] **think through the problem on your own:** think through は「…（問題や行動方針など）について考え抜く」（cf. a carefully *thought-out* plan）。on one's own は「（他人の助けを借りるのではなく）自力で」という意味でよく用いられる表現。

[14] **like the master detective in a mystery novel:**「推理小説の名探偵のように」。10章に登場する Sherlock Holmes は名探偵の代名詞。

[15] **This is basically what "doing research" is all about:** what . . . is all about は「…の本質」「…の存在意義」といった意味でよく用いられる言い回し（2章 [153]，5章 [95]）（e.g. This book will give you a very good idea of *what* cognitive psychology *is all about.*）。do research は「研究する」と言う場合の最も普通の表現。

[16] **the natural sciences, social sciences, or human sciences:**「自然科学，社会科学，人文科学」に相当する英語表現。複数形が用いられているのはそれぞれの領域に属する分野が複数あることを示す（「自然科学の諸分野」という感じを出す）ため。特にそういう意識がない場合には（無冠詞，単数の）natural science などを用いる。人文科学は the humanities とも言う。

[23] **simply take this kind of reasoning for granted:**「こういう論法をあっさり当然視する」。reasoning（「思考する」という意味の動詞 reason から派生）は「判断を下すための思考の道筋，論法」（cf. sound / faulty *reasoning*）。

[24] **ascertain:** ほぼ同じ意味の find out よりも形式張った感じの動詞で，このように疑問詞で始まる節を伴うことが多い。

came to the conclusion that "the reason this baseball field produces many home runs is *not* because balls fly farther." The text here includes only parts of the introduction and the conclusion sections to their paper, but it is still possible to understand how they reached such a conclusion. Let's try to follow their logic and experience the pleasure of breaking down the "taken-for-granted."

# Atmosphere, Weather, and Baseball

## Frederick Chambers, Brian Page, and Clyde Zaidins

Since its inauguration, Denver's Coors Field has gained national notoriety as the ultimate home-run-hitter's park — a "launching pad" of historic proportions. Indeed, Coors Field led all major-league ballparks in both total home runs and home runs per at-bat during seven of its first eight seasons. Nearly all observers, from noted physicists to veteran players to casual fans, attribute the dramatic home-run output at Coors Field to the effect of thin air on the flight of a baseball. In theory, the ball should travel about 10 percent farther in Denver (elevation 5,280 feet) than it would in a ballpark at sea level. Throughout the nation, Coors Field is viewed as a curious anomaly that distorts our cherished national pastime by transforming mediocre hitters into stars.

We put such assumptions to the test in this article. Does the ball really fly 10 percent farther in Denver, as the laws of physics would predict? And, is low air density really to blame for the large number of home runs hit at Coors Field? We address these questions through a detailed analysis of the relationships between atmosphere, weather, and baseball in Denver. The analysis is presented in four sections. We begin by discussing the physics of baseball, in order to ascertain just how far the ball should travel at mile-high elevation versus sea level. Second, we compare expected fly-ball distances to observed fly-ball distances through an examination of fly-ball-distance data

[29] **the reason this baseball field produces . . . :** The reason . . . is because . . . は正しい用法ではない(正しくは The reason . . . is that . . . と言うべきである)と考える人もいるが，実際には(日本語の「…の理由は…だからです」と同じく)よく用いられている (cf. Just *because* you're a native speaker of Japanese doesn't mean you know everything about the language.)。

[33] **experience the pleasure of breaking down the "taken-for-granted":**「『当たり前とされていること』を打破する喜びを経験する」。この場合の break down は「(障害などを)打破[克服]する」(e.g. *break down* communication barriers / cf. a *breakdown* in communications)。

[35] **Denver's Coors Field:** デンヴァー市(コロラド州の州都)にあるクアーズ・フィールドは，ナショナル・リーグ西地区所属の大リーグ球団コロラド・ロッキーズ (Colorado Rockies) の本拠地。1995年に作られた。標高5280フィート，約1マイル(＝1600メートル)にある。本塁打が多く出るこの球場で，1996年，野茂英雄はノーヒットノーランを達成した。

[35] **has gained national notoriety:** notoriety [nòutəráıəti] は「(よくない意味での)評判」「悪名」。形容詞は notorious。gain notoriety は決まった組み合わせ (cf. That sarcastic remark *earned* her considerable *notoriety*.)。

[36] **a "launching pad" of historic proportions:** launching pad は「ミサイルやロケットなどの発射台」だが，ここではホームランが驚くほど量産される球場であることを表すための比喩として用いられているので引用符に入っている。of . . . proportions は規模や重要性を述べる際によく使う表現 (e.g. a political scandal *of* colossal *proportions*)。

[37] **led all major-league ballparks:**「メジャーリーグの球場の中で首位であった」(cf. the *leading* batter on the team / The Tigers are *leading* the Giants 3–0 in the seventh inning.)。

[38] **per at-bat:**「一打席あたりの」。

[39] **Nearly all observers, from noted physicists to . . . to casual fans:** from 以下は nearly all observers の中にどんな人がいるかを具体的に述べているが，このように3つ以上の例を挙げる場合には to . . . を2回以上用いればよい。noted は「著名な」(cf. She is *noted* for her analytical skills.)。casual fans は「野球の専門知識が特にあるわけでもなく，気軽に観戦しているごく普通のファン」といった感じ。

[42] **In theory, the ball should travel:** in theory は「理論上は」「理屈の上では」。しばしば「実際には (in reality, in practice) そうならない(かもしれない)」という意味合いを伴う。should は「(理屈の上では)…のはずである」という感じ。

[45] **a curious anomaly:**「不思議で風変わりな存在」。よくある組み合わせ(5章 [238])。

[45] **our cherished national pastime:**「われわれの大切な国民的娯楽」とは(メジャーリーグの)野球の試合(観戦)のこと。

[46] **mediocre** [mìːdióukər] **hitters:**「凡庸な打者」。

[47] **We put such assumptions to the test:** put . . . to the test は「…を(妥当性，適性，実力などを判定するための)試験にかける」「…に試練を与える」。assumptions は「想定(確たる根拠があるわけではないけれども一般に正しいと思われていること)」(cf. on the *assumption* that . . . )。

[49] **is low air density really to blame for . . . ?:** blame A for B は，日本語の「BはAのせい」と同じく，B(通例望ましくないこと)の原因がA(人間とは限らない)にあることを述べる際に一般的に用いられる (e.g. The caterers *were blamed for* the outbreak of food poisoning. / cf. This cold weather *is responsible for* the influenza epidemic.)。

[50] **address these questions:** この場合の address は「(問題，課題などに)取り組む」(e.g. In this article, the author *addresses* [*herself to*] one of the hardest problems in cognitive science.)。

for fourteen National League ballparks. Our analysis of fly-ball distance spans the 1995–1998 seasons, encompassing the first four seasons in which baseball was played at the LoDo ballpark. These data show that compared to other ballparks, fly balls hit at Coors Field do not travel anywhere near as far as one would expect given the low air density in Denver. Third, we seek to explain this discrepancy through an analysis of the weather at Coors Field, using data collected inside the stadium during the 1997 season. Finally, we expand our meteorological analysis by relating ballpark-scale weather data to regional-scale weather data for northeastern Colorado.

Our overall argument is that the effect of thin air on the flight of the baseball in Coors Field is greatly overestimated, owing to the ways in which general atmospheric forces are conditioned by specific geographic circumstances. In this case, distinctive weather dynamics on the front range of the Rocky Mountains, along with topographic features of the South Platte River valley and urbanization patterns in downtown Denver, act to suppress the effect of low air density on the flight of the baseball in Coors Field. We conclude that a better understanding of the ballpark's dramatic home-run rate can be gained by examining (1) the effects of the personnel make-up of the Rockies team and (2) the effects of mile-high elevation on the act of pitching a baseball.

* * *

The laws of physics tell us that a baseball should travel 10 percent farther in the mile-high atmosphere of Denver than at sea level. Moreover, fly balls should travel 9.3 percent farther in Denver than the elevation-adjusted average of thirteen other National League ballparks. Our conclusion, however, is that these theoretical fly-ball trajectories, calculated on the basis of comparative air density, do not hold true upon the examination of fly-ball distance data. In fact, for the 1995–1998 seasons, fly balls traveled just 6 percent farther in Denver compared to the average of thirteen other National League ballparks. The results of our meteorological analysis of Coors Field and its surrounding area suggest that the key factor in this suppression of fly-ball distance is weather — specifically, the dominance of northeasterly winds in the vicinity of the ballpark during afternoon and evening hours. These wind conditions exist due to a regional-scale, diurnal, upslope-downslope wind pattern in the South Platte River valley and, we suggest, are accelerated by local topography and urban massing.

- [57] **National League:** アメリカのプロ野球組織の頂点にある大リーグ (Major League) は，2005年現在，アメリカン・リーグ (1900年創立) 14球団とナショナル・リーグ (1876年創立) 16球団の，2リーグ30球団で構成されている。したがって，14というのは，ナショナル・リーグの球場の全部ではない(全部だったら fourteen の前に定冠詞がなければならない)。

- [57] **Our analysis of fly-ball distance spans the 1995–1998 seasons, emcompassing . . . :** span は「(期間が)…にわたる」という意味の他動詞。encompassing (同じく「…にわたる」の意味)で始まる分詞節は主節の内容を言い換えたもの(3章 [6]，4章 [17]，本章 [170]，10章 [44])。

- [59] **the LoDo ballpark:** LoDo は lower downtown の略。

- [61] **do not travel anywhere near as far as . . . :**「…ほど遠くまでは飛ばない」。not anywhere near または nowhere near は比較級の形容詞，副詞などの前に用いられて強い否定を表す (e.g. He is *nowhere near* as smart as his sister.)。

- [65] **meteorological analysis:** meteorological [mìːtiərəládʒɪkəl] は「気象学的な」「気象に関する」(cf. *meteorology* [mìːtiərálədʒi] 気象学)。

- [70] **general atmospheric forces . . . :** general と specific が対比的に用いられていることに注意。

- [72] **the front range of the Rocky Mountains:** ロッキー山脈の東側地域(特にデンヴァー地域をさす)。

- [72] **topographic features:**「地形(学)上の特徴」。

- [73] **the South Platte River:** サウスプラット川は，コロラド州を縦断するロッキー山脈東部からネブラスカ州中西部へと東流している。デンヴァー市内では，クアーズ・フィールドの北西数百メートルのところを流れる。

- [77] **the personnel make-up of the Rockies team:** personnel make-up「人員の構成」とは，このチームがどんな選手から構成されているかということ (cf. *personnel* department.「人事部」/ This group *is made up of* people from all walks of life.)。

- [83] **the elevation-adjusted average of . . . :**「高度調整をした上での…の平均」。

- [84] **these theoretical fly-ball trajectories:** theoretical は「理論上の」(cf. in *theory*)。trajectories は trajectory [trədʒéktəri]「軌道」の複数形。

- [86] **hold true upon the examination of . . . :** hold true は「成り立つ」「妥当である」。upon the examination of . . . は「…を調べてみると」(cf. *On closer examination*, the painting turned out to be a forgery.)。

- [94] **diurnal** [daɪə́ːrnl]:「日ごとの，日周的な」(e.g. diurnal cycle「日内周期」)。

- [96] **urban massing:**「都市への人口集中」。

Our assessment is that these daily northeasterly winds suppress fly-ball distances at Coors Field. These winds blow up the South Platte River valley and enter the vicinity of the ballpark from the northeast. Within Coors Field, the winds blow from center field toward home plate into the face of the batter and into the path of batted balls hit to all parts of the outfield. The expected advantage of playing at mile-high elevation (as far as home runs are concerned) is decreased substantially under such conditions. However, when the winds are out of the west, the full elevation advantage can be realized. Such conditions can lead to spectacular fly-ball trajectories, especially to the right field. Thus, the effect of the wind is variable: during some games, altitude's enhancement of fly-ball distance will occur, and in other games it will be suppressed. But over the course of a season — or several seasons — wind acts to minimize the effect of low air density and thus accounts for the shorter-than-expected fly-ball distances at Coors Field.

Finally, let us return to the question raised at the outset concerning the character of baseball games played at Coors Field. While the suppression of fly-ball distance due to prevailing northeasterly winds is significant, keep in mind that the boosting effect of altitude on home-run production in Denver is further minimized by the generous outfield dimensions at Coors Field, the league's most spacious ballpark. Indeed, in order to come up with a measure of just how much more likely it is for home runs to occur at Coors Field due to low air density, one must take into consideration actual field dimensions around the league. We made this adjustment by calculating average fly-ball distance as a percentage of average outfield dimensions for fourteen National League ballparks (Table 1). This calculation yields a measure of how far the average fly ball travels relative to the average position of the outfield fence in each ballpark. As the table shows, when field dimensions are taken into account, the effective difference between Coors Field and the other National League stadiums is not even 6 percent — it is just 3 percent. Moreover, the difference between Coors Field and the stadiums in Philadelphia, Los Angeles, and Atlanta is minimal, while the average fly ball actually carries closer to the outfield wall at St. Louis's Busch Stadium than it does at Coors Field. Faced with these numbers, the facile assumption that elevation enhancement of fly-ball distance is responsible for the large number of home runs in Denver vanishes into so much thin air.

What else might account for the impressive home run statistics in Denver? After all, during the 1995 through 2002 seasons, Coors

**Table 1** *Average Fly-Ball Distance versus Stadium Dimensions in National League Ballparks*

| Stadium | Average Outfield Dimension (ft) | Difference from Coors (%) | $\dfrac{\text{Avg. Flyball Distance}}{\text{Outfield Dimension}} \times (100)$ | Difference from Coors (%) |
|---|---|---|---|---|
| Coors Field | 375.4 | | 80.7 | |
| Atlanta (composite of Turner and Fulton) | 366.7 | 2.3 | 79.3 | 1.7 |
| Chicago | 368.8 | 1.8 | 77.0 | 4.6 |
| Cincinnati | 362.8 | 3.4 | 78.5 | 2.6 |
| Florida | 369.8 | 1.5 | 76.3 | 5.4 |
| Houston | 360.0 | 4.1 | 79.6 | 1.3 |
| Los Angeles | 365.0 | 2.8 | 79.9 | 1.0 |
| Montreal | 360.8 | 3.9 | 78.0 | 3.3 |
| New York | 368.4 | 1.9 | 76.7 | 4.9 |
| Philadelphia | 362.0 | 3.6 | 80.3 | 0.4 |
| Pittsburgh | 364.0 | 3.0 | 77.5 | 3.9 |
| San Diego | 360.2 | 4.0 | 77.1 | 4.5 |
| San Francisco | 358.6 | 4.5 | 75.6 | 6.3 |
| St. Louis | 362.0 | 3.6 | 81.0 | −0.4 |
| **NL Avg. w/out Coors Field** | **363.8** | **3.1** | **78.2** | **3.1** |

[104]　**substantially:**「実質的に」とは「かなり」「相当」ということで，この場合の substantial は本文 [116] の significant とほぼ同義。

[116]　**the boosting effect of altitude on home-run production:**「高度がホームランの本数を増やす効果(をもつこと)」(cf. These measures are expected to *boost* the Japanese economy.)。

[117]　**the generous outfield dimensions:** generous はこの場合「規模や数量が普通より大きい」といった意味 (e.g. She has a *generous* travel allowance of one million yen a year.)。outfield dimensions は「外野の面積」。

[124]　**This calculation yields a measure of . . . :**「この計算によって…を測ったことになる」。yield は produce と同義 (cf. crop *yields*「作物の生産高」)。

[127]　**the effective difference:** この場合の effective は「実質的な」(cf. This *effectively* [in effect] means that there is nothing they can do about our plight.)。

[131]　**the average fly ball actually carries:** この場合の carry は「(ボールなどがある距離を)飛ぶ」(cf. His voice *carries* well even without a microphone.)。

[132]　**St. Louis's Busch Stadium:** ミズーリ州セントルイス市にあるブッシュ・スタジアム。ナショナル・リーグ創設時以来の伝統を誇る St. Louis Cardinals の本拠地。1998年，当時のシーズン最多本塁打記録70本を達成した Mark MacGwire は，カーディナルズの選手だった。

[133]　**the facile assumption:** facile [fǽsəl, fǽsàɪl] は「安易な」「いい加減な」。

[135]　**vanishes into so much thin air:** vanish into thin air は「跡形もなく消え去る」という意味の決まった表現 (cf. (appear) out of *thin air*「どこからともなく(現れる)」) だが，ここではもちろん「ホームラン量産の原因が当地の空気の薄いこと (thin air) にある」という通説が脆くも崩れ去ったことを表現するのに効果的に使われている。

[138]　**Coors Field witnessed:** 英語ではこのように see や witness が出来事の起こった場所や時を主語にして用いられることが(特にジャーナリスティックな文体で)しばしばある(2章 [115]) (e.g. Tuesday *saw* yet another startling development.)。

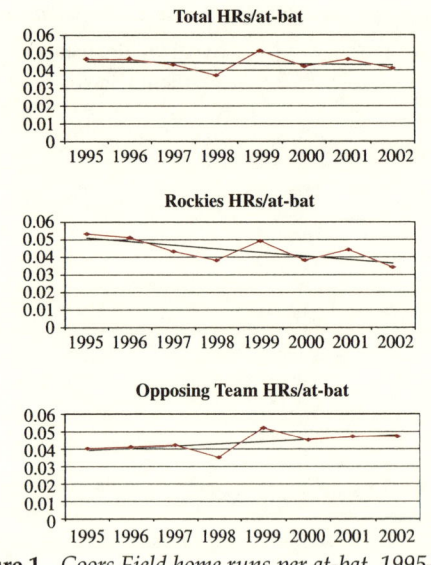

**Figure 1** *Coors Field home runs per at-bat, 1995–2002.*

Field witnessed a rate of .044 home runs per at-bat, while the combined average of the other National League parks was just .029 home runs per at-bat. In other words, home runs occur at Coors Field at a rate that is 52 percent greater than at the other ballparks — far more than would be expected even if the mile-high atmospheric enhancement was realized to its fullest. We believe that the answer to this question has to do with two factors: first, the personnel make-up of the Colorado Rockies ball club in terms of both hitters and pitchers; and second, the general problems of pitching at altitude.

During the first several seasons played at Coors Field, the Rockies team was stacked with notable power hitters. Simply put, they were a team designed to produce large numbers of home runs. However, over the past several years, these "Blake Street Bombers" have been traded or allowed to leave via free agency, as team management has shifted focus from home-run hitters to high-average hitters with less power. This personnel shift is verified in the record of Coors Field hitting statistics. Since 1995, there has been an overall downward trend in the number of home runs per at-bat — a trend that is accounted for by a reduction in the number of home runs hit by the Rockies (the trend in home runs per at-bat for the opposition at Coors Field has risen) (Figure 1). In fact, by the 2000 season, Coors Field had been surpassed in home runs per at-bat by both Busch Stadium in St. Louis and Enron Field in Houston. Thus, the large number of home runs hit at Coors Field can be attributed, in part, to the specific group of hitters assembled early on by the Rockies.

- [148] **at altitude:** at a high altitude と同義 (cf. He was proceeding *at speed*.)。
- [150] **was stacked with notable power hitters:** be stacked with ... は本来「…が積み上げられている」(e.g. One of his rooms *was stacked with* books.) だが，ここでは「…が大勢いる」といった意味 (cf. There were many notable power hitters on the Rockies team.)。
- [150] **Simply put:**「簡単に言えば」という場合の決まった表現 (cf. Let me *put* it this way.)。
- [151] **a team designed to . . . :**「…するのを目的として作られたチーム」。
- [152] **these "Blake Street Bombers":** Coors Field が Blake Street にあることから。
- [153] **leave via free agency:**「フリーエージェント制を利用して出ていく」。
- [159] **the opposition:**「(集合的に)相手チーム」。
- [162] **Enron Field in Houston:** テキサス州ヒューストン市にあるヒューストン・アストロズ (Houston Astros) の本拠地。天然芝の開閉式ドーム球場として1999年完成。他のナショナル・リーグの球場よりも，多少両翼(特に左翼)が狭い。2002年 Minute Maid Park と改称された。
- [164] **early on:**「(Coors Field でゲームをするようになった)初期の頃」(e.g. We realized *early on* that we'd have to work really hard to get the project off the ground.)。

Once the franchise changed the character of the team, the pre-eminence of Coors Field as the league's ultimate home-run ballpark was somewhat diminished.

The Rockies have also lacked successful pitching for most of their history. Colorado pitchers have had more than their share of problems over the past eight years, both at home and on the road. Between 1995 and 2002, the team was either last or next to last in most pitching categories, leading the league in home runs allowed seven times. Had the Los Angeles or New York staffs pitched at Coors Field for eighty-one games per year, the ballpark's home-run totals would most likely have been significantly less. Put Atlanta's pitching staff in Denver for half of their games and this reduction is a virtual certainty. Remember that Atlanta's Fulton County Stadium was known as the "launching pad" until the Braves put together the league's premier group of pitchers in the early 1990s.

But perhaps the most important factor in explaining the home-run numbers in Denver is the "Coors Field Effect" — the not-so-subtle influence of the ballpark on pitchers from both the home and visiting teams. Most of these professional athletes are clearly intimidated by Coors Field. As one player recently observed, the ballpark causes "an identity crisis" for pitchers, leading them to change their approach to the game, move away from their strengths, and ultimately lose confidence in their abilities (pitcher Denny Neagle of the Colorado Rockies, quoted in *The Denver Post*, 5 March 2003). Even the league's best pitchers often come unglued in Denver. Pitching is undeniably more difficult in Coors Field than in other National League ballparks because of the very limited foul ground and the cavernous outfield spaces. This field configuration gives hitters more chances, allows more balls to drop in front of outfielders, and permits more balls to find the gaps for extra-base hits. Yet beyond this, most pitchers are beset with a range of other problems once they take the mound. Chief among these are a sudden lack of control, breaking balls that do not break, and sinker balls that do not sink. The result is more pitches thrown straight and over the heart of the plate, and more balls hit high, deep, and out the park. Thus, what we suggest is that more home runs are hit at Coors Field, not because routine fly balls carry farther, but because a higher proportion of pitched balls are hit harder than in other ballparks.

These pitching problems in Denver have also been attributed to low air density. Theoretically, thin air reduces ball-to-air friction, cutting down on ball movement between the mound and home plate and thus decreasing the overall control of the pitcher and the

[165] **the franchise:** franchise は「フランチャイズ（プロスポーツリーグの加盟権）をもつチーム」，つまりここでは「プロ野球のチーム」で，もちろん the Rockies のこと。

[165] **preeminence:** ＜ preeminent:「抜群の」「傑出した」。

[169] **more than their share of problems:** more than one's share of ... は「...の数量などが普通以上に多い」(cf. Japan *has its share of* political corruption.)。

[170] **both at home and on the road:** at home と on the road はそれぞれ「本拠地で」と「それ以外の場所で」「遠征先で」ということ。

[170] **Between 1995 and 2002 ...:** leading で始まる分詞構文は主節の内容を補足したもの。このように主節の内容を別の観点から述べたり具体化したりする分詞構文の用法は非常に一般的（3 章 [6]，4 章 [17]，本章 [57]，10 章 [44]）(e.g. Over the past decade, Massachusetts' high court has expanded the legal parameters of family, *ruling* that same-sex couples can adopt children.)。

[173] **the Los Angeles or New York staffs:** ロサンゼルスにあるプロ野球チームは Los Angeles Dodgers，ニューヨークにあるのは New York Yankees と New York Mets。

[177] **Atlanta's Fulton County Stadium:** ジョージア州アトランタのフルトン・カウンティ・スタジアムは，1966 年から 96 年まで Atlanta Braves の本拠地だった。

[178] **put together:** 本文 [164] の assemble と同義。

[179] **premier:**「最優秀の」。

[181] **the not-so-subtle influence:**「それほど微妙でない影響」とは「少なからぬ影響」ということ (cf. in the not too distant future)。

[185] **"an identity crisis" for pitchers:** identity crisis は，元来，ドイツ生まれのアメリカの精神分析家エリクソン（Erik H. Erikson, 1902–94）が提唱した心理学の概念。青年期に生じる自己同一性解体の危機のこと。だが，ここではすぐ後で述べられるように「自分のピッチャーとしての能力に対する自信を失うこと」。

[187] **lose confidence in ...:**「...に対する自信を失う」という場合の決まった言い方 (cf. He doesn't *have* much *confidence in* himself.)。

[189] **come unglued:**「気が動転する」「うろたえる」という意味のくだけた表現。

[191] **the very limited foul ground:**「ファウルグラウンドが非常に狭いこと」。つまり，ファウルフライでアウトがとりにくいこと。

[192] **the cavernous [kǽvərnəs] outfield spaces:**「非常に広い外野」。

[192] **configuration:**「配置」「空間の構成」。layout と言ってもよい。

[194] **extra-base hits:**「長打」（二塁打，三塁打，本塁打）。

[195] **are beset with a range of other problems:** be beset with ... は「...に悩む」。

[195] **once they take the mound:**「いったん（ピッチャーズ）マウンドに上がると」。

[196] **Chief among these are ...:**「いろいろある問題の中でも主なものには...などがある」。倒置の構造で主語は are の後に来ている（9 章 [11]，11 章 [144]）。

[197] **breaking balls that do not break:** breaking ball は「カーブ，スライダーなどの変化球」。全体で「変化球のつもりで投げた球が変化しないこと」。

[198] **more pitches thrown straight and over the heart of the plate:**「投げたボールが（ホームベースの）ど真ん中の直球になってしまうことが他の球場よりも多い」。

[199] **out the park:** この場合の park は野球のグラウンドを指し，したがってグラウンドの外へとはホームランのこと。

effectiveness of the pitches thrown. In addition, the low relative humidity at altitude promotes evaporation from the baseball itself, making the ball lighter, drier, and slicker in Denver than in other parks around the league. Because of this, pitchers at Coors Field have a very difficult time getting a proper grip on the ball, which, in all likelihood, further reduces their control as well as the movement on their pitches. During the 2002 season, in an effort to counteract the presumed effects of thin air on pitching, the Colorado Rockies began using a "humidor" to store baseballs at Coors Field. This device maintains the balls in a controlled environment of 90 degrees Fahrenheit and 40 percent humidity. According to the Rockies organization, the intent of the humidor is to ensure that the baseballs do not shrink to a weight less than the 5.0 to 5.25 ounces specified by the league. The Rockies ball club also believes that these baseballs, not having yet lost water content to evaporation when they enter play, are easier to grip and thus will "level the playing field" for pitchers in Denver. This might just be wishful thinking, however; a comparison of the statistics for the 2002 season versus the previous seven seasons indicates that the humidor has had little, if any, effect upon games played at Coors Field.

Ultimately, these altitude-related issues may prove to be important contributors to the poor pitching in Denver. For now, however, difficulties on the mound would seem to be more the result of the fragile psychology of pitchers faced with the imagined specter of baseballs floating out of Coors Field like weather balloons. Based upon the analysis presented above, we believe that the answer to why so many home runs are hit at Coors Field lies as much on the field as it does in the air.

Coors Field

- [209] **slicker:** slick は smooth and slippery の意味。
- [211] **have a very difficult time getting a proper grip on the ball:**「ボールをきちんと握るのが非常に難しい」（cf. I *had a hard time* gett*ing* my point across.）。
- [211] **in all likelihood:**「ほぼ確実に」。
- [215] **a "humidor":**「保湿ケース」。
- [221] **not having yet lost water content to evaporation:**「（ボールに含まれる）水分がまだ蒸発していないので」（cf. I *lost* my father *to* cancer twenty years ago.）。
- [222] **level the playing field:**「競技場（この場合には野球場）を平らにする」とは「他の球場との格差をなくして Coors Field で投げるピッチャーが不利にならないようにする」ということ。「特定の人，グループなどが有利または不利になることがなく，競争が公平に行われるようになっている状況」という意味の決まった表現である a level playing field がもとになっている。
- [223] **wishful thinking:**「希望的観測」「願望的思考」(e.g. Maybe the professor will be sick today! He looked sick yesterday. No. That's just *wishful thinking*.)。
- [230] **the imagined specter of . . . :** specter は「亡霊」「妖怪」。マルケス，エンゲルスの『共産党宣言』(1848) の冒頭，"A spectre is haunting Europe — the spectre of Communism." が想起される。imagined specter は「想像が生み出した妖怪」「起きてしまうのではないかと恐れられている望ましくないこと」。「（自分の投げた）ボールが（バッターによって）気象観測用の気球（weather balloons）のように楽々と Coors Field の場外へと飛ばされてしまうのではないかという不安な想像」。

# 9
# SOUND

## Introduction
### Yoko Fukao and Ayumu Yasutomi

In the upper and middle parts of its long and winding journey to the sea, China's Yellow River passes through the Loess Plateau, an area of around 640,000 square kilometres. The river turns yellow as it runs through the plateau because of the dramatic soil erosion caused in that area by the absence of trees and grasses. The Loess Plateau region, which is about one and a half times the size of Japan, is home to approximately 70 million people. People living in the area make practical use of the heavily eroded valleys by cutting into the steep hills and constructing arch-shaped buildings, called *yaodong*, using earth and stones. This tradition has produced a unique landscape. Particularly striking is the kind of living space that is created by the way these *yaodong* and their front yards are wrapped inside the valley. This V-shaped space provides anthropologists today with some really distinctive subject matter.

This session focuses on one aspect of life in the Loess Plateau: the characteristic sounds that can be heard in the valleys today and the history of sound in the area. The idea behind the text was to listen to the lives of the people inhabiting the region and create a description of the soundscape of a typical village. The text also tries to develop an understanding of the historical transitions that have taken place in the villages by looking at how their soundscapes have changed over the years.

Almost everyone who visits and stays in one of these villages comes to appreciate and enjoy its soundscape. The various sounds from the everyday lives of the village echo throughout the valley. In the morning, there are the voices of the children, animal noises, and birdsong, as well as the sounds of fires being started with bellows and the wooden doors to the *yaodong* being opened. After the

*yaodong* in the Yellow River region

- [2] **Yellow River:**「黄河」。全長 5464 km。源を青海省に発し，四川省，甘粛省，陝西省，山東省などを経て渤海に注ぐ，中国第二の大河。中流域以下は大量の黄土を含み，黄色を呈するので，古くからこの名で呼ばれる。
- [2] **Loess Plateau:**「黄土(こうど)高原」。中国の黄河上流中流部流域に横たわる高原。小麦粉のように細かい土砂が厚く(数十メートルから数百メートル)堆積してできたもの。黄土(レス)は水による浸食を受けやすい。なお，地質学用語 loess は，loose を意味するドイツ語に由来し，1830 年代に英語に入った。
- [4] **soil erosion:**「土壌の浸食」(cf. The soil in this region has been *eroded* by wind and rain).
- [7] **is home to . . . :** be home to . . . は「…の故郷である」(cf. This city *is home to* a famous baseball team.)。
- [10] *yaodong*:「窰洞(ヤオトン)」。黄土高原地域の横穴式住居。かつては黄土の崖に横穴を掘ったが，現在の陝西省北部では，石造りのアーチ状構造物を作ってそれを住居とする。雨の少ない黄土高原の風土に適した，冬は暖かく，夏は涼しい住居。口絵参照。
- [11] **Particularly striking is . . . :**「とりわけ際立っている[目につく]のは…」。このような倒置は英語でもしばしば用いられる(8 章 [196]，11 章 [144])(e.g. *Also to be noted is* the fact that the number of applicants has been on the decline for the past several years.)。このイントロダクションの最後の文にも注目。
- [19] **soundscape:**「サウンド(sound)」と，「〜の眺め/景」を意味する接尾語「スケープ(-scape)」とを複合させた造語で，「音の風景」と訳される。視覚中心の landscape(風景，景観)に対してあえて soundscape という語を打ち出したのはカナダの作曲家 R. マリー・シェーファー(R. Murray Schafer)であり，この語の創出により，彼は環境に対する聴覚からの新たなアプローチを生み出すことになった。
- [27] **fires being started with bellows:** start a fire は「火をおこす」に相当する表現。bellows [bélouz] は「ふいご(火をおこすための送風器)」で単複同形。

morning's work in the field is over, the chattering of the villagers and the calls of peddlers echo throughout the area. These days, the sounds of motorcycles and of automobiles, too, fill the air, but thanks to the acoustic effects of the valley even these modern noises produce a lively and cheerful effect. [30]

On festival days or days on which rituals are held, the sounds of the *suona* and of drums reverberate through the air to let the villagers know that festivities are beginning. Music is an important part of the village soundscape. Even a small village has several semi-professional musicians who are experts in playing the *suona*, an instrument which requires the performer to inhale from the nose and exhale through the mouth simultaneously, in order to produce continuous sound. The sound of firecrackers, also always used on these occasions, echoes far across the surrounding valleys. [35] [40]

People's voices also travel clearly through the air across the valleys; the acoustic space here seems to be even better than that of a carefully designed concert hall. Maybe that is one reason why the area produces exceptionally good singers. But it's not only beautiful sounds that travel. On stormy days, crashing rolls of heavy thunder rock the land as if a dragon were tumbling down through the valley. When torrential rains hit, the valleys echo with the thumping sounds of falling lumps of yellow clay. [45] [50]

The text for this session was written by a scholar engaged in participant observation, an anthropological method used to study a community. However, unlike conventional participant observation, in which the anthropologist is positioned only as an observer, the writer of this text was acutely aware that she was not only observing but also being observed. She not only heard the different sounds around her, but also, as a part of the community, produced various sounds herself, that were heard by others. Out of this process of engaged participant observation came a text that tries to capture for its readers something of daily life in a remote Chinese village while inspiring them to imagine its unique and interesting soundscape. [55] [60]

Local musicians playing *suona*

[29] **the chattering:** chatter は「ぺちゃくちゃしゃべる」(cf. She's quite a *chatterbox*, isn't she?)。

[32] **the acoustic effects:**「音響効果」。acoustic の発音が [əkúːstɪk] であることに注意。

[35] ***suona*:**「嗩吶」。チャルメラに似た管楽器。

[47] **crashing rolls of heavy thunder:** crash も roll も thunder を描写するのによく用いられる語 (e.g. a great *crash of thunder* / I could hear *thunder rolling* in the distance.) で，日本語の「ゴロゴロ」や「バリバリ」という擬音語に相当する。「雷が落ちる」に当たる英語は "lightning hits [strikes]" である。

[49] **torrential rains hit:** torrential [tɔːrénʃəl] rain は「豪雨」。地震，台風などの自然の脅威が「襲う」と言う場合に英語では hit または strike を用いるのが普通であることに注意 (e.g. Another typhoon is expected to *hit* Tokyo early next week. / cf. But then tragedy *struck*.)。

[49] **the thumping sounds of . . . :**「…のドサッという音」。thump も擬音語的な語 (cf. I saw something fall off the roof and then heard *a thump* on the ground.)。以下本文でも容易に確認できるように，日本語の擬音語（onomatopoeia）が表現する音を英語では動詞（以下擬音動詞と呼ぶ）の意味に含めて表すことが多い (e.g. The rocket *roared* up into the sky.「ゴーッという音を立てて空へと飛び立った」/ A garbage truck *clanged* down the street.「ガタゴトと音を立てて通りを走って行った」)(7章 [95])。

[55] **acutely aware:**「強く意識している」と言う場合によく用いられる組み合わせ (cf. They are *painfully aware* of the gravity of the situation.)。

[59] **engaged participant observation:** engaged は「（傍観者としてではなく）積極的［直接的］に関わっている」。

# Yangjiagou Soundscape

## Junko Iguchi

The village of Yangjiagou is made up of about 300 *yaodong*, scattered across the slopes of a V-shaped space created by a river cutting between two hills. Almost a thousand people live in the *yaodong*, which are dug right into the sides of the valley. Many different kinds of sounds reverberate through the lived space of this valley community, and these are what make up the "sound of the village" for its people. Even the sound of the bell attached to a baby's foot in the front yard of a *yaodong* dug into one side of the hill can be clearly heard on the other hillside across the river, 100 meters away.

That so many small sounds, from so many corners, can be heard so clearly throughout the village is the result not only of the unique landscape here but also of the lack of any competing background noise. There is hardly any of the steady rumbling and roaring we associate with cars, factories, or machinery. Of course, since the road along the river leads to a small town, occasionally some cars pass through the village — but actually not so many. And because electricity is only available at nighttime, there are no television or radio sounds during the day. The only conspicuous sounds to be heard in the village from early morning to sunset are human voices and the sounds of animals, particularly chickens and donkeys.

Here is the typical soundscape of a day in the village, recorded on July 29, 1995:

At about five o'clock in the morning, as the sunlight slowly begins to light the valley, people begin walking towards the village wells to collect water. From the well used by the family I am living with, one can hear the sound of the pail going deep down into the hole, as well as the exchanges of greetings with the other families who have gone there to get their morning water. The area around the well gets most crowded in the summer at about six in the morning. After people return to their houses, one hears the sounds of bamboo brooms cleaning the front yard and bellows being used for cooking inside the *yaodong*.

Down around the village plaza, motor tricycles are parked, wait-

- [62] **The village of Yangjiagou:** Yangjiagou は漢字で表記すると「楊家溝」。
- [66] **reverberate:**「反響する」。
- [66] **lived space:**「生きられた空間」「生活空間」。
- [75] **There is hardly any of the steady rumbling and roaring:** hardly any... は「…がほとんどない」と言う場合によく用いられる決まった組み合わせ（cf. I *hardly ever* eat hamburgers.）。steady は「絶え間ない」「ひっきりなしの」。rumbling は「ゴロゴロ」「ゴトゴト」, roaring は「ゴーゴー」といった感じの擬音動詞派生の表現。
- [76] **machinery:**「機械類」。machines と同じものを指すのに使えるが不可算名詞であることに注意。このように，複数の異なるものを(機能などの共通性に基づいて)一括りにして指す(構成要素の個別性を捨象する)名詞は，不可算になる傾向がある (e.g. garbage / trash / furniture / luggage / stationery / cutlery / weaponry)。
- [80] **conspicuous** [kənspíkjuəs]:「顕著な」「際立った」（cf. her *conspicuous* absence）。

ing to pick up the villagers who go to work in the nearest town. At about six in the morning, these tricycles take off along the main street, leaving the purring sound of their engines behind them all along the river. Once they are gone, the street is quiet except for when the vendors appear. During the morning hours, for example, a tofu seller always comes, announcing his arrival with his distinctive tone of voice. Then the women and children appear from their *yaodong* and there is some clamor in the village for a while. But once that is over, silence prevails again. At noon, the women come out again from their *yaodong* with their children and with noodle bowls in hand and quietly eat their lunch while looking down at the highway.

Afternoon is quiet again, perhaps because it is so hot. As the evening approaches, the sound of tricycles and bicycles is heard once more, as the people working in the town return home to the village. The songs of the children and the voices of women chattering with their neighbors as they prepare their evening meal echo throughout the valley. The trilling sound of bells is heard as shepherds return from the pastures with their sheep. When the smoke from evening cooking begins to appear from each house, the quiet returns again, as people go indoors to enjoy their evening hours. After sunset, silence descends. The only sounds one can hear are those of the insects, and the occasional human voices and coughing sounds that escape from the houses.

Reflecting on the daily rhythms of this village soundscape, I started to wonder how it had changed over the lifetime of the village's older residents. I asked people what sounds they remembered. The old people started to dredge up from their memories long-gone sounds to tell me about. They told me that, in the past, the sounds that most clearly symbolized the village for them had come from three bells. The "big bell" (*dazhong*) was placed in the school ground of an elementary school and could be heard as far away as five kilometers [Figure 1]. It was only used in case of emergency, including the time when the Red Army (the Communist Army) was approaching the village. The "*pailou* bells" had been installed at the entrance to the village by the Ma family, who were the landlords of the whole area, towards the end of the Qing dynasty. Eight bells were hung from the "*pailou*," or gate [Figure 2]. The figure here shows a drawing of the *pailou* made for me by the mason of the village. When he started drawing this from his memory, he began with the bells, which suggests how intimately the *pailou* was associ-

**Figure 1**　大鐘 (*dazhong*)　**Figure 2**　牌楼 (*pailou*)。いずれも馬師元画。

- [98] **the purring sound of ...**:「…のブーン[ブルルル]という音」。この場合の purr は快調なエンジン音を表す擬音動詞。
- [100] **vendors**:「行商人」(cf. a *vending* machine)。
- [103] **there is some clamor ...**:「村はしばらくの間ちょっとガヤガヤする」。clamor は「(ガヤガヤという)喧噪」。
- [113] **The trilling sound of bells**: trill は鈴が鳴る音を表す擬音動詞。
- [123] **dredge up**:「(過去の出来事を)掘り起こす」。
- [127] **as far away as five kilometers**:「5 キロも離れたところで」(cf. We may be informed of the results *as early as* next week.「来週にも」)。
- [129] **the Red Army (the Communist Army)**:「紅軍」。正式名称は中国工農紅軍であり，現在の中国人民解放軍の初期 (1927–37) における名称。中国共産党の指揮下に成立・発展し，日中戦争期 (1937–45) は，八路軍・新四軍となって抗日戦を戦った。なお，the Red Army は，ソ連の場合は「赤軍」(ソ連軍の旧称 [1918–46]) であり，その他の共産主義国家の軍隊を指す場合もある。
- [130] ***pailou***:「牌楼」。街頭に，飾りとして，または記念・祝賀用に建てられた，屋根のある装飾門。
- [132] **the Qing [tʃín] dynasty**:「清朝」(1616–1912)。
- [134] **mason**:「石工」。

ated with the sound of the bells in his mind. By listening to the sounds of the bells, the villagers were able to detect the direction as well as the force of the wind, even from inside their houses. When the wind blew from the south, the bells made a sound like "pui tai tai, pui tai tai." A wind from the north would make a sound like "tone tone." The third bell, the temple bell, is the only one still present and audible today. It is located on the top of the hill and produces a dry sound. The sound does not linger much but echoes throughout the village when the villagers go to the temple to pray. All three of these bells used to be heard by all of the villagers, and sometimes served to convey information. They were the sounds that symbolized the village community.

Another interesting group of remembered sounds are more modern: the sounds produced by electrical equipment. The earliest of these was the sound of movies, which started to be shown in the village in the mid-1950s. At that time, because there was no electricity running in the village, an electric generator was used. After that, the sounds of cable broadcasting came to the village. Villagers installed small speakers inside their houses and listened to the news, everyone at the same time, three times a day. The broadcasting service was started by the soldiers of the Red Army and ended soon after the death of Mao Zedong in 1976. During the Cultural Revolution, a large loudspeaker was set up on the hillside. This was only there for ten years, during the period of the Cultural Revolution. The speaker was used to convene meetings but it also blasted political messages many times a day, and was actually a great nuisance for many of the villagers. Compared to the general quietness that wraps itself around the area today, the soundscape of that era can hardly be imagined. Cable broadcasting was replaced by the radio in the 1980s. Electricity had come to the village in 1985 and along with it, gradually, black and white television. But there are quite a few villagers who do not own television sets even today, and the number of hours they can watch television is limited, anyway.

A third group of sounds from the soundscape memories can still be heard today. In a village like this, environmental sounds are shared by all the residents. People always seem to have been particularly attuned to bird sounds. Another notable sound for them has been the river sound. The river that runs through the village is narrow and shallow and the sound of the water cannot be heard unless one goes quite close to it. But even that small sound is, for some reason, not much liked by the villagers. What they like instead is the sound of the water coming up from the well. This seems

- [150] **electrical equipment:**「電気製品」。equipment が不可算名詞であることに注意（cf. electric(al) appliances）。
- [158] **Mao Zedong:**「毛沢東」。中国の政治家（1893–1976）。湖南省出身。1921 年の中国共産党創立に参加，31 年に中華ソヴィエト政権が樹立されたとき主席に選ばれ，35 年に党の主導権を掌握。49 年，中華人民共和国の成立とともに政府主席になり，54〜59 年には国家主席の地位にあった。
- [158] **the Cultural Revolution:**「文化大革命」。1966 年から 76 年にかけて，中国全土で展開された権力闘争のことで，正しくは「プロレタリア文化大革命」，略して「文革」とも呼ばれる。資本主義復活への修正主義を阻止する目的をもって毛沢東が発動したもので，この運動の尖兵として高校生・大学生のあいだに全国規模で紅衛兵が組織され，また闘争の手段としての大字報(壁新聞)が各地に氾濫した。その後，文化大革命は，文革派と脱文革の実務派官僚グループとの権力闘争を経て，76 年秋の毛沢東の死と江青ら文革派のリーダー「四人組」の逮捕をもって実質的に終結した。
- [161] **convene** [kənvíːn] **meetings:**「会議を招集する」。
- [161] **blasted:** この場合の blast は「がなりたてる」。
- [162] **a great nuisance:**「大いに迷惑なもの」「大迷惑」（cf. It's *a nuisance* having to get his approval every time we want to start something new.）。
- [172] **have been particularly attuned to . . . :** be attuned to . . . は「(…)になじんでいる，慣れている，適応している」。

to be because the water in the river represents potentially bad times for their small farms. When there is not enough water, there is a [180] drought. But when there is too much water, the river floods the nearby fields, destroying the crops. The sound of the river water reminds villagers of the bad experiences of the past and of the possibility of further misfortunes in the future. On the other hand, the sound of the water coming up from the well reminds people of [185] social occasions, because that is where people have always gathered and socialized with each other.

These environmental sounds are a part of daily life and for that simple reason it is rather difficult for the residents to be really aware of the way they have changed over time. But clearly, in the past fifty [190] years, various sounds have appeared and disappeared in this village. Interestingly, it seems that the village has become quieter in recent years. The population has remained more or less the same but the site of the local government has been moved from this village to another. Electricity is available, but there are no phones [195] here. Villagers say "now is the quietest time" they can remember.

[187] **socialized with . . . :** socialize with . . . は「…と打ち解けてつき合う」(cf. He doesn't do much *socializing*.)。

[193] **more or less the same:**「大体同じ」「ほぼ同じ」と言う場合の決まった表現のひとつ(12章[30])(cf. (pretty) much the same, essentially the same)。

# 10

# EMPIRE

## Introduction

### Yoshiki Tajiri

At the beginning of the novel *A Study in Scarlet* (1887), which marks the very first appearance of Sherlock Holmes, Dr. Watson recounts how he met Holmes for the first time. After completing his studies in medicine, Dr. Watson was attached to a regiment and sent to India as an assistant surgeon. This was soon after the second Afghan war broke out. During the campaign in Afghanistan, Watson was injured in the shoulder, and while in hospital was struck down by typhoid fever, "that curse of our Indian possessions". Being of no use to the army, he was sent back to England to recuperate.

Having nothing to do, Dr. Watson "naturally gravitated to London, that great cesspool into which all the loungers and idlers of the empire are irresistibly drained". He was well aware that he was one of those "loungers and idlers". There, he happens to meet an old friend, who introduces him to Sherlock Holmes as a possible fellow lodger. The memorable first meeting between them takes place in a chemical laboratory in a London hospital. As soon as they meet, Holmes characteristically astonishes Watson by remarking, "You have been in Afghanistan, I perceive".

Now we can see how their encounter is coloured by Britain's imperial projects. Dr. Watson, the narrator of almost all the Sherlock Holmes stories, is himself a kind of foreign object imported from the empire, just like all the other strange people, animals and diseases from abroad that Holmes copes with. By competently solving all manner of problems involving exotic elements both fascinating and disturbing, perhaps Holmes (and his stories) had the symbolic effect of alleviating the anxiety of people living in an over-expanded empire.

In his 1985 article in the *Journal of Geography*, "The Landscapes of

[1] ***A Study in Scarlet* (1887), which marks ...**: *A Study in Scarlet*（邦訳名は『緋色の研究』）はArthur Conan DoyleによるSherlock Holmesものの記念すべき第一作。動詞markはこのように物事を主語にして「(重要な出来事や変化など)を示すものになる」という意味で用いられることが多い (cf. 2章 [38]) (cf. This round of talks is expected to *mark* a turning point in the relations between the two countries.)。

[2] **Dr. Watson recounts:** recount は「(自らの経験などを)物語る」。

[4] **was attached to a regiment:**「ある連隊に配属されていた」。

[5] **the second Afghan war:** 1838年から42年の第一次アフガン戦争以来，インドを拠点とするイギリスとロシアの間でアフガニスタンをめぐる領土争いが続いた。第二次アフガン戦争 (1878–80) では，国王の親露政策に反発し，イギリス軍が侵攻。戦争中に結んだ条約により，イギリスはアフガニスタン外交へ介入できるようになった。1919年，第三次アフガン戦争の後，アフガニスタンは正式に独立する。

[6] **During the campaign in Afghanistan** [æfgǽnəstàːn]: この場合のcampaignは「軍事行動」(cf. launch an aggressive *campaign* against smoking in public buildings / an election *campaign*「選挙運動」)。

[7] **was struck down by typhoid fever:** ここでの be struck down by ... は「…(病気)に倒れる」(cf. His whole family *came down with* the flu.)。typhoid fever は「腸チフス」。

[8] **that curse of our Indian possessions:**「わがインド領のあの呪うべきもの」とは typhoid fever のこと。our Indian possessions と言っているのは当時インドが英国の植民地だったため。

[9] **recuperate:**「療養する」。

[10] **gravitated to London, that great cesspool into which ...:** gravitate to ... は「引力に引かれるように，…(魅力のあるもの)に引きつけられていく」。cesspool は「汚水貯め」だが，ここではもちろん be drained into ... (「(水などの液体が)…の中へと吸い込まれていく」) とともに比喩的に用いられている。汚水に喩えられているのは all the loungers and idlers of the empire「大英帝国のすべての無為徒食の輩(やから)」。

[17] **Holmes characteristically astonishes Watson:** ここでの characteristically はいわゆる文副詞で「いかにも(ホームズ)らしく」という感じ。ホームズはその人並みはずれた推理力と観察力でワトソンを驚かせるのが常であった。ここでホームズが初対面のワトソンに対してアフガニスタン帰りであることを言い当てたのは，物語の設定されている1881年時点では，「軍医が熱帯で肩に負傷するほどの苦難に遭う場所は，明らかにアフガニスタンである」という推測による。

[24] **all manner of ...:**「さまざまな(種類の)…」という意味の決まった言い方。manner が単数形であることに注意 (7章 [160])。

[26] **alleviating:** alleviate [əlíːvièɪt] は「(苦痛や問題を)軽減する」。

Sherlock Holmes", the geographer Yi-Fu Tuan explains why he believes Arthur Conan Doyle's well-known stories about the detective Sherlock Holmes can provide readers today with useful insight into Victorian England. Finding many parallels between the fictional world inhabited by Sherlock Holmes and the real world known to Doyle, his creator, Tuan argues that we can deduce a great deal about the social and cultural geography of Victorian England from the texts. For example, Tuan explains, "Holmes's world exudes confidence in science and rationality, but also self-doubt and misanthropy". Similarly, in the real Victorian England, "on the one hand, the English exhibited enormous confidence in material progress; on the other hand, they were aware that society had grown unmanageably large and complex, with seething unassimilable elements that might erupt in violence". Tuan explains how the stories show that a "'dark London' (the analogy being 'dark Africa') was thought to exist in the heart of the imperial capital, threatening to unsettle the even tempo and polite surfaces of bourgeois life". The appeal of the competent and resourceful Holmes to Victorian readers thus becomes obvious: "If only England had someone, endowed with almost supernatural intelligence, who could penetrate the gloom. If only there were a court of final appeal to which bewildered people could go when the established institutions of order and justice failed". Sherlock Holmes was just such a man, his rooms in Baker Street just such a court of final appeal.

In this article on the late Victorian landscapes, both literal and imaginary, depicted in the Sherlock Holmes stories, Tuan focuses on a wide range of topics including the geographical reach of Victorian England, Victorian views of the natural world and of the relationship between character and physical appearance, and the ways in which Victorians understood the environment to influence human institutions, behaviour, and mood. In the text for this session, he first deals with the geographical imagination of the late Victorians at the height of the British Empire, and then with Victorian attitudes towards the city and the natural world.

[31] **provide readers today with useful insight into ...:** provide (someone with) insight [an insight / insights] into ... は give someone insight [an insight / insights] into ... や gain insight into ... (2章[156], 7章[65])と並ぶ insight を用いた頻出表現で,「(人に)…の本質を理解させてくれる」といった意味 (e.g. Her latest book has *given* us a real *insight into* how our mind works.)。

[34] **deduce:** シャーロック・ホームズと言えば必ず出てくる動詞(名詞は deduction)で,「推理する」という意味。推理の材料が from 以下に来て, 結論が目的語で表現される。

[36] **exudes** [ɪgzjúːdz] **confidence:**「信頼にあふれている[を発散させている]」。

[37] **misanthropy:**「人間嫌い」。anthrop(o) は「人間の」「人類の」という意味の連結形 (e.g. anthropology)。

[41] **with seething unassimilable elements that might erupt in violence:** seething のもとになっている seethe は「(心に秘めた)怒りに体を震わせる」。unassimilable は「(社会に)同化することができない」(cf. Some immigrants find it difficult to *assimilate* into the community.)。elements は「社会や組織の中で(しばしばその集団外では受け入れられにくい)特定の主義, 目的, 習慣などを共有する集団」(e.g. discontented *elements* in the party「党内の不満分子」)。erupt in violence は「暴動を起こす」(cf. go up in flames [smoke])。

[43] **the analogy being 'dark Africa':** analogy は「類推」「類比」。'dark London' が当時よく使われた 'dark Africa' を模した表現であることに注意を促している。(cf. the *dark* Continent「暗黒大陸」。この表現は H. M. Stanley, *Through the Dark Continent* (1878) 以来, アフリカ大陸の呼び名として定着)。

[44] **the imperial capital:** 当時の英国が大英帝国であったため, その首都ロンドンを指す。

[44] **threatening to unsettle the even tempo:** 主節の内容をより具体的に述べるための分詞構文の用法(4章[17], 8章[170])。threaten to ... は「…するぞとおどす」という意味 (e.g. He *threatened* to call the police.) だが, ここではよくない事態が発生しそうであることを表すために助動詞的に使われている (e.g. Typhoon No. 11 is *threatening* to hit Tokyo early tomorrow.)。even tempo は「規則正しい[安定した]テンポ」の意味で, 平穏無事な生活を表している。

[46] **resourceful:**「問題を解決したり, 事態に対処したりする能力に優れた」という意味。快刀乱麻を断つごとく難事件を解決する名探偵シャーロック・ホームズにはまさにぴったりの表現。

[47] **If only England had ...:**「…であったらよいのに」という(叶えられない)願望を, if only の後にこのように仮定法の節を続けて表現することはよくある (e.g. *If only* I *had* more money.)。only が使われているのは日本語の「…でさえあれば(よいのに)」と同様の発想によるもの。

[47] **endowed with almost supernatural intelligence:**「ほとんど超自然的な(常人をはるかに越えた)頭脳に恵まれた」。(be) endowed with ... は「生まれつき, または自然に…という能力, 才能, 特性などを備えた」(5章[51])。

[49] **a court of final appeal:** appeal は「上訴」「控訴」「上告」「抗告」)で, court は「裁判所」。したがって全体として「終審裁判所」の意味だが, ここでは, すぐ後を読めばわかるように,「事件の解決に警察などの公的な機関が失敗した時に最後の頼みの綱として助けを求めるところ」という比喩的な意味で用いられている。

[51] **his rooms in Baker Street just such a court of final appeal:** Baker Street と just の間に were が省略されている。動詞を共有する同じ構造の文が連続する時には, このように2つ目以降の文ではその動詞がしばしば省略される。

[61] **at the height of ...:**「…の絶頂期に」。

# The Landscapes of Sherlock Holmes

## Yi-Fu Tuan

### Geographical Scope

An empire is made up of many ethnic groups and cultures. When they come to England, they add color and life to the country but also — to xenophobic natives — a vague sense of threat. This sense is heightened when not only strange people but strange, and possibly dangerous, animals and diseases find their way into the carefully tended, cozy landscapes of England. In "The Speckled Band" an ominous mood is created over the Surrey estate of Dr. Grimesby Roylott when we are told not only of the mysterious events taking place there but, in addition, that Roylott, although extremely antisocial, allowed gypsies to roam over the grounds, as also a cheetah and a baboon that he had brought back with him from India. Surrey is a part of England that calls up images of civilized calm and quintessential English ways. Yet, on the Roylott estate there lurked these alien presences from the distant corners of the empire including — the reader discovers at the end of the story — India's deadliest snake, the swamp adder. In "The Adventure of the Dying Detective," we are informed that Chinese sailors worked in the London docks. Holmes claimed to have caught a painful disease there, for the alleviation of which he pretended to seek the help of a Mr. Culverton Smith from Sumatra, a specialist on Oriental microbes and Holmes's enemy.

In the stories, these signs of alien presence, in themselves, are able to project an atmosphere of impending chaos and doom. Victorians, for all their show of confidence, deeply doubted that they could comprehend, much less control, a world so large, turbulent, and strange. There was so much that they did not know. Who in Europe had the power of mind to grasp the myriad linkages of actors and events in distant parts of the world? Who, moreover, had the physical stamina to go to these places and investigate in person, should the occasion demand it? The answer is, of course, Sherlock Holmes. Unlike another mental giant, his brother Mycroft, Sherlock was a

[66] **xenophobic natives:** xenophobic [zènəfóubik] は「外国人嫌い[恐怖症]の」。「外国人嫌い[恐怖症]」は xenophobia (cf. acrophobia, agoraphobia, claustrophobia)。

[68] **find their way into . . . :**「…に入り込む」(13章 [89]) (e.g. I wonder how your passport has *found its way into* my bag. / cf. Are you sure you can *find your way* home?)。

[69] **"The Speckled Band":**「まだらの紐」("The Adventure of the Speckled Band," 1892)。ロンドンの南側に隣接するサリー州で起きた，インド帰りの軍医 (Grimesby Roylott) の屋敷を舞台にした殺人事件。

[70] **ominous** [ámənəs]:「不吉な」(cf. omen [óumən])。

[73] **gypsies:** gypsy は今日，蔑称とされているので，Roma という呼称が用いられることが多い。

[73] **roam over the grounds:**「敷地内を徘徊する」。「敷地」の意味の grounds はこのように複数形で用いる (e.g. I used to live on the *grounds* of a temple.)。

[73] **as also a cheetah and a baboon:** as he also allowed a cheetah and a baboon to roam over the grounds ということ。

[75] **calls up images of . . . :**「…のイメージを呼び起こす」。

[76] **quintessential:** quintessence (「精髄」「本質」「典型」) の形容詞形。

[76] **there lurked these alien presences:** lurk は「(好ましくないものが)潜んでいる」。このように (be 動詞以外でも) 存在や出現を表す動詞は，there で始まる構文でよく用いられ，人やものを新たに導入する役割を果たす (e.g. *There remain* three major issues to address.)。

[79] **"The Adventure of the Dying Detective":**「瀕死の探偵」(1913)。

[81] **Holmes claimed to have caught a painful disease there:** claim はこのように to 不定詞を伴って「…であると主張する」という意味を表すことがある。Holmes claimed that he had caught . . . という言い方も可能。ちなみに，ここで言う "a painful disease" は，より具体的には「スマトラのクーリー病 (a coolie disease from Sumatra)」と呼ばれている。

[81] **for the alleviation of which . . . :** which の先行詞は a painful disease だから，「その病気の症状を緩和するために」。alleviation < alleviate: make less severe.

[82] **a Mr. Culverton Smith:** 固有名詞に a がついているのは (日本語の「…という人」と同じく) 読者にとって未知の人物であることを表示するため (cf. It's *a* Sony.)。

[86] **impending chaos and doom:** impending は「(通例よくないことが) 間もなく起こりそうな」。chaos は「渾沌」「カオス」だが，英語の発音は [kéɪɑs] であることに注意 (cf. chaotic [keɪɑ́tɪk])。

[87] **for all their show of confidence:**「自信があるように見せかけてはいても」。for all . . . は in spite of . . . とほぼ同じ意味の表現 (e.g. *For all* his credentials, he is clearly incompetent)。

[87] **deeply doubted that . . . :** doubt that . . . はこのように「…ではないと思う」という that 節の内容を否定する意味を表すことに注意。much less は let alone 同様，このように (理解できないのだから支配はなおさら不可能，といった) 否定の文脈で用いられる。

[92] **in person:**「(他人にやらせたり，他人から聞くのではなく) 本人自ら (が行う，行く)」(e.g. They told me how much fun they had at the party. I wish I had been there *in person*.)。

[92] **should the occasion demand it:**「必要とあらば」。このように仮定法の仮定を表す節で if を用いない場合には倒置 (yes-no 疑問文と同じ語順) になる (13章 [198]) (e.g. *Had I* stayed there longer, I would probably have been killed.)。「必要があれば」の意味の表現としては他に if necessary / if need be / if the need arises などがある。

[94] **Mycroft:** Sherlock Holmes の7歳年上の兄。弟よりも優れた頭脳の持ち主だが，実際的な行動力には欠けるという設定になっている。

At the Reichenbach Falls
(drawing by Sidney Paget)

man of action and an indefatigable traveler who could make himself thoroughly at home, whatever the social setting, in all countries of the world. Consider the almost offhand way with which Holmes described his itinerary to Watson after the near fatal combat with Professor Moriarty at Switzerland's Reichenbach Falls:

"I travelled for two years in Tibet and amused myself by visiting Lhasa, and spending some days with the head lama. You may have read of the remarkable explorations of a Norwegian named Sigerson, but I am sure that it never occurred to you that you were receiving news of your friend. I then passed through Persia, looked in at Mecca, and paid a short but interesting visit to the Khalifa at Khartoum, the results of which I have communicated to the Foreign Office. Returning to France I spent some months in a research into the coal-tar derivatives, which I conducted in a laboratory at Montpellier."
("The Adventure of the Empty House")

## LOCAL KNOWLEDGE
If the empire and the world seemed at times to consist of turbulent human masses beyond the capacity of the mind to order and understand, so did (at a smaller scale) the sprawling cities of Europe. The unbounded variety of a metropolis made it seem a great mystery. What thoughts and passions lurked behind the myriad of impassive faces, or behind the facades of the interminable rows of houses, tenements, and buildings? An insistent curiosity, driven by malaise, already existed in the eighteenth century. As early as 1707, in the first significant urban novel, Alain-René Lesage suggested that only

- [95]　**indefatigable** [ɪndɪfǽtɪgəbl]:「不屈の」「疲れを知らない」(cf. fatigue [fətíːg])。
- [95]　**could make himself thoroughly at home . . . in all countries of the world:**「世界のどの国にあってもくつろぐことができる」。at home は「(ある場所にいて，ある人と一緒にいて，あることを行っていて)緊張しない，くつろいでいる，心地よい」という状態を表す表現 (e.g. It took me a while before I began to feel *at home* working on the new team.)。来客に対して「どうぞくつろいで下さい」「楽にして下さい」と言う時の決まり文句としての"Make youself *at home*" も参照。
- [97]　**the almost offhand way:**（普通に考えると大変なことなのに）「大したことではないかのように」「こともなげに」という感じ。
- [98]　**the near fatal combat:** 悪の天才，宿敵モリアーティ教授 (James Moriarty) と戦ってもう少しで死ぬところだったことを指す。作者のドイルは「最後の事件」("The Final Problem," 1893)でホームズをモリアーティとともにスイスのライヘンバハ滝で転落死させたのだが，読者の強い要望などもあって，10年後，「空家の冒険」(1903) で「復活」させた。ホームズが実は死んでおらず，モリアーティ一味から姿を隠すために世界を旅行していたという設定にしたのである。ところで，チベットのラサで「ラマの頭」（ラマはチベット仏教の僧）に会い，ペルシャを通ってメッカを訪れ，ハルツーム（スーダンの首都）でカリフ (Muhammad の後継者; イスラム教国の教主，首長) に会った，というホームズの「旅程」は，同時代のイギリスの帝国主義的活動と密接に結びついた地名を辿っていることに注意。
- [103]　**I am sure that it never occurred to you that . . . :**「…だとは夢にも思わなかっただろうね」(cf. Didn't it *occur to* you to call me?)。
- [107]　**the coal-tar derivatives:**「コールタールの誘導体」。「誘導体」とは化学用語。ある化合物の一部分が変化して生じた化合物を，もともとの化合物に対して「誘導体」と言う。
- [108]　**Montpellier:** モンペリエはフランス南部の都市。
- [112]　**beyond the capacity of the mind to order and understand:**「人間の秩序立ててものを理解する能力を超えた」。order はこの場合「整理する」「秩序 (order) を与える」という意味の動詞。理解しようとする対象がいかに chaotic (< chaos) であるかがわかる。
- [113]　**the sprawling cities of Europe:** sprawling は都市などがだらしなく広がっている様子を表すのによく使われる (cf. urban *sprawl*)。
- [115]　**impassive faces:**「(感情が表出されていない)無表情な顔」。
- [116]　**facades** [fəsáːdz]:「建物の正面」。
- [117]　**tenements:**「(通例都市の貧しい地域に建てられた)大型の共同賃貸住宅」。
- [117]　**malaise** [məléɪz]:「何となく不安な気持ち」。
- [119]　**Alain-René Lesage:** アラン゠ルネ・ルサージュ (1668–1747)。フランスの小説家，劇作家。ここでいう 1707 年のルサージュの「都市小説」とは，『跛の悪魔』(*La Diable boiteux*) を指す。松葉杖をつき山羊の足に顎のとがった黄色い顔といった異様な風体の悪魔アスモデがマドリードの夜空をさまよい，家々の屋根を剥ぎながら人々の生活を次々に暴露していく風俗風刺小説。

devils and demons could penetrate the facades and expose all the frivolities and vices of city life. Because Holmes demonstrated a talent for seeing behind the surface, he was frequently suspected of possessing devilish powers, although Watson — the most common target of these demonstrations — was too polite to say so. "You cunning, cunning fiend!" was all that the enraged Colonel Moran, the most dangerous criminal in England, could say to Holmes when he had been captured following the death of Moriarty.

What goes on in a large city? We would like to know because ignorance is frightening. We do find out a little about what takes place behind the walls of strange houses, and in strange neighborhoods, through the reports and gossipy stories of newspapers, radio, and television, but what we know is secondhand. In daydreams, perhaps, we see ourselves as possessing the freedom of the devil to move about, penetrate, and see; or the freedom of a man like Sherlock Holmes, clever, daring, energetic and with the social position to enter and be welcomed in all layers of society. Holmes felt as comfortable in a London drawing room as in a Turkish bath, a boxing gymnasium, or an opium den. He could speak on equal terms with a nobleman and a semiliterate prizefighter.

> "Good day, Lord St. Simon," said Holmes, rising and bowing. "Pray take the basket chair. This is my friend and colleague, Dr. Watson. Draw up a little to the fire, and we will talk this matter over."

When the nobleman suggested that Holmes was not used to having a member from his class of society as client, the proud denizen of Baker Street responded smoothly:

> "No. I am descending."
> "I beg pardon."
> "My last client of the sort was a king."
> ("The Adventure of the Noble Bachelor")

When the porter of Pondicherry Lodge, in *The Sign of Four*, refused to admit Holmes on the ground that he did not know him, Holmes cried genially.

> "Oh, yes you do, McMurdo. I don't think you can have forgotten me. Don't you remember the amateur who fought three rounds with you at Alison's rooms on the night of your benefit four years back?"
> "Not Mr. Sherlock Holmes!" roared the prizefighter. "God's truth! how could I have mistook you?"

- [121] **frivolities:** frivolity は「軽薄さ」。形容詞は frivolous「軽薄な」。
- [122] **he was frequently suspected of possessing devilish powers:** suspect [səspékt] someone of . . . で「人が…ではないかと疑う」「人に…の嫌疑をかける」(e.g. She is *suspected* of murder.)。そのような嫌疑をかけられる人のことも suspect [sʌ́spèkt] と呼ぶ。
- [125] **Colonel** [kə́ːrnl] **Moran:** モラン大佐は，ホームズの宿敵モリアーティの参謀。かつてインド陸軍に所属していたので，こう呼ばれている。「我々の東方の帝国が生んだ猛獣狩りの達人 (the best heavy-game shot)」という設定。"You cunning, cunning fiend!" は「空家の冒険」からの引用。
- [135] **daring:**「勇敢な」「危険を顧みない」。
- [136] **all layers of society:**「社会のあらゆる層」。
- [137] **a Turkish bath:**「トルコ風呂(浴場)」。トルコ風呂はサウナのような蒸し風呂のこと。「有名な依頼人」("The Adventure of the Illustrious Client," 1913) は，ホームズとワトソンが 1902 年 9 月 3 日にノーサンバーランド・アヴェニューのトルコ風呂の寝椅子に心地よく寝転がっている場面から始まる。
- [137] **a boxing gymnasium:** ホームズものの作品に「ボクシング・ジム」という言葉が出てくる場面はないが，ホームズがボクシングの名手であったことは，さまざまな箇所で言及されている。
- [138] **an opium den:**「阿片窟(阿片を吸わせる場所)」。「唇のねじれた男」("The Man with the Twisted Lip," 1891) でホームズはある事件の調査のために変装して阿片窟に潜入する。
- [138] **He could speak on equal terms with . . . :**「…と対等の立場で話ができた」(cf. He and I are now *on first-name terms*.)。
- [139] **semiliterate:**「かろうじて読み書きができる」(cf. literate, illiterate)。
- [141] **Pray take the basket chair:** Pray は Please と同義。basket chair は「柳枝製の肘掛椅子」。
- [145] **the proud denizen of Baker Street:**「ベーカー街の誇り高き住人」とはもちろんホームズのこと。
- [147] **I am descending:** 先回の同種の事件よりも社会的に下の階層の顧客を相手にしているということ。
- [150] **"The Adventure of the Noble Bachelor":** 1892 年に発表されたこの作品のタイトルの邦訳は「独身貴族」あるいは「花嫁失踪事件」。
- [151] *The Sign of Four*:『四つの署名』(1890)。ポンディシェリ荘の門番マクマードは，かつてプロボクサー (prizefighter) だったという設定。
- [153] **genially:**「朗らかに」。
- [154] **I don't think you can have forgotten me:**「まさか私のことを忘れてしまったわけではないだろう」。否定的な内容の推量を表現する場合に，英語ではこのように "I don't think + 肯定平叙文" という形式を用いることが多い (e.g. *I don't think* you should contact her.「彼女に連絡しない方がいいと思う」)。
- [156] **benefit:** 一般には「慈善興行試合」だが，ここでは引退記念試合で，利益は引退する者に渡される。
- [158] **how could I have mistook you?:** もちろん正しくは how could I have mistaken you? で「どうして見間違えたりしたんでしょうか」という驚きの気持ちを表している。

For all the material progress made in the course of the nineteenth century, Victorians suspected that, not only their understanding of society was imperfect, but their control over nature might be more illusory than real. A striking feature of the Holmes stories is the sense of isolation even in London. Houses are fragile shelters. Families and individuals tend to fend for themselves, surrounded by hostile nature and society. The atmosphere is one of siege. Here is an example from one of Watson's narrations:

> "As we drove away, I stole a glance back, and I still seem to see that little group on the step — the two graceful, clinging figures [of Mrs. Forrester and Miss Morstan], the half-opened door, the hall light shining through stained glass, the barometer, and the bright stair-rods. It was soothing to catch even that passing glimpse of a tranquil English home in the midst of the wild, dark business which had absorbed us." (*The Sign of Four*)

But of course the key image in almost all the stories (particularly those that readers love) is 221B Baker Street. Repeatedly, Conan Doyle depicts it as an oasis of comfort and coziness in the midst of threatening chaos, human and natural.

The Sherlock Holmes Museum, Baker Street, London

- [160] **Victorians suspected that . . . :**「ヴィクトリア朝の人々は…ではないかと思っていた」。このように suspect that . . . は（[87] の doubt that . . . と異なり）「…ではないかと思う」という，that 節の内容を肯定する意味であることに注意(7 章 [189])。
- [161] **might be more illusory than real:**「現実と言うより幻想と言った方がよいかもしれない」(cf. He is *more* a politician *than* a statesman.)。
- [164] **fend for themselves:** fend for oneself は「(他人に頼らずに)自力でやっていく」という意味の決まった言い方。
- [165] **The atmosphere is one of siege:** ホームズの物語にたちこめているのは，「なにか(敵対的なもの)に包囲されているという雰囲気」である，ということ。
- [171] **It was soothing to . . . :**「…すると心が和んだ」。

# 11 ART

## Introduction
### Eiko Imahashi

For art lovers, an exhibition that focuses on certain individual artists or themes is a wonderful opportunity to see at one time works that are usually scattered around the world. I wonder how many people, when seeing an exhibit like that, purchase the catalog as they leave and take it home. Many may think it doesn't make sense to purchase a catalog after they have already seen the exhibit.

Surprisingly, however, these exhibition catalogs are "secret best sellers" that sell hundreds and thousands of copies. Unlike the situation in the United States or Europe, most exhibition catalogs sold in Japan do not have ISBN numbers and therefore are not marketed through bookstores. This makes many of these colorful and professionally designed catalogs quite affordable. Good catalogs also include academically oriented explications and plenty of bibliographic information. Thus, even though these catalogs may be difficult to obtain, they are definitely worth buying. It can even be argued that these catalogs serve as the basis for art-related research. Moreover, as art exhibits are currently being transformed from mere sequences of famous artworks to theme-based explorations of the association of art with non-art fields (such as literature, history, ethnology, anthropology, history of science, and others), the catalogs for such exhibits also enable people to reflect on the purpose of the project.

The first reading below develops this point about the significance of art catalogs and themed exhibits. The second reading approaches the topic from a slightly different angle. Taken from an article published in an English-language Japanese newspaper, it deals with the visit made to Japan in 2002 by a London-based art specialist who had come to view the exhibit "Christopher Dresser and Japan."

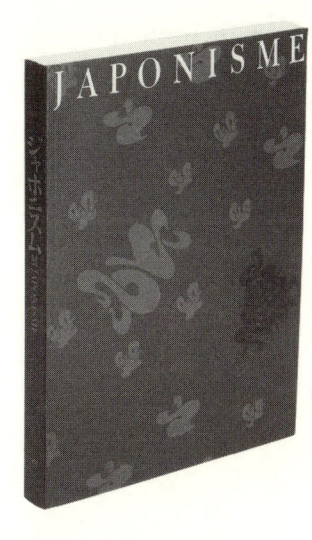

『「ジャポニスム」展カタログ』
（国立西洋美術館，1988 年）

- [5] **make sense:**「道理にかなっている」「なるほどと思える」(cf. That *makes* a lot of economic *sense*.)。
- [8] **sell:**「…(本など)がよく売れる」といった意味を表す場合，このように売れた部数を目的語として表現することもよくある (cf. Her latest novel *is selling like hot cakes*.)。
- [10] **ISBN:**「国際標準図書番号」。International Standard Book Number の略。
- [13] **academically oriented explications:** ... oriented は「…指向[志向]の」「…優先の」(e.g. Do you think the Japanese are as *group oriented* as many scholars have claimed?)。explication < explicate [éksplәkèıt]「解説する」。
- [18] **theme-based explorations ...:** ある共通のテーマに基づいて芸術と芸術以外の分野の結びつき[関連性]を研究すること。
- [19] **ethnology:**「民族学」。
- [28] **Christopher Dresser:** イギリスのデザイナー，著述家 (1834–1904)。植物図案を得意とし，壁紙を始め，家具，金属製品，陶器，ガラス，テキスタイルなど，あらゆる種類の家庭用品のデザインを手がけた。『デザイン原理』(*Principles of Decorative Design,* 1873) など，装飾デザインに関する本の著者でもある。日本の美術に興味をもち，1876 年，日本を訪れた最初のヨーロッパのデザイナーとなった。

Having loaned some of the key art works featured in both the exhibit and its related catalog, Andrew McIntosh Patrick came to Japan to view those objects in a new theme-based exhibit setting.

# The Pleasures of Exhibition Catalogs

## Eiko Imahashi

A former student of mine once asked me a surprising question. She said, "why is it necessary to purchase a catalog when I have already looked at the exhibit carefully?"

For this student, the event, or the exhibit, was understood to be the same as the book, or the catalog. The catalog is regarded in this view as something those who were unable to see the actual exhibit would purchase. In any case, the catalog is often too expensive for students to buy. Moreover, many people express a sense of disappointment with exhibition catalogs because they are unable to replicate, for readers, the sense of wonder that visitors experience in the presence of the "real" artworks. Unlike literary works, artworks are something that can only be encountered "here and now."

But can we simply dismiss exhibition catalogs as something unnecessary for art exhibits? The presence of a large number of high-quality catalogs that have been published recently clearly shows that such is not the case. The reason for having catalogs is not simply to reproduce beautiful artworks. These catalogs provide new light on the art pieces in the exhibit by connecting them organically with various kinds of information such as data regarding the works on display, their cultural context, the life of the artist, the background or the purpose of the exhibit, and other relevant resources.

Catalogs make it possible for people to reminisce over good exhibits. The information they contain can also be a source of some new discovery that might lead to a totally new interest. I once happened to go to an exhibit on Hungarian applied art. I was deeply impressed by the wonderfully rich culture of central Europe, which I knew nothing of at the time. As I read through the catalog, I almost

[30] **Andrew McIntosh Patrick:** 本文 [155] 参照。

[40] **replicate** [répləkèɪt]: 「再現する」（cf. They've been trying to *replicate* the results of their earlier experiments, so far without success.)。

[43] **"here and now":** 「今ここ」は現在目の前で生じている出来事の一回性，再現不可能性などを表現する際によく用いられるが，日本語の対応表現との語順の違いに注意 (cf. black and white / left and right / here and there)。

[44] **dismiss:** このようにしばしば目的語の後に as ... を伴って，「～を…であるとして簡単に片付ける[まともに扱わない]」という意味で用いられる (cf. I don't think it's a good idea to *dismiss* his proposal *out of hand*.)。

[47] **such is not the case:** 「そうではない」「それは正しくない」。「事実」「実情」という意味の the case を用いた決まった言い方のひとつ (cf. *Is it* really *the case that* a lot of teenagers simply can't live without their cell phones even for a single day?)。

[48] **provide new light on ... :** cf. Recent findings *cast new light on* life in ancient Greece. / I find her new book very *illuminating*.

[53] **reminisce** [rèmənís] **over ... :** 「…を楽しく[なつかしく]思い出す」。前置詞として about を伴うことも多い。reminiscence「回想」「追憶」から逆成 (back formation) によって作られた動詞 (cf. This tune is somehow *reminiscent of* another song I used to enjoy listening to years ago.)。

[56] **applied art:** 「応用芸術」とは，日常生活での利用を前提とした芸術のことで，たとえば壁紙やカーテンなどのデザイン，陶磁器，家具など。

decided that I had to learn Hungarian. I also went to an exhibit on Sergei Diaghilev, a ballet producer active in the 1920s in Paris, where he was living in exile. Because the exhibit had too much information on display and I felt it difficult to gain an overall picture, I purchased the catalog to study the significance of the exhibit later.

Catalogs should be considered on their own, even though it is true that they cannot be separated from the exhibits. Recent catalogs have been released in media other than printed books, such as CDs and DVDs, which enable their producers to experiment with the idea of reconstructing the whole exhibit three-dimensionally. But most catalogs are published, and it is published catalogs that I would like to consider a little further here.

Even among those people who really enjoy looking at art, there are probably only a few who regularly visit exhibits based on special themes. I have to admit that I am not one of those few. However, this is quite unfortunate, because Japanese museums are actually rather good at mounting exhibits centering on particular themes. For example, every year, there are excellent exhibits displaying the *ukiyo-e* painting collections of foreign museums and the treasures of famous temples. These exhibits hardly ever disappoint their visitors. In that respect, these quality exhibits based on certain themes should not be missed.

Another equally important theme often repeatedly exhibited in Japanese museums is Japonisme. Japonisme has already generated considerable research in the academic field, not only in art history but also in comparative culture, intercultural exchange and comparative art. Most people probably know something about the relationship of *ukiyo-e* composition to Van Gogh paintings, for example. However, current Japonisme research is now at some distance from that of the early stages, when scholars were simply investigating the mutual influence and impact of modern Western paintings and Japanese art.

The move away from this kind of study is related to the recognition that comparative literature and comparative culture can no longer be understood simply in terms of a "comparison between A and B." This trend away from rudimentary comparative study has been especially strong since Edward Said's work on Orientalism, which urged scholars to shift away from the conventional comparative study of Japonisme to the analysis of the phenomenon within the more rigorous conceptual framework of the "Orient as other, under the gaze of the West." Japonisme studies in Japan are now

[60] **Sergei Diaghilev:** ディアギレフ (1872–1929)。ロシアのバレエ興行主。貴族に生まれ，ペテルブルグで進歩的な芸術家のグループに入った後，パリへ移る。1909 年に，パリでロシア・バレエ団「バレエ・リュッス (Ballet Russes)」の旗揚公演を実現。以後 20 年間，一級の美術家，作曲家，文学者の協力を得て，バレエ界のみならず，20 世紀初頭の芸術運動全体を牽引した。

[61] **he was living in exile** [égzàɪl, éksàɪl]: live in exile は「(国外追放者として) 亡命生活を送る」。政治的な理由などで自国にいられなくなった者が国外で暮らすこと。ディアギレフの場合，かならずしも国外追放されたわけではないが，貴族としての出自ゆえに革命後のロシアに帰国できなかった事情を指しているのだろう (cf. political *exiles*)。

[62] **gain an overall picture:**「全体像をつかむ」。このように picture が「像」「イメージ」という意味で用いられるのは非常に一般的 (e.g. Politicians are finding it difficult to *paint a rosy picture of the economy* / cf. I'm finally beginning to *get the picture*.)。

[64] **on their own:** on one's own は「(他のものの付属物としてではなく) それ自体 [独立した存在] として」(cf. It's hard to believe that he wrote the essay *on his own*.)。

[66] **in media other than . . . :**「…以外の媒体で」。

[75] **mounting exhibits centering on . . . :** この場合の mount は「(展覧会などを) 開く，催す」(cf. hold an exhibition)。center on . . . は「…を中心とする」(cf. Our discussion *revolved around* what to do to make the project a success.)。

[82] **Japonisme:** ジャポニスムは，日本趣味，すなわち日本の物品，美術品に対する関心のことであり，特に，19 世紀後半に日本美術の影響をうけてフランスを中心として欧米で盛んになった美術の傾向。それは絵画，版画，彫刻，工芸など美術のあらゆる分野にわたるが，とくに印象派の画家に対する浮世絵の影響などが典型的な例として挙げられる。

[93] **in terms of . . . :**「…という観点から」「…に基づいて」という意味の重要な表現 (e.g. We are hardly ever conscious of the tacit assumptions *in terms of* which we make sense of our day-to-day experiences.)。

[94] **rudimentary** [rùːdəméntəri]:「初期段階の」(cf. rudiments「基本原理」「初歩」)。

[95] **Edward Said:** エドワード・サイードはパレスチナ生まれのアメリカ人文学者・批評家 (1935–2003)。コロンビア大学で長年教鞭をとるかたわら，活発な西洋文明批判を繰り広げた。主著 *Orientalism* (『オリエンタリズム』1978 年) は，いかに西洋が「東洋＝野蛮・未開」という〈他者〉表象を生み出すことで自らを文明として定義し，帝国主義を正当化していったかを論じた記念碑的著作で，20 世紀後半の文学・文化研究に多大な影響を与えた。

[98] **the "Orient as other, under the gaze of the West":** 西洋のまなざしのもとで東洋が西洋と異なる「他者」として色眼鏡付きで表象されてきたということ。オリエンタリズムとはその結果生じてきた虚構の表象の体系にほかならない。

[99] **are now under strong pressure to . . . :** be under pressure to . . . は「…するよう迫られて [強制されて] いる」という意味の重要な表現型 (e.g. We *were under tremendous pressure to deliver on our mission*)。

under strong pressure to be self-reflexive, in order to avoid the pitfall of a distorted nationalism that ingratiates itself with Euro-Americanism and tries to confirm its identity by being recognized by the West.[1]

This new research trend has meant that especially in the last fifteen years or so Japonisme exhibits in Japan have become recognizably more sophisticated, even "profound." The first notable exhibit of this new era was the large-scale Japonisme exhibit held in Paris and Tokyo in 1988, the result of major collaborative work between the French and Japanese. This exhibit produced a 400-page catalog that is not unlike the major catalogs published in Western Europe and America.

After this major exhibition, two significant trends appeared in Japonisme exhibits. Both engage in a reinvestigation of the notions of the "West" and "paintings" as well as "Japan." In other words, they necessitate a fresh look at the concept of Western Europe and at this style of paintings.

The first trend attempts to clarify particular aspects of Japonisme, as it turns out that it was surprisingly variable in areas outside of Western Europe. The focus of study has been expanded to include the United States, Britain, Vienna, and Prague, and the study of Japonisme has consequently become more detailed and interesting. In the United States, particularly after 2000, scholars began focusing their attention on the works of print artist Arthur Dow, who was influenced by Japonisme at the turn of the century and developed it into a unique educational system. Since the fall of the Berlin Wall there has also been increasing recognition of the value of studying the art of central Europe, and this has also had a clear impact on the recent trend in Japonisme exhibits.

The other major trend in recent Japonisme exhibits has been a broadening of scope to include genres other than paintings. The 1988 Paris-Tokyo exhibit mentioned above pioneered this trend by including ceramics, prints, furniture, and photographs. In the 1990s, Japonisme exhibits focusing on decorative arts and crafts have become the mainstream. There have been several small but solidly executed exhibits. The 1994 "Mode Exhibition" attracted attention because of its innovative approach. In the past few years, several exhibits have put crafts at the center, as their main theme. We have also seen not only art nouveau exhibits but also good exhibits focused on the works and the styles of skilled decorative artists such as Arthur Liberty, Charles Rennie Mackintosh and Christopher Dresser. Various exhibits on Japonisme, in this way, offer an exciting

- [100] **self-reflexive:**「内省的な」「自省的な」。
- [100] **avoid the pitfall of . . . :**「…という落とし穴を避ける」(e.g. This kind of *pitfall* is easy to fall into and very hard to climb out of.)。avoid と pitfall との結びつきは非常に一般的。
- [101] **ingratiates itself with . . . :**「…に取り入る」「…のご機嫌取りをする」(cf. an *ingratiating* smile)。
- [105] **recognizably more sophisticated:** recognizably は「目に見えて」「はっきりと」(cf. appreciably)。sophisticated は「洗練された」「高度な」で，ここでは [94] の rudimentary の反意語。
- [110] **that is not unlike . . . :** not unlike . . . は結局「…に似ている」という意味になる決まった組み合わせ (cf. In some countries, it's *not uncommon* for unmarried couples to live together.)。
- [123] **Arthur Dow:** アメリカの版画家（1857–1922）。アメリカ・ジャポニスムの担い手。ボストン美術館で日本美術を担当していたフェノロサと知り合い，日本美術に内在する抽象性に注目，それを西洋美術に応用する可能性を示唆した。浮世絵や着物デザイン見本帖などの収集も行った。1899 年に著した *Composition: A Series of Exercises in Art Structure for the Use of Students and Teachers* は，20 世紀初頭の美術教科書の古典として，現在でもリプリント版が出版されている。
- [124] **at the turn of the century:**「世紀転換期に」「世紀の変わり目に」という意味の決まった言い方であるが，ここではもちろん 19 世紀から 20 世紀初頭にかけてのこと。
- [125] **the Berlin Wall:**「ベルリンの壁」。東西の冷戦期の 1961 年に東ドイツが，拡大しつつあった自国民の西側への流出を阻むため，東西ベルリンの境界に築いた障壁。冷戦によるドイツおよび欧州の東西分断の象徴であったが，89 年 11 月，東欧の民主化運動の波を受けて破壊され，90 年のドイツ統一後，撤去された。
- [130] **genres:** genre は日本語の「ジャンル」に相当するが，発音は [ʒɑ́ːr] であることに注意。
- [131] **pioneered:** pioneer は「…の先駆け［先駆者］となる」。英語ではこのように名詞をそのままの形で関連する意味を表す動詞として用いることが多い (e.g. She *lectures* in American studies. / Have you *mopped* the floor yet? / The police will *dust* the room for fingerprints.)。
- [132] **ceramics, prints:**「陶磁器」と「版画」(cf. woodblock *prints*)。
- [133] **arts and crafts:**「美術工芸品」と言う場合の決まった組み合わせ。
- [134] **solidly executed exhibits:**「堅実に［しっかりと］行われた展覧会」(cf. There is no *solid* evidence that he was involved in any wrongdoing.)。
- [138] **art nouveau** [àːr nuvóʊ]:「アール・ヌーヴォー」。19 世紀末から 20 世紀初頭にかけて，西欧諸国を中心に開花した芸術様式。フランス語で「新しい芸術」の意味。波状曲線，植物的曲線による特異な装飾性を特徴とするこの様式は，宝石デザイン（ルネ・ラリック）からガラス工芸（エミール・ガレ），家具や建築（ヘンリ・ファン・デ・フェルデ）にいたるさまざまな装飾芸術・応用芸術の分野に波及した。
- [140] **Arthur Liberty:** イギリスのリバティ商会の創立者（1843–1917）。リバティ商会は，日本，中国，インドの陶器や絹といった東洋の物産を扱うことから始め，次第にアーツ・アンド・クラフツ運動の工芸作家と提携して染織や家具その他のオリジナル商品を販売するようになった。リバティ・スタイルは，アール・ヌーヴォーと同義のものとして人気を博した。
- [140] **Charles Rennie Mackintosh:** イギリスの建築家，家具デザイナー（1868–1928）。1893 年頃からグラスゴーでポスター，家具，工芸品のデザイナーとして活発な活動を始め，ヨーロッパ大陸のアール・ヌーヴォーに呼応する動きとして注目された。建築家・室内装飾家としての代表作はグラスゴー美術学校（1896 年の競争設計に当選）。

means for reconceptualizing our understanding of the various aspects of intercultural exchange.

Of particular value to us as viewers has been the fact that the catalogs of these decorative arts-and-crafts-related exhibits have been sympathetically rendered through sophisticated design and have included a wealth of vivid photographs. It is also good to see that things such as sketchbooks, books, and other materials relevant to the exhibits and the catalogs are now being given equal weight with the actual art works. I was impressed to see many visitors carefully looking at these related materials at the various exhibits. Exhibition catalogs, in this way, can play just as important a part as the actual exhibit in enhancing the appreciation and understanding of a significant artistic phenomenon.

# Christopher Dresser and Japan

## Angela Jeffs

Andrew McIntosh Patrick is managing director of the Fine Art Society, located in London's Bond Street. He is also an avid collector. Which is why he was in Japan in late April [2002], seeing items loaned to a museum in Fukushima Prefecture. This landmark exhibition will come to Tokyo on May 25, and then move on to Toyama and Tochigi. For the first time, Japan can see the work of the world's first industrial designer, Christopher Dresser.

Dresser was born in 1834 in Glasgow, Scotland. Trained as a botanist, it was an interest in organic forms that led him into design. He was also fascinated by the industrial revolution, which meant objects could be mechanically reproduced. He was a contemporary of William Morris, who was determined that craft techniques should not be lost. Yet their interests — ceramics, metalwork, furniture, furnishings and wallpapers — had much in common.

"Dresser had an extraordinary career," Patrick explains. "He saw no reason why mass-produced goods should not be well designed. After visiting Philadelphia's 1876 Expo, where he met the

[144] **Of particular value to us as viewers ...**:「見物するわれわれにとって特に価値があるのは…」。the fact that ... を主語とする倒置表現（8章[196]，9章[11]）。of particular value は particularly valuable とほぼ同じ意味（cf. of [the] utmost importance / of little consequence）。

[147] **a wealth of vivid photographs**:「たくさんの生き生きとした写真」。a wealth of ... は数や量が豊富にあることを表す際によく用いられる（cf. This site provides *a wealth of* information about your favorite cartoon characters.）。

[155] **the Fine Art Society:** the Fine Art Society (FAS) のホームページには，以下のような説明がある（http://www.faslondon.com/pages/home.html）。The Fine Art Society is one of the world's oldest art galleries, with premises in both London and Edinburgh. The company specializes in British art and design from the 17th to the 21st centuries and has traded from 148 New Bond Street, London, since its foundation in 1876.

[156] **an avid collector:** avid [ǽvəd] は通例限定的に用いて「(趣味などについて)熱心な」（e.g. an *avid* fan of Japanese movies）。

[162] **botanist** [bátənɪst]:「植物学者」（< botany / cf. zoology）。

[165] **a contemporary of ...**:「…と同時代人」。

[166] **William Morris:** イギリスの詩人，小説家，工芸家，社会改革家（1834–96）。D. G. ロセッティにひかれて画家を志望したが，のち工芸家に転向。1861年ロセッティ，バーン・ジョーンズらとともに，ステンド・グラス，家具，タイル，壁紙，染織など室内装飾のいっさいを扱うモリス・マーシャル・フォークナー商会を設立。「彼は産業革命によって可能となった大量生産で市場に氾濫する俗悪な製品を嫌悪し，作る人にとっても使う人にとっても喜びとなるような製品を作るべきであるという信念から，中世を範とし，手仕事と共同作業による，労働および工芸品の質に変革が必要なことを主張した。これはアーツ・アンド・クラフツ・ムーブメントの推進力，ひいては近代デザイン誕生の布石となるものである」（『平凡社世界大百科事典』）。

[168] **had much in common:**「共通点が多々あった」。have something [nothing / a lot / (very) little] in common のような表現は「共通点がある[ない，多い，少ない]」などに相当する意味を表すのに非常によく用いられる（5章[12]，6章[196]）（e.g. They seem to *have* an awful lot *in common*.）。

[169] **He saw no reason why ... should not ...**:「…すべきではないという理由がわからなかった」とは「ぜひ…すべきだと考えた」ということ。see no reason why ...（または not see any reason why ...）はよく用いられるパターン（cf. Shall we go for a drink? — I *don't see why not*.）。

[171] **Philadelphia's 1876 Expo:** アメリカ建国100年を記念してフィラデルフィアで開催された万国博覧会。このときベルの電話がはじめて一般に公開されたことで有名。

American artist designer Tiffany, he traveled to San Francisco for the boat to Yokohama. In an audience with the Emperor Meiji, he was offered the chance to tour Japanese factories and craft outlets, all expenses paid, in return for a report on the potential for trade to the West."

Dresser brought 2,000 items to Japan from the U.K., one of which — a blue-and-white glass vase — can be seen in the Tokyo National Museum. He took back 8,000 objets d'art from Japan, which he presented to London's Victoria and Albert Museum. Having gained tremendous support from industries throughout Britain, he returned here with a party that included a group of Tiffany's craftsmen.

Andrew became interested in Dresser through his mentor, the pioneer collector Charles Handley-Read. Since then FAS has always had something of Dresser's on show or for sale. Initially Patrick bought ceramics, but because they were always getting broken by cleaning ladies, moved into metalwork. "In 1985 I was lucky enough to buy the teapot shown on the cover of the catalog. After a sleepless night before auction, it cost me £40,000."

He did have to sell a few things to afford it, but since it is the only surviving sample known to date, he believes it worth every penny. He also thinks so few of the Japanese-influenced teapots and tea sets survived because they were useless for tea as drunk socially in Britain.

Currently the silver-plated geometric teapot shares the cover of the catalog for the Koriyama exhibition with a curved vase nicknamed "the Hokusai wave" after the famous print. "Thirty percent of the Milan show came from my personal collection. Here my loans number nine items, including some sets." After Japan the exhibition will go to America in 2003. "I don't expect to see it [his teapot] for several years. If I get lonely, I can always go and visit."

---

1 Shigemi Inaga, *Kaiga no Toho* [The Orient in Paintings], Nagoya University Press, 1999.

『「クリストファー・ドレッサーと日本」展カタログ』より
（郡山市立美術館，2002 年）

- [172] **Tiffany:** L. C. Tiffany（1848–1933）は，アメリカのアール・ヌーボーのガラス工芸家，デザイナー。ニューヨークの有名な宝石商の息子として生まれた彼は，はじめは印象派スタイルの風景画家として名をなしたが，自らの作品を出品したフィラデルフィア万博において，日本美術，とりわけ工芸品の展示品と出会ったのをきっかけに，その後工芸の道へ転じた。彼の活動は，1892 年に設立したティファニー・ガラス装飾会社（通称ティファニー・スタジオ）を中心にして，ガラス，金工，宝飾，皮革，家具，インテリア・デザインなど工芸品一般にわたって広範に展開された。
- [173] **an audience with ... :**「…との謁見」。
- [175] **all expenses paid:**「費用は全額支払ってもらって（自分は全く費用を出さなくてよくて）」という意味の決まった言い方（e.g. an *all-expenses-paid* trip）。
- [175] **in return for ... :**「…のお返し［お礼］に」。
- [178] **the Tokyo National Museum:** 上野公園内にある東京国立博物館のこと。日本を中心とする東洋諸地域の美術工芸，考古遺物を保管・展示している。創設は 1872 年。
- [179] **objets d'art** [ɔbʒe daːr]: フランス語で「芸術品」「骨董品」「芸術的な価値をもつ物」。
- [180] **London's Victoria and Albert Museum:** ロンドンのサウス・ケンジントンにある世界最大の工芸美術館。1851 年ロンドンで開催された万国博覧会を契機とし，イギリスの産業美術，工芸，工芸教育を発揚するために 52 年に創設された産業博物館を母体とする。その後，ヴィクトリア朝時代の植民地拡大により，内外の美術工芸品を多く収集。57 年博物館の複合体として建設されたサウス・ケンジントン博物館に移った。ヴィクトリア女王と夫君アルバート公の名を連ねた現在の名称は，1899 年，ヴィクトリア女王によって定められた。
- [184] **Charles Handley-Read:** 英国の美術史家，美術収集家（1916–71）。
- [191] **known to date:**「今までのところ知られている」。
- [191] **worth every penny:** be worth every penny は「たいへん値打ちがある」。
- [195] **the silver-plated geometric teapot:** silver-plated は「銀めっきされた」。口絵参照。
- [199] **number ... :**「総数が…になる」（e.g. The casualties of the train accident *numbered* more than one hundred.）。

# 12
# SCULPTURE

## Introduction
### Ryoji Motomura

The sun was shining in the blue sky, but the warmth was fading. A cool wind was starting to blow. As the temperature dropped, I started to feel anxious. It was getting darker.

It was August 11, 1999, and central Europe was experiencing an eclipse of the sun — a very rare event. I was in London at the time. Even there, it was close to a total eclipse — 96%. This was the first eclipse in England since 1927 and the next one wasn't due until 2090.

Another year famous for its eclipse was 1764. And the same year, a horse with a big white spot on his face was born. One of his legs was also white. He was named "Eclipse" after the big event.

The four-legged Eclipse grew up to be the best racehorse ever in the history of horse racing. Even before his first race, there were rumours about his speed and endurance, and, indeed, he won his first race resoundingly. The power of Eclipse was overwhelming. He won all eighteen of the races for which he was entered. He was invincible.

The rare solar eclipse was not the only event in Europe that summer connecting past to present and serving as a memorial to a great horse — an invincible crowd-pleasing favourite. In London, the summer of 1999 will probably be remembered as the summer of the eclipse. But in Milan, it was the summer that an American horse-lover's 100-to-1 shot came off and Leonardo da Vinci's horse finally came home. On September 10, 1999, an equine statue designed by Leonardo da Vinci 500 years earlier finally took up residence in all its bronze magnificence in a park across from Milan's famous race-track.

As you walk around a sculpture like the great bronze horse of

- [1]  **was fading:** fade は「衰える」(cf. This program's popularity is quickly *fading*.)。
- [4]  **an eclipse of the sun:**「日蝕」(cf. a *solar / lunar eclipse*)。
- [11] **He was named . . . :** name A B after C は「C にちなんで A を B と命名する」(3 章 [212])(cf. This pond *is named after* the main character of one of Soseki Natsume's novels.)。
- [13] **horse racing:**「競馬」(cf. horse (back) riding)。
- [15] **resoundingly:** resounding [rɪzáʊndɪŋ] は「(勝利[敗北]，成功[失敗]などが)決定的な，圧倒的な」(cf. a landslide / a landslide victory)。
- [16] **He won . . . he was entered:**「出走した 18 のレースすべてで勝った」。この場合の enter は「(競技などに)参加させる」。
- [17] **invincible:**「無敵の」(cf. unrivalled)。
- [19] **serving as a memorial to . . . :** serve as . . . は「…の役目を果たす」。a memorial to . . . は「…(過去の重要な出来事や今は亡き有名人など)を記念するもの(像，石碑など)」(cf. a collection of essays *in memory of* . . .「…追悼論文集」)。
- [20] **favourite:**「競馬の本命」「競技の優勝候補」。
- [23] **100-to-1 shot:**「100 分の 1 の見込み」ということで，後 ([33]) に出てくる long shot 同様，favourite と反対の意味となる。
- [24] **an equine statue:** equine [íːkwaɪn] は「馬の」(cf. bovine, canine, elephantine, feline)。
- [25] **took up residence:** take up residence は場所を表す表現を伴って「…に居を定める」。
- [26] **a park across from . . . :** across from . . . は「(通りなどをはさんで)…の真向かいにある」(cf. The post office is just *across* the street.)。

Milan, you find that each position gives you a slightly different angle and a different view. In much the same way, the readings for this session tell the story of Leonardo's horse from four different perspectives and in four rather different styles of writing, providing us with four versions of one story — the story of a long shot that paid off. The first story introduces us to the man who was most instrumental in reviving Leonardo da Vinci's vision. It is followed by an account of the festival atmosphere surrounding the sculpture's departure from the United States for Italy. The third story is taken from a children's book and provides us with a vivid account of the horse's arrival in Milan. Finally, the readings conclude with a personal reflection written by Nina Akamu, the Japanese American sculptor responsible for making a 20th-century work of art out of a 15th-century plan.

# Leonardo's Horse

## A Long Shot Pays Off
### Nancy Mohr                              September 1998

In the days when Milan was one of the richest and most powerful city-states in northern Italy, its duke, Ludovico Sforza, liked to do things in a grand way. In 1482 he commissioned Leonardo da Vinci to create the biggest horse statue ever. Made to honor the duke's father, it was to be 24 feet high. Leonardo spent years sketching a great charger, eventually sculpting a full-sized model in clay and leaving notes about how to cast it — the bronze would weigh 80 tons! But then a French army threatened and the metal was needed for cannon. When Milan fell in September 1499, Leonardo fled. French archers used the clay horse for target practice. For more than four centuries it was lost to history.

Then a most unlikely thing happened. United Airlines pilot Charles Dent, a lover of Italy and an amateur sculptor, saw copies of the Leonardo sketches that had been rediscovered in Spain in 1966. Dent sculpted a rough clay model of Leonardo's charger, and resolved that somehow he would build the famous animal as a gift from the American people to the people of Italy. Such a horse looked like a 100-to-1 shot, but Dent persevered. He created an organiza-

- [30] **much the same:**「ほぼ同じ」と言う場合に非常によく用いられる組み合わせ(9 章 [193])（cf. more or less the same / essentially the same / virtually the same）。
- [33] **a long shot:** 元来競馬用語で「ほとんど勝ち目のない馬」。一般的に「成功する見込みがほとんどないもの，人」の意味で用いることも多い (e.g. Your plan might work, but I'm afraid it's *a long shot*.)。
- [34] **paid off:** pay off は「うまく行く」「(努力などが)報われる」(e.g. I'm sure your hard work will *pay off*.)。
- [34] **was most instrumental in:** be instrumental in . . . (…はしばしば -ing 句)は「…の実現に重要な役割を果たす」(e.g. She *was instrumental in* making this project a big success.)。
- [40] **Nina Akamu:** 日系アメリカ人彫刻家。アカムの主要な彫刻作品としては，1999 年の「レオナルドの馬」の他，近年建てられたワシントン DC の日系アメリカ人記念碑（The National Japanese American Memorial）の地に置かれたモニュメント「鶴」がある。

- [44] **city-states:**「都市国家」。
- [44] **Ludovico Sforza:** ルドヴィーコ・スフォルツァ（1452–1508）。ルネサンス期ミラノの君主。レオナルド・ダ・ヴィンチをはじめとする芸術家のパトロンとして有名。1494 年に甥から権力を強奪する形で実権を掌握してミラノ公となるが，公位を要求したフランス王と争った末，1500 年に捕らえられ，幽閉されたまま没した。
- [45] **in a grand way:**「はなばなしく」「派手に」。
- [45] **he commissioned Leonardo da Vinci to . . . :** commission は「(人に)…するように依頼する」。
- [46] **the biggest horse statue ever:** ever は最上級の意味を強調するために用いられている (e.g. This is one of *the most* thought-provoking books that I've *ever* read.)。
- [48] **charger:**「騎馬」「軍馬」。
- [49] **how to cast it:** cast は「型（mold）に溶かした金属などを流し込んで作る」(e.g. a statue *cast* in bronze)。
- [53] **it was lost to history:** be lost to history は「歴史から消える」という意味の決まった言い方。
- [57] **and resolved that . . . :** resolve は「固く心に決める」(cf. New Year's resolutions)。
- [60] **Dent persevered:** persevere は「困難にもめげず努力し続ける」(cf. It takes *perseverance* to learn a foreign language.)。

tion, Leonardo da Vinci's Horse, Inc., which raised $4 million.

The job of making the horse was given to the Tallix foundry in Beacon, New York. Charles Dent died in 1994, but the work went on, most recently under the direction of sculptor Nina Akamu, who created the eight-foot master model. From it, a larger, clay version was made and will be cast in bronze. On September 10, 1999, five hundred years to the day after the archers shot Leonardo's model to pieces, the bronze horse — broken down into seven manageable sections and flown for free from the United States by Alitalia — will take its place on a pedestal in the ancient city of Milan.

## Buon Viaggio

### June 1999

Charles Dent loved people. He loved parties where he would engage in a favorite pastime: talking to people. Charlie would have come away from the Buon Viaggio weekend feeling happy, surprised, and excited by how many people his idea attracted. To tell the truth, the organizers were a bit unprepared for so many people. Perhaps we should have taken a hint when, on Wednesday and Thursday, crowds of people caused traffic jams on Beacon's Fishkill Avenue by literally stopping their cars on the road and jumping out to take pictures of the now-assembled Horse gleaming in the sunlight on the lawn inside Tallix's entrance. The foundry had to post security just to keep people off the grounds until the 10:00 a.m. Friday 25 June opening. It had been estimated perhaps 8,000 to 10,000 might show up. In expectation of that number, the organizers had 10,000 pamphlets printed, and 1,500 Leonardo T-shirts. The pamphlets were gone by mid-Saturday, as were the T-shirts, and the crowds kept streaming across the street, directed by community police who were themselves overworked for a few days.

Definitely a family affair, the event drew people of all ages, backgrounds and expectations, from people who had just read the front-page *New York Times* article and caught a train out of the city to see The Horse to donors who had been following the project for 10 years and wanted to celebrate The Horse's imminent journey to Milan. One couple was from Los Angeles. Having read a front-page *Los Angeles Times* article about The Horse, they flew East just to see it in person. One elderly gentleman of Italian-American heritage was in tears as he viewed the magnificent sculpture, moved deeply by a gift to be sent to "the old country" by America, and surprised

[61] **raised $4 million:** raise は「(資金を)調達する」(cf. a *fund-raiser*「資金調達係」「資金調達のための催し」)。

[62] **foundry in Beacon, New York:**「ニューヨーク州ビーコン市の鋳造所[鋳物工場]」。

[66] **five hundred years to the day:**「(一日と違わず)ぴったり500年目に」。

[68] **broken down into seven manageable sections:** break down にはいくつかの意味があるが、ここでは break down A into B で「A (全体)を B (部分)に分解する」(cf. *a breakdown* of the costs「費用の内訳」)。manageable sections とは空輸しやすい大きさに分けられた部分のこと。

[69] **flown for free:** fly が「空輸する」という他動詞で用いられていることにも注意 (e.g. The wounded soldier *was flown* to a hospital.)。for free は「無料で」。

[69] **Alitalia:** アリタリア航空はイタリアの航空会社(本社はローマ)。

[70] **a pedestal** [pédəstl]:「台座」。

[73] **Buon Viaggio:** イタリア語で(旅行に出かける人に)「気をつけて行ってらっしゃい」と言う場合の決まり文句(英語に直訳すると good trip)。

[76] **have taken a hint:** take a hint は「(ほのめかされて)感じ取る」という意味の決まった言い方 (e.g. Can't you *take the hint*? She wants you to leave her alone.)。

[81] **post security:**「警備員を配備する」。この場合の security は security guards (「警備員」)のこと (e.g. Call *security*!)。

[81] **keep people off the grounds:**「人々を構内[敷地内]に入れない」(cf. *Keep off* the grass.「芝生に立ち入り禁止」/ An apple a day *keeps* the doctor *away*.)。「敷地」という場合には grounds と、必ず複数形になることにも注意 (cf. The police are searching *the premises* for evidence.)。

[83] **show up:**「(しばしば待っていた人が)現れる、やって来る」(cf. There were quite a few *no-shows* at the theater last night.)。

[87] **community police who were themselves overworked:** police は常に複数扱いであることに注意。overworked は「働きすぎの」「過剰労働の」という意味の形容詞。

[89] **a family affair:** ここでは「家族向きの催し」といった感じ。

[93] **celebrate The Horse's imminent journey to Milan:**「馬がこの後すぐに (imminent) ミラノへと旅立つことを祝う」。

[96] **in person:**「(他人に頼んだりするのではなく)自分で、本人自らが」(e.g. I didn't expect him to show up *in person*.)。

[96] **One elderly gentleman of Italian-American heritage:** of ... heritage はすぐ後の of ... ancestry と同じく「…系の先祖をもつ」という意味の表現 (cf. a woman *of Irish descent*)。

[97] **was in tears:** be in tears は「泣いている」「涙を流す」と言う場合の決まった言い方のひとつ (cf. He was *in* a lot of *pain*.)。

[97] **moved deeply by ...:** be moved by ... は「…に感動する」「…に心を動かされる」という意味の頻出表現 (cf. a *moving* experience)。

to learn that neither a single member of the Board nor Charlie Dent was of Italian ancestry. He was told of Charlie's passion for Italy and the Renaissance.

Just how many people saw The Horse? A conservative estimate is that The Horse had more than 35,000 visitors over the weekend. The police told us that "at least" an additional 15,000 people drove by Wednesday and Thursday, and the three nights during which The Horse was lighted.

Charlie loved people. He would have been thrilled that over 50,000 people came to see The Horse; he would have tried to talk to every one of them!

## The Horse Arrives in Italy
## Jean Fritz

### 2001

If Leonardo had finished his horse, he would only have had to move it from the vineyard where he worked to the front of the duke's palace. Charlie's horse had to cross the ocean to Italy. But he was too big.

So he was cut up into separate pieces, crated, and flown to Milan, where the Tallix people waited to reassemble him. Workers would crawl through a trapdoor in the horse's belly to fasten the pieces together.

He would stand on a pedestal in a small park in front of Milan's famous racetrack, within whinnying distance of the racing stable.

On June 27, 1999, the horse took off.

September 10, 1999 was the date set for the unveiling of the statue, exactly five hundred years to the day since the French invaded Milan and destroyed Leonardo's horse.

An enormous cloth was spread over the horse so he couldn't be seen. Two huge clusters of blue and white balloons were attached to either end of the cloth. On the pupil of one eye of the horse, Nina had written in tiny letters *Leonardo da Vinci*. On the other eye she had written *Charles Dent*. She had put her own name in the curly mane of the horse.

As a large crowd of Italians and Americans took their seats, the horse stayed in hiding. Speeches were made. The Italian national anthem was sung. Then the American national anthem.

Finally, the strings anchoring the balloons were cut and the cloth rose into the sky.

Leonardo's Horse in Milan

- [102] **A conservative estimate is that ...**:「控えめに見積もっても…」。a conservative estimate / guess という結びつきは非常に一般的。
- [104] **"at least" an additional 15,000 people:** at least が引用符に入っているのは警察による発表からの直接引用であることを示すため。additional の前に不定冠詞が必要なことにも注意 (cf. He has *another five years* before retirement.)。

    **The Horse Arrives in Italy:** 口絵参照。
- [114] **crated:**「梱包用の(大きな)箱」を意味する名詞 crate から派生した同じ形の動詞で,「梱包する」。
- [116] **a trapdoor:**「はね上げ戸」(床や天井の一部になっている扉)。
- [119] **within whinnying distance of ...**:「…から馬のいななきが届く距離の」。whinny は「(馬が)いななく」。within がこのように of 句を伴って「(距離や時間が)…から…の範囲内に[で]」という意味を表すパターンには慣れておきたい (e.g. *within* a hundred kilometers *of* the center of Tokyo / *within a stone's throw of* ...「…の目と鼻の先に[で]」)。
- [121] **the date set for ...**: set a date for ... は「…の日程を定める」という意味の決まった組み合わせ。
- [126] **the pupil of one eye:** この場合の pupil は「瞳」「瞳孔」(cf. iris「虹彩」)。
- [128] **the curly mane:** mane は「たてがみ」。

*Ahhhhhhh!*
At last Leonardo's horse was home.

## Sculptor's Statement
## Nina Akamu

## May 1999

During the 17 years Leonardo da Vinci worked on his plans for the Sforza Monument, he made numerous small sketches of horses to help illustrate his copious notes on the complex technological procedures for molding and casting the monument in bronze. Due to the lack of systematic order in his notetaking, none of the existing drawings reveal the final position of the Horse or the appearance of the finished monument. However, experts suggest that enough studies remain to provide evidence of Leonardo's intentions. Was the information contained in these small 1"–3½" sketches sufficient to substantiate the creation of a life-sized equine sculpture and the final 24-foot colossal Horse?

The unavailability of exact visual references necessary to a project of this magnitude created a wide latitude for interpretation. I relied on several sources of relevant information to gain more insight into the sculpture's possible position, proportion and aesthetic character. Leonardo's drawings and notes for other projects, as well as his thoughts on anatomy, painting, sculpture and natural phenomena were carefully studied. Other visual and literary sources including the contributions of his teachers and their influence on his work were also investigated. Finally, discussions with experts, colleagues and writings of scholars in the field were respectfully considered.

The complex artistic challenges of creating the eight-foot master model involved an understanding and sculptural translation of design, structure, anatomy, character, and movement combined with grace and harmony.

The sculpture which I created for the Leonardo da Vinci's Horse Inc. pays homage to the creative genius of Leonardo. It is not intended to be a recreation of his sculpture. However, it has been significantly influenced by certain works of art and writings from that period, and specifically Leonardo's notebooks and accompanying drawings with great emphasis on his involvement with the Sforza Monument.

It is my hope that the duality of knowledge and imagination and the creative problems which have challenged this project have

The sculptor Nina Akamu with a model of Leonardo's Horse

- [139] **his copious** [kóupiəs] **notes:** copious は「夥しい」「大量の」。
- [140] **molding and casting the monument:** mold は「型に入れて作る」（名詞としては「型」），cast は「鋳造する」（名詞としては「鋳型」「鋳造物」）。
- [145] **these small 1″–3½″ sketches:**「1インチから3.5インチまでの小さなスケッチ集」。「1″」は 1 inch の省略表記。「小さい」は実際の彫像の「巨大」さと対比されている。
- [146] **substantiate the creation of a life-sized equine sculpture:** substantiate は「実現させる」。life-sized は「実物大の」。
- [147] **colossal** [kəlásəl]:「巨大な」（cf. a *colossus*「巨像」）。
- [149] **latitude:**「（行動，発言，解釈などに関する）自由度，許容範囲」。
- [158] **The complex artistic challenges:** challenge は「自らの能力や技能を試すことになるような（特にやりがいのある）課題」。本文 [170] の have challenged this project の challenge は対応する動詞用法（cf. a *challenging* job「（自らの能力や技能を試すことになるような）難しいがやりがいのある仕事」）。
- [163] **pays homage to . . . :** pay homage [hámɪdʒ] to . . . は「…に敬意を表する」という意味の決まった言い方。homage は日本語化したフランス語の「オマージュ」(hommage) に相当する。
- [169] **the duality of knowledge and imagination:**「知識と想像力の二重性」とは，ダ・ヴィンチの馬の彫像を実際に創作しようという試みが知識と想像力の双方を必要とする仕事であるということ。
- [170] **have resolved themselves in an image . . . :**「力強く，魅力的で，象徴的意味を伴うひとつの彫像（image）に結実した」（cf. The distant shapes in the sky gradually *resolved themselves into* a group of airplanes. / high-*resolution* images.）。

resolved themselves in an image which is powerful, intriguing and symbolically significant.

During the two years of my involvement with this project, I have been deeply inspired by the richness of information encountered in my investigations. Moreover, the profound dedication and tenacious creative efforts of those who have supported the 20-year vision of Charles Dent have also been an inspiration and have strengthened my resolve to help in fulfilling his dream.

Perhaps the modern Leonardo da Vinci's Horse can be seen as a symbol for the power and momentum of creative energy and a vision which is directed and focused on a distant goal. The Horse's awesome size stands as a testament to the magnitude of Leonardo's colossal creation. Our gift to Italy may be viewed as a metaphor for the immense genius of Leonardo, a paragon of creativity, and the great epoch in which he lived, the Renaissance.

- [173] **I have been deeply inspired by . . . :**「私は…に深く感化されてきた[大いにインスピレーションを与えられてきた]」(7 章 [101], cf. 2 章 [156]) (cf. a deeply *inspiring* work of art「深い感銘を与える芸術作品」)。
- [175] **tenacious** [tənéɪʃəs]:「粘り強い」「不撓不屈の」(cf. tenacity)。
- [178] **my resolve to . . . :** この場合の resolve は名詞で,「(…しようという)決意」。
- [180] **momentum:**「勢い」「推進力」「発展し続ける力」(e.g. Our project is steadily gaining *momentum*.)。
- [182] **a testament to . . . :**「…の証(あかし)」。
- [183] **a metaphor for . . . :** metaphor は「隠喩」だが,ここでは「抽象概念などを具体的に表現したもの」といった感じ。
- [184] **a paragon of creativity:**「創造性の鑑(かがみ)[手本]」。
- [185] **epoch** [épək; íːpɔk]:「(特に重要な出来事や変化が起こった)時代」(cf. an *epoch-making* event)。

# 13
## LAW

## Introduction
### Hiroshi Okayama

Most of us, I imagine, are repeatedly told as we grow up that we must "follow the rules." We are surrounded by all sorts of rules that have different forms, objectives, and often, sanctions. And we all know, or at least are supposed to know, that it is important to observe whatever rules govern a society. But remaining faithful to rules is very often boring and tiresome. This is especially true when one cannot understand what good the particular rule serves, or when the rule seems plain silly, or both.

Perhaps we would be better off without rules. After all, many historic inventions and discoveries were made precisely by ignoring or even going against the existing rules, as the case of the original Copernican Revolution that involved Galileo Galilei's confrontation with the Catholic Church suggests. Such a statement may sound perverse, but it might not be too much to say that man-made rules need a reality check from time to time. It might reveal some unnoticed reality about the world within which we live, just as Copernicus and his followers did.

The passage that follows is part of a large-scale reality check for one of the most well-known, formal (in the sense that its enforcement is institutionalized), and admired sets of rules: the United States Constitution, the world's oldest written constitution still in force today. In 1994, prominent constitutional law scholars were asked what they thought was its "stupidest" provision, that is, the provision that was "at the same time most nonsensical and most harmful for today's polity" of the United States. And they indeed had a lot to say about the Constitution, a document once praised as "a machine that would go of itself" (James Russell Lowell, 1888). In addition to those regarding slavery and Prohibition, which do not

- [3] **sanctions:**「制裁」(cf. impose economic *sanctions* on . . . )。
- [4] **at least are supposed to know:**「(実際には知らないまでも)少なくとも知っていることにはなっている[知っていてしかるべきである]」(cf. You're *not supposed to* smoke in here.)。
- [5] **observe:**「(法律,規則などを)遵守する」(cf. *law-abiding* citizens)。
- [7] **what good the particular rule serves:**「その特定の規則が何の役に立つのか」(cf. *What good* is money when you don't have the time to spend it?)。
- [8] **plain silly:**「全くばかげている」(cf. He's *plain* wrong.)。
- [9] **we would be better off without rules:** be better off without . . . は「…などない方が幸せだ,うまくいく」(cf. He'd *be better off* quitting his current job.)。
- [9] **After all . . . :** after all が日本語の「結局」に対応すると思っていると,このような典型的な用法のひとつが正しく理解できないし,自分で使うこともできなくなる。この場合の after all は直前の発言内容に対する根拠や理由になる——その内容を受け入れてもらうのに役立つ——ことを述べる際の合図として用いられている。「だって[何と言っても]…なのですから(今言ったことは正しいですよね)」という感じ(e.g. Don't be too hard on him. *After all*, he started working here just last month.)。
- [11] **the existing rules:**「現行の規則」。
- [11] **original:** この但し書きは,Copernican Revolution「コペルニクス(Copernicus [koupɚ́ːrnikəs])的転回」が(コペルニクスによる天動説から地動説への転回のように)「ものの考え方が根本的に変わること」という意味で,比喩的に(figuratively)用いられることが多いのに対して(e.g. a *Copernican revolution* in psychology),ここでは文字どおり(literally)地動説から天動説への転回が話題になっていることを明確にするため。
- [14] **perverse:**「ひねくれた」「つむじ曲がりの」。
- [15] **a reality check:**「(自分の考えや想像などを)現実と照合して適切かどうかを確認する機会」。
- [19] **its enforcement is institutionalized:** enforcement < enforce:「(法律などを)実施[施行]する」(cf. law *enforcement* officer「法執行官(警察官など)」)。institutionalize (< institution)は「制度化する」。
- [20] **the United States Constitution:**「アメリカ合衆国憲法」。1787 年に発議され,1788 年に批准成立した。現在までに 27 の修正条項が成立しており,そのうち 1791 年に成立した第 1〜10 修正条項は連邦政府が侵すことのできない基本権を保障したもので,「権利章典(the Bill of Rights)」とも呼ばれる。
- [21] **in force:**「実施[施行]されている」「実効力をもっている」(cf. enforce(ment))。
- [23] **provision:**「(法律などの)条項」。
- [25] **polity:**「政治組織体(としての国家)」。
- [27] **a machine that would go of itself:** of oneself は「(ほうっておいても)ひとりでに」。古い言い方で,現代の英語なら a machine that would work [operate] all by itself [on its own] と言うところ(cf. in and of itself)。J. R. Lowell はアメリカの詩人,随筆家(1819–91)。ハーヴァード大学教授,駐スペイン公使,駐イギリス大使を歴任した。
- [28] **Prohibition:** 1919 年に成立した合衆国憲法第 18 修正条項は「禁酒」条項と訳されることが多い。しかし,そこで「禁止(prohibit)」されていたのは,酒類の製造,販売,そして輸送であって,飲酒ではなかった点が注意を要する。すこぶる評判の悪かったこの「高貴な実験(noble experiment)」は,1933 年に第 21 修正条項の成立によって終わりを迎えた。

exist anymore, the provisions named included those relating to the Electoral College, now world-famous after the debacle in the 2000 Presidential election.

But, as the old adage goes, rules are there to be broken. And, sure enough, some contributors to *Constitutional Stupidities, Constitutional Tragedies*, the end product of this exercise, evaded the original question. Instead of asking themselves which specific constitutional provision could now be called "stupid," they asked themselves what kind of constitutional assumption seems no longer to be valid. Harvard professor Frederick Schauer was one of these contributors and, as was the case with several others who productively subverted the assignment, he not only points out what might be one weakness of the U.S. Constitution, but also makes us think about why there are rules and why it is important to reflect on them.

# The Constitution of Fear

## Frederick Schauer

At various places along the Massachusetts Turnpike, a limited-access toll road with a speed limit of sixty-five miles per hour in most places, there are signs cautioning drivers not to back up on the turnpike if they have missed their desired exit. These signs tell us much about the Massachusetts drivers, since in most other states we could not imagine the need for such signs, precisely because we could scarcely imagine the possibility of drivers even contemplating the behavior that Massachusetts sees a need to warn against.

The phenomenon on the Massachusetts Turnpike is hardly unique, for with some frequency we learn about the proclivities of a population by learning about the behavior that it is necessary explicitly to prohibit. There are numerous "No Spitting" signs in Hong Kong, but few in Switzerland; and when I saw a sign on a supermarket cash register in Woodstock, Vermont, announcing that discount coupons would not be accepted unless the customer purchased the item for which the coupon was designated, my initial reaction was

[30] **the Electoral College:** アメリカの大統領選挙は間接選挙制をとっており，最も注目される 11 月の一般投票は，実は翌月行われる「本選挙」で投票する大統領選挙人を各州が選出するためのものである。こうして選出された選挙人全体が electoral college と呼ばれる。

[30] **the debacle in the 2000 Presidential election:** debacle [deɪbáːkl] は「大失敗」。2000 年の大統領選挙では，フロリダ州で一般投票の集計結果に関して争いが生じた。同州選出の選挙人が選挙全体の帰趨を左右しえたため，2 人の大統領候補の間で訴訟合戦となり，約 1 ヶ月遅れで，合衆国最高裁判所の判決によって勝者が確定するという異例の結果となった。

[32] **as the old adage goes, rules are there to be broken:**「古い格言にもあるように，規則は破られるためにある」(cf. That's *how* the story *goes*. / Teachers *are there to* facilitate the students' learning process.)。adage [ǽdɪdʒ] は「格言」。

[39] **as was the case with . . . :**「…の場合にそうであったように」という意味の決まった言い方 (cf. *as is the case with . . .*「…の場合と同じように」)。

[39] **productively subverted the assignment:** 与えられた課題を巧みに読みかえることでよい結果を生み出した，ということ。

[43] **At various places . . . :** turnpike は「有料高速道路」。limited-access toll road も「有料高速道路」。limited-access は出入り口が限定されているところから (cf. *Access* to the bridge is *limited* to passengers' cars only.)。toll は「使用料金」(cf. a *toll*-free call)。caution はこのように (warn と同じく) 動詞として用いられることも多い (e.g. Patients taking this medicine are *cautioned* [*warned*] against drinking alcohol.)。この場合の back up は「車をバックさせる」。

[49] **we could scarcely imagine . . . :** contemplate は名詞句や -ing 形を伴って「…しようかと考える」という意味を表す (cf. *I'm thinking of applying* for this job.) が，think of . . . ing と同じく，否定の文脈で用いて「…することなど考えもしない」，つまり「…することなどありえない」「絶対に…しない」という，行為の可能性を強く否定する場合に用いられることも多い (1 章 [132]) (e.g. *Don't even think of* smoking.)。

[52] **unique:** この場合の unique は本来の「他に例がない」「特有の」という意味 (5 章 [4])。このように否定の文脈で用いることも多い (14 章 [2]) (cf. This is *not* a *uniquely* Japanese problem.)。

[53] **the proclivities of a population:** proclivity は「(しばしばよくないことをする)傾向」。population はこのように「特定地域に住む人々全体」という意味で用いられることもよくある (e.g. Half the *population* of this city lives in the downtown area.)。

[57] **discount coupons:**「割引クーポン」。coupon は [kúːpàn] の他に [kjúːpàn] と発音されることもあるので，聞いた時にはわかるようにしておきたい。

surprise, for just like the out-of-state driver on the Massachusetts Turnpike, it had never occurred to me that anyone would engage in the behavior that the supermarket was prohibiting. Just as an assertion presupposes the plausibility of its negation — "You are sober" is not a compliment — so too does a prescription presuppose the empirical likelihood of its violation.

As they tell us about Massachusetts drivers, the signs on the turnpike also instruct us about constitutional jurisprudence. Like the signs on the turnpike and the warnings in the supermarket, constitutional provisions tend to presuppose the likelihood of the behavior they prohibit. Just as there are no signs on the turnpike prohibiting throwing Molotov cocktails at other vehicles, and no signs on the Hong Kong ferries prohibiting fare avoidance, so too do we rarely see constitutional provisions addressed to theoretically or logically possible occurrences that are in practice unlikely to occur within the relevant domain. Just as the signs on roads and ferries prohibit what the sign posters believe is actually likely to happen, so too do the drafters of constitutions go out of their way to address what they see as genuine threats. Given, for example, South Africa's recent history of abuse of power by the police and prosecutors, it is not surprising that the new South African Constitution is extraordinarily detailed in its regulation of police and prosecutorial practices. Similarly, it is only to be expected that discrimination on the basis of language is prohibited in the constitution of multilingual Canada but not in the constitution of monolingual Mexico.

Yet what is a genuine threat or possibility at one time may be less so at another. Few students of American history fail to understand the perceived need, in 1791, for the Third Amendment, prohibiting the quartering of troops in private houses, yet for the same reason it is unlikely that the Third Amendment would find its way into a constitution newly written in 1997. That the Fourteenth Amendment makes no mention of discrimination on the basis of gender or sexual orientation is historically unsurprising, just as it is historically unsurprising that gender discrimination is now explicitly prohibited in virtually every one of the new constitutions now emerging throughout the world, and that discrimination on the basis of sexual orientation is prohibited by some, such as the aforementioned Constitution of the Republic of South Africa.

From this perspective, the imperfections of the Constitution of the United States, in 1997, are likely to be imperfections of two types: guarding against problems that no longer exist and not guard-

[62] **an assertion presupposes the plausibility of its negation:**「何かが真であると（わざわざ）主張するということはそれが偽であっても不思議はないということが前提になっている」。plausibility の元になっている plausible は「もっともらしい」と訳されることが多いが，否定的な意味合いを伴うことなく，「道理にかなっている」という，reasonable の類義語としてもしばしば用いられることに注意。

[64] **so too does ...:** この場合の倒置の用法は，話し相手が例えば "I really admire the director of this movie." と言ったのに対して "So *do* I." 「私もです」と言うような場合に近い。prescription は「処方箋」(cf. *prescribe* a medicine / e.g. *prescription* drugs) という意味がよく知られているが，ここでは「規定」「指示」。empirical likelihood「経験的な蓋然性」とは「実際に起こる可能性があること」といった意味(この場合の empirical は「実際の経験に基づく」)で，plausibility の言い換え。

[67] **jurisprudence:** 法学をさして用いられる場合が多いが，ここではより広く，法学自体がその一部であるところの，法の体系一般をさす。

[71] **Molotov** [múlətɔ̀f] **cocktails:**「火炎瓶」。

[72] **fare avoidance:** fare は「乗り物の料金」。

[73] **constitutional provisions addressed to ...:** A addressed to B は「B（問題，課題など）に取り組むための A（努力，政策，研究など）」。本文 [78] に出てくる address の用法と比較するとよい（cf. This paper *addresses* a long-standing problem in cognitive psychology.）。本文 [116] の the problem toward which ... was ... directed という表現も参照。

[77] **the drafters of constitutions:**「憲法の起草者」。

[77] **go out of their way to ...:** go out of one's way to ... は（「...するために遠回りする」という文字どおりの意味から）「...（普通はしないようなこと）を特に努力して[わざわざ]する」と言う場合によく用いられる表現。

[82] **it is only to be expected that ...:** すぐ前の it is not surprising that ... と同じく，「...ということがあっても全く不思議はない」「いかにもありそうだ」といった意味を表す決まった言い方としてよく用いられる（cf. It is *only natural* that ... / It *should come as no surprise* that ...）。

[88] **the quartering of troops:** quarter は「(軍隊を)宿泊させる」。

[89] **find its way into ...:** find one's way into ... は，「(意外なものや望ましくないものが)...に入り込む」「...(意外なところ)で見つかる」という感じの表現(10 章 [68])（cf. I managed to *find my way to* the conference site.）。

[90] **the Fourteenth Amendment:**「第 14 修正条項」（1868 年に成立）は，市民がもつべき権利に関する規定。

[92] **sexual orientation:** 異性愛（heterosexual），同性愛（homosexual）などの「性的志向」を表す，非常によく用いられる表現（e.g. the "don't ask, don't tell" policy on *sexual orientation* / cf. sexual preference [inclination]）。

ing against problems that exist now but did not exist, or were not then perceived as existing, at earlier times. As examples of the former, we have not only the Third Amendment, whose prohibition of a nonproblem is relatively costless, but also the more costly efforts to guard against dangers now perceived as less dangerous than they were in other times, such as the Seventh Amendment right to trial by jury in civil cases and the Second Amendment right to keep and bear arms. The cost of the Seventh Amendment comes not only from the expense and delay of a civil jury trial but also from the possibility of more suboptimal verdicts from juries than from judges. The cost of the Second Amendment comes from the way it has legitimated a certain rhetoric and politics that probably makes gun control more difficult or more limited than would otherwise be the case. If this is so, and if guns are dangerous, then the costs of the Second Amendment are apparent. In both the Second and Seventh Amendment examples, therefore, it is at least arguable that the problem toward which the provision was originally directed is now less pressing and that the costs of the provision itself are not insignificant. Such provisions, in 1997, may by the excess imposition of constraint entail costs no longer justifiable by even the long-term benefits.

The converse problem exists with respect to the erroneous nonimposition of constraint. As examples here, we might think of the lack of (textual) protection for the right to privacy or the right to be free of discrimination on account of gender or sexual orientation. And many people believe (although I am not one of them) that the lack of term limits and the lack of a constitutional requirement of a balanced budget are perfect examples of the eighteenth-century Constitution's failure to anticipate all of the problems of the twenty-first-century United States.

Yet although it is evident that there are existing constitutional provisions that are no longer necessary, and nonexisting constitutional provisions which would now be beneficial, the difficulties created by guarding against what are now nonproblems and not guarding against what are now problems are not restricted to particular constitutional provisions. Rather, the eighteenth-century Constitution, in the large, adopts a certain attitude about the state itself, an attitude not unlike the one that Massachusetts appears to adopt with respect to people who are armed with automobiles. This attitude is best characterized as one of risk aversion, for with respect to exercises of governmental power, the overwhelming perspective of

[103]　**a nonproblem:**「問題であるかのように扱われているが実際には問題ではないこと」．ここではa problem that no longer exists のこと（cf. Do you mean to say sexual orientation is a *nonissue* in this debate?）．

[106]　**the Seventh Amendment:** 民事訴訟について陪審員をおくことを求める権利は，民事訴訟では裁判官が法理を，陪審員が事実認定を審理するという分業を徹底し，裁判官による事実認定という越権行為を防ぐという（今日ではあまり必要性がないとみられる）発想から生み出された．

[107]　**the Second Amendment:** 市民兵（militia）を維持するために，銃器所持の権利（right to bear arms）を保障したもので，今日の銃規制論争を複雑化させる要因のひとつとなっている．

[111]　**The cost of the Second Amendment . . . :** come from . . . はこのように由来や出所を表す場合に一般的に用いられる（e.g. Further evidence *comes from* a recent clinical study.）．legitimate はここでは「正当化する」「適法にする」という意味の動詞で，発音は [lɪdʒítəmèɪt]（cf. legitimize）．a certain rhetoric and politics は「ある種のレトリックや政治的な駆け引き」．このように通常不可算の名詞でも a certain とともに用いることができる場合がある（e.g. It takes *a certain tenacity* to make things happen in this organization.）．gun control は「銃規制」．than would otherwise be the case は「そうでない（ここでは the Second Amendment が適法化したある種のレトリックや政治的な駆け引きがない）と仮定した場合よりも」．仮定法とともに用いられる otherwise のこうした用法にも慣れておきたい（cf. This theory helps make sense of some *otherwise* puzzling phenomena.）．

[116]　**it is at least arguable that . . . :** it is arguable that . . .「…と主張することができる」は，it could be argued that . . . と同じく，「…が妥当であると考える根拠が十分にある」と，that 節の内容が正しいという意見を控えめに述べる場合に用いられる表現（cf. He is *arguably* one of the greatest philosophers of all time.）．

[118]　**pressing:**「速やかに対処する必要のある」「緊急性のある」（cf. urgent）．

[119]　**by the excess imposition of constraint:**「過度に制約を課すことによって」（cf. by imposing too many constraints）．

[122]　**the erroneous** [eróuniəs] **nonimposition of constraint:**「課すべき制約を課さないという過ち」．

[127]　**term limits:**「任期制限」．連邦議会議員などについては，ある政治家が再選されつづけ，数十年にわたって公職に留まることも珍しくない．それが政府の肥大化や国民との乖離の元凶だとして，任期を制限しようとする運動が一部で展開されている．

[128]　**a balanced budget:**「均衡予算」．赤字公債に依存せず，財政支出を経常収入によってまかなう予算（cf. The governor has pledged to *balance the budget* within five years.）．

[131]　**existing constitutional provisions:** existing は「既存の」「現行の」という意味を表す限定用法の形容詞（[11]）（e.g. The *existing* support system needs revamping.）．

[137]　**in the large:**「大規模に」という意味もあるが，ここではすぐ上の particular（「特定の」）の反意表現として「一般に」の意味で用いられている．

[139]　**people who are armed with automobiles:**「自動車という凶器を運転している人々」．

[140]　**risk aversion:**「リスク回避」（cf. risk averse「リスク回避的な」）．aversion < avert:「避ける」「防ぐ」．ここでは，政府が不適切に行動する危険を防止するために，政府の権限を限定したり，三権の抑制均衡（checks and balances）に代表される，政策の形成や変更を困難にするような制度を導入したりといった態度をさす．

the eighteenth-century Constitution, not surprisingly, is that risk aversion is preferable to risk preference or even risk neutrality in thinking about the inevitably uncertain consequences of any form of governmental behavior.

When we think of the Constitution as risk-averse, we associate it in some ways with skepticism about human motivation. This is not inconsistent with a Lockean and rights-based understanding of the Constitution's inspirations, but it is also not inconsistent with a Hobbesian perspective on officials, for the risk-averse Constitution has as dim a view about concentrations of state power as Hobbes had about human nature in general. An underlying theme of the Constitution is and has always been that the dangers of mistaken governmental action are more to be feared than the dangers of mistaken governmental inaction. The philosophy of the Constitution appears to be that, in a world of uncertainty about the consequences of any governmental action, it is better that ten good things go undone than that one bad thing be permitted.

Perhaps such a libertarian, risk-averse, and government-distrusting view of the state is still appropriate. Although we hear much talk of governmental "gridlock" these days, perhaps that talk is misguided, and perhaps now, just as in the eighteenth century, the expected danger of governmental overreaching may be far greater than the expected danger of governmental impotence. Indeed, it is not implausible to suspect that modern technological developments — consider how much easier modern technology has made it to invade someone's privacy — have increased rather than decreased the expected danger of governmental error, and thus increased rather than decreased the appropriate degree of risk aversion toward governmental action with uncertain consequences and uncertain application.

But perhaps not. Perhaps the greatest dangers come from governmental inaction, dangers that we see when we look, for example, at governmental inaction with respect to health care and many other issues of social policy. If we were in 1997 to redraft the Constitution, knowing what we know today about the world and the history of this country, would we be as concerned as our forebears were in 1787 about guarding against the excesses of another George III, or would we be, comparatively, less concerned about that problem and more concerned about the problem of governmental inaction?

Thus, no amount of attention, however appropriate it might be, to individual clauses and individual constitutional doctrines can

- [143] **risk preference:** ここでは，政府が不適切に行動する危険性をあえて受け入れつつ，政府に大きな行動の権限を与える態度をさす。際限なくリスクを求めるわけではないので，risk seeking「リスク志向」とはニュアンスが異なる。
- [143] **risk neutrality:** risk preference と risk aversion の中間で，「リスクに対して中立的であること」。政府の行動の余地を明示的・積極的に拡大することも制限することもしない態度をさす。
- [148] **Lockean:** < Locke。John Locke（1632–1704）はイギリスの哲学者。人間は生命，自由，財産に対して天賦の権利（自然権）を持ち，それを実効ならしめるために協力して国家をつくったのであり，政府が人民を裏切って専制を働いたならばそれへの抵抗が正当化される（革命権）とする社会契約説を唱えた。
- [150] **Hobbesian:** < Hobbes。Thomas Hobbes（1588–1679）はイギリスの哲学者。政府のない「自然状態」は，利己的な個人の間で闘争が展開する悲惨な状態であり，それを脱するべく社会契約を通じて生み出される政府は，秩序の形成と維持を重視する強力なものとなる（他ない），とする社会契約説を唱えた。
- [151] **has as dim a view about ...:** have [take] a dim view of ... は定型的な言い方で「…に対して否定的な見方をする」「…を好ましくないと思う」という意味。
- [152] **An underlying theme:** underlying は「根底にある」という意味の限定用法の形容詞（cf. This is the most important assumption *underlying* his argument.）。不定冠詞は他にも underlying theme(s) があることを含意する。
- [155] **inaction:** lack of action ということ。「行動すべき時にしないこと」「手をこまねいていること」。
- [158] **go undone:** go + un-過去分詞は「（本来…されるべきものが）…されない」という意味を表す定型表現（e.g. I'm afraid many more errors have *gone unnoticed* than we care to admit.）。
- [159] **libertarian:** ノジック（Robert Nozick, 1938–2002）に代表される，個人の自由と財産の保護を第一に考え，そのために最小限必要なもの以外政府権力の行使を一切認めない，政府への徹底した懐疑の立場をとる思想。
- [160] **much talk of ...:** このように「…が取沙汰されている」とか「…が（大いに）話題になっている」という場合に用いられる talk は不可算名詞扱い（e.g. *There's a lot of talk* these days *about* how to be environmentally friendly. / cf. You're used to *giving talks* like this, aren't you?）。
- [161] **gridlock:**「道路網全体が交通渋滞で麻痺している状態」という意味から派生して，「（議会などで）意見が対立して膠着状態になること」（cf. The issue left the Senate *in gridlock*.）。
- [162] **misguided:**「（意見や考えが）見当違いの」（cf. He is often well-intentioned but *misguided*.）。
- [163] **governmental overreaching:**「政府がやりすぎること」。
- [164] **Indeed:** このように文頭で用いた indeed は，「それどころか」「もっと言うならば」と，直前で述べた内容を強調する働きがある。
- [166] **how much easier:** how で始まる疑問文や感嘆文の疑問詞句や感嘆詞句の中で比較級を用いる場合にはこのように much が必要になることに注意（e.g. *How much longer* do you think it'll take us to get there?）。
- [175] **social policy:** 社会保障や福祉のように，20世紀に発達した福祉国家の取り組んできた，社会全体の厚生を向上させるべくとられる政策一般をさす。
- [178] **George III:** アメリカ独立革命時のイギリスの国王（在位 1760–1820）。強い王権の回復を図り，逆に北米の植民地を失った。
- [182] **constitutional doctrines:**「憲法上の原理」。個々の条項を背後で支えている，個人の自由や権力分立といった原理原則。

transcend the fact that the degree of distrust of government in the United States appears to exceed that of most other countries in the world, including many in which the citizens have far more reason to distrust their government than we have to distrust ours. And it is not implausible to hypothesize that this degree of distrust is not only reflected in the Constitution and in particular constitutional decisions but is also, in part, a product of the Constitution and a particular form of risk-averse and government-distrusting constitutional culture.

The overarching theme of the Constitution of the United States, and the "who's to say/where do you draw the line/parade of horribles/foot in the door/thin edge of the wedge/camel's nose in the tent/slippery slope" rhetoric it has engendered, is one of fear, a fear which in 1787 or 1791 was quite properly aimed at the state. Yet just as the signs on the Massachusetts Turnpike would be misguided were Massachusetts drivers to become more sensible, so too would the target of the eighteenth-century Constitution — governmental tyranny — be misguided if the target had shifted. Whether the target has so shifted is a question that is both political and empirical. But the measure of the imperfection of the Constitution is the extent to which the entire Constitution, as written, as interpreted, and as understood, is aimed at a danger that occupies a different position on the spectrum of all dangers than it did more than two centuries ago. If that is the case, then the imperfections of American constitutionalism should not be trivialized by identifying the occasional flaws in this or that clause, or this or that interpreting case. To pick out a clause or two, or a case or two, as imperfect is implicitly to endorse the remainder. But whether the remainder, in the large and not in the small, is worthy of endorsement is an issue, in an era of constitutional transformation throughout the world, that cannot safely be ignored.

[192] **The overarching theme:** overarching は「全体を支配する」「全体に影響を及ぼす」という意味の限定用法の形容詞。

[193] **"who's to say ...":** 容認できる範囲とそうでない範囲の線引きをきちんとしておかないと(あるいは，しておいても)事態がずるずると悪い方向に進んでしまう，という警句を発する際によく用いられる一連の決まり文句。ここで批判されている政府による専制への恐れが，いかに頻繁に，しかしあまり考えなしに表明されているかを皮肉っている。

[195] **engendered:** engender は「(状況，感情などを)生じさせる」。

[198] **were Massachusetts drivers to ... :** if Massachusetts drivers were to ... と言っても同じ意味。このように仮定法の if 節の if を省略すると残りの部分が倒置になることに注意(10 章 [92])(e.g. *Were it not for* your constant encouragement and support, I wouldn't be doing what I'm doing.)。

[205] **the spectrum of all dangers:** spectrum は「スペクトル」の意味から，このように「(考え，意見などの)範囲」を表すことも多い (e.g. This textbook covers *a wide spectrum of* topics ranging from babies to art to Eurocentrism.)。

[207] **American constitutionalism:** 一般に constitutionalism は「立憲主義」と訳され，政府権力は法の制約を受け(うるものであり)，また法に従う限りで正当とされる，という考え方をさすが，ここではより広く「合衆国憲法を中核とするアメリカの法システム全体について広く受け入れられた考え方」というほどの意味で用いられている。

[207] **should not be trivialized by ... :**「…することによって矮小化されるべきではない」。trivialize は「実際よりも重要[深刻]でない(= trivial である)かのように扱う[思わせる]」。

[209] **pick out:**「(慎重に)選ぶ」「選び出す」。この意味で(日本語のピックアップにつられて) pick up を使うのは誤り。pick には単独でも「選ぶ」という意味がある (e.g. *Pick* a card, any card.)。

[210] **implicitly:**「暗黙のうちに」(cf. explicitly)。

[210] **endorse:**「支持する」「是認する」。

[213] **cannot safely be ignored:**「無視するわけにはいかない」。この場合の safely はいわゆる文修飾の副詞で「…しても差し支えない」といった感じ (cf. I believe it is *safe* to say things are finally looking up.)。

# 14

# EUROCENTRISM

## Introduction
### Motoo Furuta

The binary way of imagining global space that divides the world into an "east" and a "west" is not unique to the western world. When France colonized Vietnam in the late nineteenth century, it named the area it then controlled, which included the adjacent Cambodia and Laos, "Indochina." This was not without some justification, as Vietnam had long been under the influence of Chinese civilization, while in Cambodia and Laos the important impact had come from Indian civilization. Still, it was France that created and named this historically unprecedented region. But from the early twentieth century, the Vietnamese themselves began to refer to Indochina as "Dong-duong," which is the Vietnamese way of reading the Chinese characters 東洋. In Japanese, of course, these characters are used to mean "the Orient." But in China, the word 東洋 has been used to refer to Japan. As a result, at the time of the Chinese movement to resist the import of Japanese products, in the 1920s, Vietnamese products carrying labels which read "made in 東洋" were mistakenly banned as well. In modern Japan, it is this word 東洋 that is used to refer to Asia in binary contrast with the West (西洋). So it is not surprising that when a Vietnamese historian came to Japan, he was surprised to find a whole list of 東洋 history books in the library. He was mistakenly impressed by the intense interest in "Indochina Studies" in Japan.

People everywhere in the world view global space in a way that reflects their own location and concerns. But the reason why "Western centeredness" in particular is such a problem is that it has become the dominant way of thought in the modern world. In Edward Said's terms, this is "Orientalism," a global framework in which the west and east are polarized: the East is identified through

- [1] **binary** [báɪnəri]:「二つの要素からなる」「二項(対立)的な」(a *binary* opposition) (cf. [33])。
- [2] **is not unique to ...** : be not unique to ... は「…に特有のものではない」(13章[52]) (cf. This kind of problem is *not peculiar to* Japan.)。
- [3] **When France colonized Vietnam:** フランスは19世紀半ばからヴェトナムに介入を始め，1867年に南部に直轄植民地コーチシナを作り，次いで，中部をアンナン保護国，北部をトンキン保護領として徐々に権益を拡大し，1887年，このヴェトナム3地域にカンボジア保護国を加えて，フランス領インドシナ連邦を建設した。この連邦組織は，1893年にさらにラオスを加えるが，最終的に1945年に消滅した。
- [5] **This was not without some justification:**「これにはそれなりに妥当な理由がなかったわけではない」(cf. She was, *with some justification*, quite upset about the way he treated her.)。
- [9] **unprecedented:**「先例のない」[ʌnprésɪdèntɪd] (cf. without *precedent* / set a *precedent*)。
- [13] **But in China, the word 東洋:** 中国語での「東洋」について Chinese-English Dictionary を引くと，「東洋」= "the Eastern Sea; Japan" とある。つまり，「東洋」とは，中国の東に広がる海であり，そこに浮かぶ日本を意味する。
- [24] **Western centeredness:**「西洋中心主義」(cf. *self-centered*)。
- [27] **Edward Said:** エドワード・サイード (1935–2003) はパレスチナ生まれのアメリカ人文学者・批評家。コロンビア大学教授。主著 *Orientalism* (1978年，邦訳『オリエンタリズム』)は，西洋が東洋を「オリエント」という虚構の他者像へとつくりあげることによって，みずからを文明として定立してきたこと，そしてそのことが西洋の帝国主義の正当化に重要な役割を果たしてきたことを論じた記念碑的な大作であり，1980年代以降の文学・文化研究に多大な影響を与えると同時に，現在のポストコロニアル批評(本章[194])の基盤を築いた(11章[95])。
- [28] **are polarized:** polarize (< pole「極」) は「分極化させる」「(対立する意見や信念をもつ複数の集団に)分裂させる，対立させる」(5章[59]) (cf. He is a *polarizing* figure.)。

a negative image of non-progressive passivity while the West, in contrast, assumes a more positive image. Said's critical analysis of Orientalism identified this way of thinking as part of a system of cultural dominance generated by colonialism.

The binary logic of Orientalism was an essential part of the West's invention of itself. In order for the West to identify itself with civilization and progressiveness, it had to create an Other, the "regressive Orient," that could stand in contrast. This way of creating a binary between the west and east in the modern world was a way of splitting global space into one part identified as "how the world should be" and another identified as "how the world should not be." It is easy to understand how as a result the multiplicity and hybridity of the origin of western culture itself was deemphasized or even ignored.

When modern Europe "rediscovered" its origins in ancient Greece, it was "pure Greek culture" that was emphasized, and the Oriental aspects of ancient Greece were ignored. Attention was focused on ancient Athens, which had itself made a point of its cultural purity in opposition to "others." Aristotle, for example, distinguished the Greeks from the *barbaroi*, "the barbarous," using a term that had originally meant "those who have unpleasant words" and which was used as a derogatory way of referring to other ethnic groups. Aristotle argued that the *barbaroi* could be distinguished from the Greeks by the fact that they had an inherently subservient nature. In contrast, in his controversial *Black Athena* (1987), the historian Martin Bernal located the origins of Athens in Egypt, arguing that the history of this link had been erased only by modern European racism.[1]

This kind of controversy over "purity" is paradoxically a reflection of the fact that Europe is a spatial and cultural composition with multiple origins. The desire to claim cultural purity starts from a deeply buried consciousness of hybridity. Accordingly, the challenge for the twenty-first century, sometimes referred to as the Asian century, is not so much to replace existing Eurocentrism with a newly dominant Asia-centrism as to overcome the binary that was created in the modern world of Occident versus Orient, or Europe versus Asia.

I am a scholar of Vietnamese studies and have for some time been insisting that the University of Tokyo should actively promote scholarly exchanges with other Asian countries. When I gave a paper

[29] **a negative image of non-progressive passivity:**「遅れていて受動的という負の［否定的な］イメージ」。これは後にくる西洋の positive image「正の，肯定的なイメージ」と対照されている。

[30] **critical analysis:**「批判的な視座から繰り広げられる分析」。

[31] **a system of cultural dominance generated by colonialism:**「植民地主義によって生成された文化支配のシステム」。

[33] **The binary logic of Orientalism:**（世界を東洋と西洋に二分する）「オリエンタリズムの二項対立的論理」。

[33] **the West's invention of itself:**「西洋が自らを創り出すこと」。invention は発明だが，ここでは「創出」という感じ。

[35] **the "regressive Orient":** regressive「退行的」は progressive の反意語で，数行上の [29] non-progressive の言い換え。

[38] **splitting global space into ...:** 西洋と東洋という概念に基づいて世界を二分し，一方を先進的で文明的なものとして，もう一方を野蛮で遅れているとみなすこと。

[40] **multiplicity and hybridity:** multiplicity「多様性」と hybridity「雑種性」（hybrid の名詞化）はほぼ同じ意味で用いられている。この2語は近代以降の文化理解のための重要な概念として，今日，盛んに文化研究で用いられている。

[41] **deemphasized:** deemphasize は emphasize の反意語（cf. downplay [dáʊnpleɪ]）。

[43] **When modern Europe "rediscovered" its origins in ancient Greece:**「近代ヨーロッパが自らの起源を古代ギリシアに『再発見』したとき」。引用符は，その「再発見」というのが近代ヨーロッパの一方的な見方であり，必ずしも事実ではないという含みを暗示している。

[46] **cultural purity:**「文化的純粋性」。前に出てきた multiplicity / hybridity と対照されている。

[47] **Aristotle** [ǽrɪstɑ̀tl]: アリストテレス。言うまでもなく古代ギリシアの哲学者。ここで指摘されているように，『政治学』などにおいて，異邦人（バルバロイ＝自分たちに通じない言語を話す者）をギリシア人より劣った存在と見なしていた。

[50] **ethnic groups:** ethnicity は一般的に「民族(性)」と訳されることも多いが，最近ではカタカナの「エスニシティ」「エスニック」という言い方も増えている。エスニシティを簡潔に定義するのは難しいが，言語，歴史，慣習，伝統などを共有すると考える人々によって形成されるアイデンティティと言えよう。

[52] **an inherently subservient nature:** inherently は「本来」「元来」「元々」。subservient は「従属的な」「卑屈な」。

[54] **Martin Bernal:** マーティン・バナール。コーネル大学政治学部名誉教授。専門は中東，アフリカ，アジアなどの比較政治学。主著 Black Athena: The Afroasiatic Roots of Classical Civilization (The Fabrication of Ancient Greece 1785–1985)（邦訳『黒いアテナ：古典文明のアフロ・アジア的ルーツ』）において，ギリシア文明はアフリカのエジプト，およびフェニキアのユダヤに大きな影響を受けていたと主張することで，ギリシア文明は白人が生み出したものとする考えを否定した。

[58] **a spatial and cultural composition with multiple origins:**「空間的に見ても文化的に見ても多様な起源から合成されたもの」。

[60] **a deeply buried** [bérid] **consciousness of hybridity:**「心の深層に埋め込まれた雑種性の意識」。

[60] **the challenge for the twenty-first century:**「21世紀に取り組むべき課題」（cf. a challenging session）。

entitled "The University of Tokyo looks towards Asia" at a joint symposium of the University of Tokyo and the University of Munich in 2003, an American scholar who was present criticized me for deploying the familiar "Europe versus Asia" format, arguing that it was not an appropriate framework for the twenty-first century. I argued in response that the point is not that the University of Tokyo is trying to shift its focus in international exchange from a Euro-American orientation to an Asian one but instead that, by strengthening its currently relatively inactive exchanges with Asia, the university is trying to encourage exchanges with universities and other research institutions in Asia *as well as* in Europe and America. In so doing, I indicated, our university is attempting to go beyond the binary that contrasts Europe and Asia and creates an Occident and an Orient. This is an issue that universities in the twenty-first century worldwide must face head on.

# The Myth of the West

## Ella Shohat and Robert Stam

When Captain Mac, in King Vidor's *Bird of Paradise* (1932), repeats Kipling's nostrum that "East is East, and West is West, and never the twain shall meet," he receives the joking response: "Hey, Mac, what's the dope on the North and South?" This apparently frivolous exchange calls attention to the geographic imaginary that imposes neat divisions, along a double

[70] **the University of Munich** [mjúːnɪk]: ドイツのミュンヘン大学。正式名は Ludwig-Maximilians-Universität München という。

[71] **criticized me for deploying the familiar "Europe versus Asia" format:**「よくある東対西の図式を用いていると私を批判した」。deploy は「部隊を展開する」などを意味する軍事用語だが，このように議論などを展開するという意味で用いられることもある。

[75] **a Euro-American orientation:**「欧米指向」。Euro-America は基本的に西ヨーロッパと北米の価値観などを合わせて表現するときに用いられる。

[80] **our university is . . . :**「東京大学は，ヨーロッパとアジアを対照させることで西洋と東洋を生み出してしまう二項対立を超えようとしている」。ここで contrasts は動詞。

[83] **face head on:**「真っ向から取り組む」(cf. a *head-on* collision「正面衝突」)。

**Ella Shohat and Robert Stam:** 本章の題材となっている *Unthinking Eurocentrism: Multiculturalism and the Media* は，1994 年に出版され，同年 Katherine Kovacs Singer Best Film Book Award を受賞した。著者の Shohat はニューヨーク市立大学教授。専門はメディア論，女性学。Stam はニューヨーク大学教授。専門は映画論。ちなみに，"Unthinking Eurocentrism" というタイトルは，「ユーロセントリズムを考え直す」と「ものを考えないユーロセントリズム」の両方の意味が込められている。これは unthinking を動名詞ととるか，現在分詞の形容詞的用法ととるかの違いによる（cf: Visiting relatives can be a nuisance. / Flying planes can be dangerous.）。

[84] **King Vidor:** アメリカの映画監督（1894–1982）。本文にもあるとおり，Captain Mac は，彼の 1932 年の作品 *Bird of Paradise*（邦題『南海の劫火』）の登場人物の一人。

[85] **Kipling:** Rudyard Kipling はイギリスの小説家，詩人（1865–1936）。少年向き動物文学の古典 *The Jungle Book* は彼の作品（1894）。本文に引用されている "East is East, and West is West, and never the twain shall meet"（「東は東，西は西，両者会うことなかるべし」）は彼が書いた "The Ballad of East and West" という有名な詩の冒頭にある。twain は two の古形。

[85] **nostrum:**「実際には効かない妙薬[万能薬]」。

[87] **what's the dope on the North and South?:**「じゃあ，北と南はどうなんだい」と茶化している。dope は「麻薬」だが，口語表現として what's the dope on . . . ? は「いったい…は何なんだ」という問いかけになる。*Bird of Paradise* は「南」とされる地を舞台にした映画だから，「東と西」ではなく，「北と南」はどうなんだ，と冗談めかして問うているのである。

[88] **This apparently frivolous exchange calls attention to . . . :**「この一見軽薄（frivolous）なやりとりが…に注目することを促す」。apparently はこのように形容詞の前に用いられて「一見…（であると思われる）」という意味を表すことがよくある。call attention to . . . は attention を用いた数ある頻出表現のひとつで「…に注目させる」「…に関心を向けさせる」といった意味を表す (cf. This paper is intended to *draw attention to* the growing importance of cross-cultural communication skills. / Over the years some politicians have been trying to *focus* public *attention on* the disputed islands.)。

[88] **the geographic imaginary that imposes neat divisions:** ここでいう geographic imaginary は geographic reality と対立する概念ではなく，われわれが reality と自然視する空間や地理そのものがひとつの imaginary（「想像されたもの」「虚構」）であるということ。本文後出の the Eurocentric imaginary [144] も参照。impose A on B は「A を B に押しつける」。neat divisions は「明確な境界線，区分」。

axis (East/West, North/South), on a globe inhospitable to such rigidities. Like its orientalizing counterpart the "East," the "West" is a fictional construct embroidered with myths and fantasies. In a geographical sense, the concept is relative. What the West calls the "Middle East" is from a Chinese perspective "Western Asia." In Arabic, the word for West (*Maghreb*) refers to North Africa, the westernmost part of the Arab world, in contrast to the *Mashreq*, the eastern part. (In Arabic, "West" and "foreign" share the same root — gh.r.b.) The South Seas, to the west of the US, are often posited as cultural "East."

Furthermore, the term "West" comes overlaid, as Raymond Williams has pointed out in *Keywords*, with a long sedimented history of ambiguous usage.[2] For Williams, this history goes back to the West/East division of the Roman Empire, the East/West division

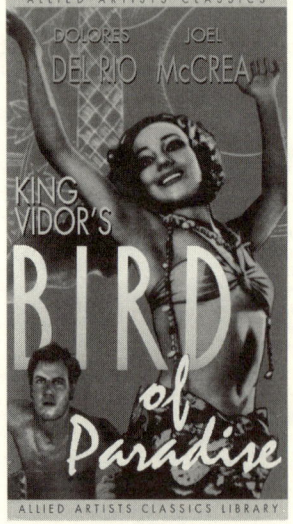

*Bird of Paradise* (1932)

[90] **a globe inhospitable to such rigidities:** 地球はそもそも東西南北で厳密に区分けすることはできないものなので,「そのような硬直した区分」には「無愛想」(inhospitable) なのである。hospitable [hɑ́spɪtəbl, hɑ̀spítəbl] は「愛想の良い」(cf. an *inhospitable* climate)。

[91] **Like its orientalizing counterpart the "East":** counterpart はこのように所有代名詞とともに用いて「(役割, 機能などにおいて)…に相当[対応]するもの, 人」という意味でよく用いられる (e.g. How do Korean college students compare with *their Japanese counterparts* in terms of motivation?)。orientalize は「東洋化する」だが, ここでは「ある国や地域を東洋 (the East) と呼ぶ[見なす]」といった意味。

[92] **a fictional construct embroidered with myths:** fictional は「架空の」。construct [kɑ́nstrʌ̀kt] は「頭の中で組み立てたもの」(7章 [156])(e.g. a theoretical *construct*)。embroider は本来「刺繍する」(cf. embroidery「刺繍」) だが, ここでは「潤色する」という比喩的な意味。with 以下が潤色の内容。myth は「神話」だが,「多くの人が信じているが, 事実に反する考え」という意味で用いることが多い (e.g. the *myth* that Japanese society is homogeneous)。

[93] **the concept is relative:**「『西』という概念は相対的なものである」。the concept は前文の the "West" を指す。relative「相対的」(cf. absolute) の内容はこの直後で述べられている。

[98] **The South Seas:**「南太平洋」。

[98] **are often posited as cultural "East":**「…はしばしば文化的には『東』であると考えられている」。posit は「措定する」だが, ここでは posit A as B で「A を B であると考える」という意味。

[100] **the term "West" comes overlaid ... with a long sedimented history of ambiguous usage:**「『西』という用語は, 昔から多義的に使われてきた結果, それらの意味が定着して重なり合った概念を表すようになっている」。comes overlaid は is overlaid としてもほぼ同じ意味 (cf. These days most computers *come* complete with basic software.)。be overlaid with... は (「…に表面を覆われている」「…を上にかぶせられている」という原義から比喩的に)「…(特性, 意味合いなど)を帯びる」。sedimented のもとになっている名詞 sediment [sédəmənt] は「沈殿物」。ambiguous は「ひとつの表現が複数の異なる意味に解釈できる」(e.g. The title "Unthinking Eurocentrism" is *ambiguous*. / cf. ambiguity)。

[100] **Raymond Williams:** 20世紀のイギリスを代表する批評家 (1921–88)。マルクス主義批評家として知られるが, 文化と生産様式の関連を従来のマルクス主義より柔軟に捉えることで, カルチュラル・スタディーズの創始者のひとりとなる。主著は *Culture and Society* (『文化と社会』) や *The Country and the City* (『田舎と都会』) など。1976年に出版された *Keywords* (『キーワード辞典』) は文化を考えるうえで不可欠な用語を簡便に説明する解説書の体裁をとっているが, 実はこれらの短い各項目そのものが優れた文化批評にもなっている。

[102] **goes back to ... :** go back to... は「…にさかのぼる」という起源を表す表現 (cf. This school *dates back* over a century.)。

[102] **the West / East division of the Roman Empire:** 395年テオドシウス1世の死後, 帝国東方は長子アルカディウス, 西方は次子ホノリウスに引き継がれる。以後全帝国を実質的に支配する単独帝は現れず, 東方と西方は別個の発展をたどり始めるので, 一般にはこの年をもってローマ帝国が〈分裂〉したと言われる。

[103] **the East / West division of the Christian Church:** 1世紀の原始キリスト教は4世紀に入ってローマ帝国内の制度的教会となる。しかし, その後, ローマ教会が西方, コンスタンティノープル教会が東方の教会を代表することになると, 両教会の関係はしだいに悪化し, 1054年に決定的分離を迎えることになる。

of the Christian Church, the definition of the West as Judeo-Christian and of the East as Muslim, Hindu, and Buddhist, and finally to the postwar division of Europe into the capitalist West and the communist East. Thus politics overdetermines cultural geography. In contemporary parlance Israel is seen as a "Western" country while Turkey (much of which lies to the west of Israel), Egypt, Libya, and Morocco are all "Eastern." At times the "West" excludes Latin America, which is surprising since most Latin Americans, whatever their ethnic heritage, are geographically located in the western hemisphere, often speak a European tongue as their first language, and live in societies where European modes remain hegemonic. Our point is not to recover Latin America — the name itself is a nineteenth-century French coinage — for the "West," but only to call attention to the arbitrariness of the standard cartographies of identity for irrevocably hybrid places like Latin America, sites at once Western and non-Western, simultaneously African, indigenous and European.

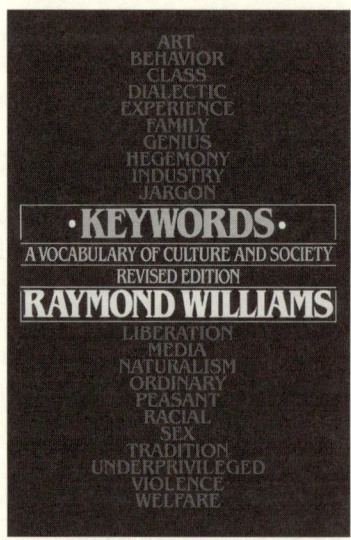

Raymond Williams, *Keywords* (1976)

EUROCENTRISM●177

[104] **the definition of the West as Judeo-Christian:** define the West as Judeo-Christian を名詞句化したもの (cf. categorize [characterize / classify / describe / portray] A as B)。Judeo-Christian は「ユダヤ教とキリスト教の」。

[106] **the postwar division of Europe:** 第二次世界大戦後の米ソ対立の冷戦構造のもと，ヨーロッパはアメリカを中心とする西側ブロックの資本主義諸国と，ソ連を中心とする東側ブロックの共産主義諸国に，政治的経済的軍事的イデオロギー的に分断される。

[107] **Thus politics overdetermines cultural geography:** thus は「このように」。overdetermine は「重層決定する」という意味。「重層決定」とは，あることが決定されるのに様々な要因がそこに関係しているという場合に用いられる。この場合の politics は権力関係を含む広い意味での「政治」。

[108] **In contemporary parlance:**「現代の用語法では」(cf. in common *parlance*)。

[108] **Israel is seen as a "Western" country:** be seen as . . . は，be regarded as . . . / be viewed as . . . などと同じく，「…と見なされている」「…であると考えられている」という意味の頻出表現型。本来視覚を表す動詞が判断の意味で用いられることがあるのは日英語共通。

[110] **At times:** sometimes と同義。

[112] **whatever their ethnic heritage:** whatever their ethnic heritage may be の may be が省略された形。このような省略は非常に一般的 (6章 [142]) (e.g. We've got to talk to him, *whatever* the consequences.)。

[112] **are geographically located in the western hemisphere:**「地理的には西半球に位置している」。be located は場所を表す表現と組み合わせて「…に位置する，ある」という意味で用いるのが一般的 (e.g. She was born in a small town *located* ten miles north of London.)。be situated も同じように用いられる (cf. The department store is very *conveniently located* [*situated*].「便利な場所にある」)。geographically がついているのは(比喩的ではなく)実際の空間的な位置について語っていることを強調するため。

[114] **societies where European modes remain hegemonic:**「ヨーロッパ的な生活習慣 (modes) が依然として支配的な (hegemonic) 社会」(cf. a new *mode* of behavior)。hegemonic の名詞形 hegemony [hɪdʒéməni, -gém-] は，control by one country, organization, etc., over other countries, etc. などと一般的には説明され，ここでもそのような意味で使われている。文化論においてヘゲモニーは，社会全体を包含し，反対勢力までを巧みに取り込む，圧倒的な権力を指す。

[115] **recover Latin America . . . for the "West":**「ラテンアメリカを再び『西洋』にする」。この場合の recover は「取り戻す」。

[116] **a nineteenth-century French coinage:**「19世紀フランスの造語 (coinage)」(cf. *coin* a word)。

[117] **the arbitrariness of the standard cartographies of identity . . . :**「(東，西 というような)標準的な地図上の区分をラテンアメリカのようなどうしようもないほど混成の地域に適用しようとすることの恣意性」。arbitrariness < arbitrary:「根拠のない」「恣意的な」。irrevocably < irrevocable [ɪrévəkəbl]:「戻ることのでない」「取り返しのつかない」。

[119] **sites at once Western and non-Western . . . :** すぐ前の hybrid places の言い換え。at once および simultaneously は，日本語の 「同時に」と同じく，「二つのことが『同時に』成り立つ」ことを表すために用いることがある (cf. You have to work hard, but *at the same time* you should learn to take it easy sometimes.)。indigenous [ɪndídʒənəs] は「その土地に固有の」(cf. *indigenous* peoples)。

Although the triumphalist discourse of Plato-to-NATO Eurocentrism makes history synonymous with the onward march of Western Reason, Europe itself is in fact a synthesis of many cultures, Western and non-Western. The notion of a "pure" Europe originating in classical Greece is premised on crucial exclusions, from the African and Semitic influences that shaped classical Greece itself to the osmotic Sephardic-Judeo-Islamic culture that played such a crucial role in the Europe of the so-called Dark Ages (a Eurocentric designation for a period of oriental ascendancy) and even in the Middle Ages and the Renaissance. As Jan Pieterse points out, all the celebrated "stations" of European progress — Greece, Rome, Christianity, Renaissance, Enlightenment — are "moments of cultural mixing."[3] Western art has always been indebted to and transformed by non-Western art, whence the Moorish influence on the poetry of courtly love, the African influence on modernist painting, the impact of Asian forms (Kabuki, Noh drama, Balinese theater, ideographic writing) on European theater and film, and the influence of Africanized dance forms on such choreographers as

Edward Said, *Orientalism* (1978)

[121] **the triumphalist discourse of Plato-to-NATO Eurocentrism . . . :**「プラトンから NATO までというヨーロッパ中心主義の（自分だけが正統であるという）勝利主義的（triumphalist）言説によると，歴史とは西洋的な理性が前へ前へと行進してきた過程に他ならないことになる」。Plato-to-NATO は Plato [pléɪtoʊ] と NATO [néɪtoʊ] が二重韻（double rhyme）を踏んでいる。synonymous はこのように「二つの表現の意味が実は同じである」ことを表すためによく用いられる (e.g. Many of us mistakenly believe that affluence *is synonymous with* happiness.)。

[123] **a synthesis of many cultures:**「多くの文化を合成してできたもの」。

[124] **The notion of a "pure" Europe . . . :**「『純粋な』ヨーロッパの起源が古典ギリシアにあるという考え方は，（ヨーロッパの形成にとって）決定的に重要（crucial）であった要因を排除してはじめて成り立つ」。be premised on . . . は「…を前提にして成立する」（premise は名詞では「（議論の依って立つ）前提」）。その要因が直後に from A to B「A から B まで」という形で列挙されている。

[127] **the osmotic Sephardic-Judeo-Islamic culture:** osmotic「浸透性（osmosis）の」は，ここではこれらの文化がヨーロッパに深く浸透していることを表す。Sephardic < Sephardi:「セファルディ」（スペイン，ポルトガル，北アフリカ系のユダヤ人）。cf. Ashkenazi「アシュケナジ」（ドイツ，ポーランド，ロシア系のユダヤ人）。

[128] **the so-called Dark Ages:** 世界の歴史を古代・中世・近代の3つに区分する歴史区分法のもとで，キリスト教信仰が支配的だった中世は古典古代とルネサンスにはさまれた「暗黒時代」と呼ばれることがある。ただし，ここでは「暗黒時代」は「中世」とイコールではなく，そのなかで特に東洋が西洋に対して文化的に「優勢」であった時代を指している。

[128] **a Eurocentric designation for a period of oriental ascendancy:**（the Dark Ages という名称について）「東洋が優勢（ascendancy）になった期間に対するヨーロッパ中心主義的な名称（designation）」。

[130] **Jan Pieterse:** イリノイ大学アルバナ校社会学部教授。

[131] **all the celebrated "stations" of European progress:** celebrated は「有名な」「名高い」（cf. *celebrity*「有名人」）。"stations" は key stages in a narrative of progress という意味（cf. *stations* of the cross「十字架の道行きの留（りゅう）」。受難のキリストが体験した 14 の主要な出来事のひとつひとつを「留」と呼ぶ。第 1 留が最後の晩餐で，第 14 留が復活）。

[133] **Western art has always been indebted to and transformed by non-Western art:**「西洋の芸術は，これまでずっと西洋以外の芸術によって恩恵を受け，また変容させられてきた」。be indebted to . . . は「…の恩恵を受ける」という意味の決まった言い回し。

[134] **whence the Moorish influence on the poetry of courtly love . . . :** whence はあまり使われない古い表現だが，ここではすぐ前の節の内容を受けて「そこから[それゆえに]（…が生じた）」。Moorish は「ムーア人[式]の」。ムーア人（Moor）は北西アフリカに住むイスラム教徒。courtly love「宮廷風恋愛」とは，貴婦人への絶対的献身を理想化した中世ヨーロッパの騎士道的恋愛の理念。modernist painting「モダニズム絵画」とは 20 世紀初頭に出現してきた，キュビズムをはじめとする革新的な絵画（運動）の総称。パブロ・ピカソの芸術とアフリカ部族のマスクの関係などでよく指摘されているように，モダニズム絵画は当時ヨーロッパの植民地であったアフリカの伝統芸術に影響を受けた。Balinese theater は「バリの伝統劇」だが，本来，バリには複数の伝統劇があるのでここで何を指すかは不明。ideographic [ìdiəɡrǽfɪk] writing は「表意文字」（cf. ideogram, phonogram）。

Martha Graham and George Balanchine.⁴ The "West," then, is itself a collective heritage, an omnivorous mélange of cultures; it did not simply "take in" non-European influences, "it was constituted by them."⁵

An idealized notion of the West organizes knowledge in ways flattering to the Eurocentric imaginary. Science and technology, for example, are often seen as "Western." The correlative of this attitude in the realm of theory is to assume that all theory is "Western," or that movements such as feminism and deconstruction, wherever they appear, are "Western"; a view that projects the West as "mind" and theoretical refinement and the non-West as "body" and unrefined raw material. But until recent centuries Europe was largely a borrower of science and technology: the alphabet, algebra, and astronomy all came from outside Europe. Indeed, for some historians the first item of technology exported from Europe was a clock, in

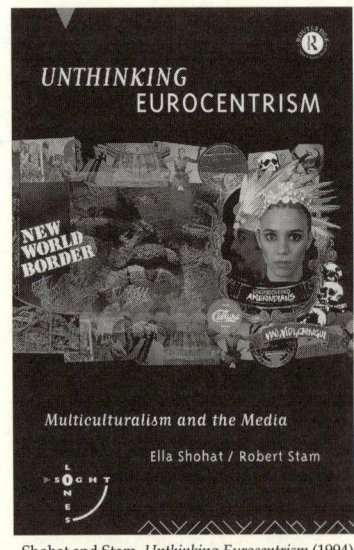

Shohat and Stam, *Unthinking Eurocentrism* (1994)

[139] **Martha Graham:** アメリカ史上最高のダンサー，振付師とされる女性（1894–1991）。

[139] **George Balanchine:** ロシア生まれのアメリカのバレエ振付師（1904–83）。

[140] **a collective heritage:**「集合的な遺産」は前出の a synthesis of many cultures と同じ趣旨で，「西」がその成立過程で様々な異質の文化の影響を受けてきたことを強調するための表現。ここでの collective の意味は，family, committee などが文法用語で collective noun「集合名詞」と呼ばれていることなどを参照するとわかりやすいかもしれない。

[140] **an omnivorous mélange of cultures:** omnivorous [ɑmnívərəs] は「雑食性の」（cf. carnivorous「肉食性の」，herbivorous「草食性の」）だが，ここでは比喩的に「何でも取り入れる」といった意味。mélange [meɪlɑ́:nʒ] は「混合物」「ごたまぜ」。全体で直前の a collective heritage の言い換え。

[140] **it did not simply "take in" non-European influences . . . :**「『西洋』は単に非ヨーロッパの影響を『取り入れた』だけではなく，『そうした影響を構成要素として成立した』のである」。constitute [kánstətjù:t] は「構成する」「作り上げる」（cf. the U.S. *Constitution*）。つまり，著者は今日の「西洋文化」が，非西洋とされた地域の文化なくして存立することはありえないと主張している。

[143] **An idealized notion of the West:** idealized は「理想化された」で，このように「あるものを実際よりもよいかのように捉えたり提示したりする」という意味で用いることが多い。

[143] **in ways flattering to . . . :**「…にとって実際よりもよく思われる仕方で」。An idealized notion of the West の内容を具体化した表現。flatter は「お世辞を言って喜ばせる」が基本的な意味だが，「（写真，文章などが）…を実物よりもよく見せる」の意味でも用いられる（e.g. a *flattering* photo）。

[145] **The correlative of this attitude in the realm of theory:**「理論の領域（realm）でこの態度と相関関係がある考え方（correlative）」。

[146] **assume that all theory is "Western":**「理論はすべて『西洋』のものであると想定する」。assume は「想定する」「決めてかかる」「当然視する」「前提にする」（cf. an implicit *assumption*「暗黙の前提」/ on the *assumption* that . . .「…が正しいと仮定すると」）。

[147] **feminism:**「フェミニズム」。女性参政権の獲得などの制度的な平等を求める政治的・思想的運動としてスタートした近代のフェミニズムは，1960 年代後半のウーマンリブを経て，あらゆる種類の女性の問題をあつかうことになる。フェミニズムやジェンダー・スタディーズがあつかう性差は，民族，階級とともに，現代の政治的批評の中核的主題となっている。

[147] **deconstruction:**「脱構築」。フランスの哲学者ジャック・デリダ（Jacques Derrida, 1930–2004）の造語。音声／文字，内部／外部，自己／他者などの階層秩序を伴う一連の二項対立の不安定性や相互依存関係（文字なき音声，外部なき内部，他者なき自己の成立不可能性）を暴露することによって，最終的にこのような二項対立の基盤を揺るがすことにいたる批判的思考法。男性／女性，西洋／非西洋の二項対立の脱構築は，したがってフェミニズムやポストコロニアリズムの理論的な根拠を提供することになる。

[148] **a view that projects the West as "mind" . . . :** "mind"「心」と "body"「身体」を対立させる，「西洋」に典型的な発想を踏まえた表現（cf. the mind-body problem「（哲学などにおける）心身問題」）。脳と心の関係を考えればわかるように，こうした単純な対立の図式の妥当性自体が疑問視されるようになって久しい。

[150] **largely:** to a great extent / mostly / mainly とほぼ同義。

1338.⁶ Even the caravels used by Henry the Navigator were modeled after lateen-sailed Arab dhows.⁷ From China and East Asia Europe borrowed printing, gunpowder, the magnetic compass, mechanical clockwork, segmental-arch bridges, and quantitative cartography.⁸ But quite apart from the historical existence of non-European sciences and technologies (ancient Egyptian science; African agriculture; Dogon astronomy; Mayan mathematics; Aztec architecture, irrigation, and vulcanization), we should not ignore the interdependence of the diverse worlds. While the cutting edge of technological development over recent centuries has undoubtedly centered on Western Europe and North America, this development has been very much a "joint venture" (in which the First World owned most of the shares) facilitated by colonial exploitation then and neocolonial "brain draining" of the "Third World" now. If the industrial revolutions of Europe were made possible by the control of the resources of colonized lands and the exploitation of slave labor — Britain's industrial revolution, for example, was partly financed by infusions of wealth generated by Latin American mines and plantations — then in what sense is it meaningful to speak only of "Western" technology, industry, and science? The "West" and the "non-West" cannot, in sum, be posited as antonyms, for in fact the two worlds interpenetrate in an unstable space of creolization and syncretism. In this sense, the "myth of the West" and the "myth of the East" form the verso and recto of the same colonial sign. If Edward Said in *Orientalism* points to the Eurocentric construction of the East within Western writing, others, such as Martin Bernal in

- [154] **the caravels used by Henry the Navigator:**「カラベル船」は，15, 16世紀頃にスペイン，ポルトガルなどで使われた小型の軽快帆船のこと。エンリケ航海王子（Henry the Navigator, 1394–1460）の時代に多用された。エンリケ航海王子は，その名が示すように，ポルトガルの海外進出最大の貢献者と言われる。
- [154] **were modeled after lateen-sailed Arab dhows:**「大三角帆（lateen）を用いて航行するアラブのダウ（沿海貿易用帆船）をモデル[手本]としていた」。
- [157] **segmental-arch bridges:** アーチ型の橋の一種。
- [157] **quantitative cartography:**「定量的地図法」。
- [158] **quite apart from the historical existence of non-European sciences and technologies:**「西洋以外にも科学技術が歴史上存在したことは別にしても」。apart from は「…は別にしても」「…に加えて」。sciences and technologies が複数形になっているのは西洋以外の科学技術の多様性を強調するため。
- [160] **Dogon astronomy:** Dogon「ドゴン族」は西アフリカの山地に住む農耕民。天地創造の神話をはじめとする壮大な宇宙観・世界観で，西欧世界に衝撃をあたえた。
- [161] **vulcanization:**「加硫（処理）」。
- [162] **the cutting edge of . . . :**「…の最先端」(cf. technology *at* [*on*] *the cutting edge* / *cutting-edge* technology / *state-of-the-art* technology)。
- [165] **a "joint venture":**「ジョイントベンチャー」。喩えであることを示すために引用符に入れてある。すぐ後の shares「株」はこの喩えの続き。
- [165] **the First World:** ここではいわゆる「先進国」。
- [166] **facilitated by . . . :**「…によって促進された」。facilitate: make it easier for . . . to happen or proceed. cf. with great *facility*「いともたやすく」。colonial exploitation then は西洋が非西洋を植民地として搾取した過去。then は文末に来る now と対照されている。
- [167] **"brain draining":**「頭脳流出」。
- [167] **the "Third World":** いわゆる「第三世界」（アジア，アフリカ，ラテンアメリカなどの発展途上国）。命名者はフランスの人口学者ソーヴィー（Alfred Sauvy）。
- [171] **infusions of wealth:**「富の注入」。
- [172] **in what sense is it meaningful to speak only of . . . ?:**「『西洋』の技術，産業，科学という言い方ばかりをすることにどういう意味があるというのであろうか？」。speak of . . . はこのように「…という言い方をする」「…という表現を使う」という意味を表すことが多い（e.g. You often hear politicians *speak of* globalization these days.）。
- [173] **The "West" and the "non-West" cannot, in sum, be posited as antonyms:**「要するに（in sum），『西洋』と『非西洋』を反意語（antonyms）であると考えることはできないのである」。
- [174] **the two worlds interpenetrate in an unstable space of creolization and syncretism:**「二つの世界はクレオール化と混合主義という不安定な空間の中で互いに浸透し合っている」。creolization and syncretism は，全体として，様々な人が交流しあうことによって，宗教，文化，信念などが混ざりあうことを意味する。
- [177] **the verso and recto of the same colonial sign:**「植民地時代の同じ記号の裏と表」。verso は「本の左ページ」「紙などの裏」，recto は「本の右ページ」「紙などの表」。「西洋という神話」と「東洋という神話」が植民地時代の表裏一体の産物である，ということ。
- [178] **Edward Said in *Orientalism* points to . . . :** point to . . . は「…（重要だと思う物事）を指摘する」「…に言及する」（cf. All the evidence *points to* her innocence.）。

*Black Athena*, point to the complementary Eurocentric construction of the West via the "writing out" of the East (and Africa).

The fact is that virtually the entire world is now a mixed formation. Colonialism emerged from a situation that was "always already" syncretic (for example among Jews, Christians, and Muslims in Moorish Spain, among African nations before colonialism, among indigenous "Americans" before 1492), and the post-independence era has projected its own diasporas and crisscrossing migrations into a fluid cultural mix. Within this flux, "majorities" and "minorities" can easily exchange places, especially since internal "minorities" are almost always the dispersed fragments of what were once "majorities" elsewhere, whence the various "pan"-movements. The expanding field of "comparative intercultural studies" (North/South border studies, pan-American studies, Afro diasporic studies, postcolonial studies) recognizes these dispersals, moving beyond the nation-state to explore the palimpsestic transnationalisms left in colonialism's wake.

---

1 Martin Bernal, *Black Athena: The Afroasiatic Roots of Classical Civilization (The Fabrication of Ancient Greece 1785–1985)* (London: Free Association Books, 1987).
2 Raymond Williams, *Keywords: A Vocabulary of Culture and Society* (New York: Oxford University Press, 1976).
3 Jan Pieterse, "Unpacking the West: How European Is Europe?," unpublished paper given us by the author, 1992.
4 On the African influence on modern dance, see Brenda Dixon, "The Afrocentric Paradigm," *Design for Arts in Education*, No. 92 (Jan./Feb. 1991), pp. 15–22.
5 Pieterse, "Unpacking the West," p. 16.
6 See C. M. Cipolla, *Before the Industrial Revolution: European Society and Economy 1000–1700* (New York: W. W. Norton, 1980), p. 222.
7 Pieterse, "Unpacking the West," citing J. Merson's *Road to Xanadu* (London: Weidenfeld and Nicolson, 1989).
8 See Joseph Needham, *The Grand Titration: Science and Society in East and West* (Toronto: University of Toronto Press, 1969).

[180] **the complementary Eurocentric construction of the West via the "writing out" of the East (and Africa):** ここの writing out とは西洋が東洋を描かないで西洋を作り上げた，つまり東洋を徹底的に排除した西洋観を西洋が勝手に作ったということ。西洋というのは東洋を描くことで作られたというサイードの主張と相補的（complementary）に，バナールは西洋が東洋を描かないことで作り上げられたと主張している。

[183] **"always already":**「常に，既に」。脱構築批評の典型的な言い回し。つまり「純粋」な文化などいつの時代にも存在などしなかった。文化とは必ず「混交」しているものなのであるということ。

[184] **syncretic:** < syncretism.

[186] **1492:** コロンブスが今日の西インド諸島に到着した年。つまりアメリカの「インディアン」が「発見」された年である。アメリカ先住民はひとつのまとまった集団ではなく，そのなかには様々な文化が存在し，その間で様々な交流が起こっていた。

[186] **the post-independence era:** 第二次世界大戦後に起こったアジア・アフリカ諸国の「独立の時代の後」。

[187] **diasporas:** 大文字 Diaspora は，紀元前597年および586年のバビロン捕囚以後，多数のユダヤ人がパレスチナから離散したことをさす。普通名詞化した diaspora は「（民族の）集団移住，離散」「（家族の）離散」のこと。

[187] **crisscrossing migrations:**「様々な方向に人々が移住すること」。

[188] **a fluid cultural mix:**「複数の文化が混じり合い変化しつづける状態」。すぐ後の this flux「この流動」はこれを言い換えた表現。

[189] **internal "minorities":**「ある集団内の『マイノリティ』」。

[190] **the dispersed fragments of what were once "majorities" elsewhere:**「以前別の場所で『マジョリティ』であった人々が拡散してばらばらになったもの」。

[191] **whence the various "pan"-movements:**「そこから様々な『汎』運動が生じる」。"pan"-movements というのは，拡散してばらばらになった人々をふたたび「全体（pan＝all, universal）」へと統合しようとする運動。

[193] **Afro diasporic studies:**「アフリカン・ディアスポラの研究」。主にアフリカと南北アメリカ間の人口・文化移動と交流の研究。

[194] **postcolonial studies:** post は「…以降の」という意味。したがって，postcolonial という語は，帝国主義時代の列強の植民地支配のあとに独立した国々の政治的・経済的・文化的状況に関して用いられる。postcolonial studies はそのような状況に関する研究一般を指すが，文化と帝国主義の「対位法的な」歴史記述・テキスト分析を確立したサイードの Culture and Imperialism (1993, 邦訳『文化と帝国主義』) はその金字塔と位置づけられる。

[195] **the nation-state:** 日本語では「国民国家」と訳される。絶対主義の時代に成立した主権の概念は，君主主権から国民主権へと転換し，その結果，近代国民国家が形成されたといわれる。国民国家の成立には国民的自覚を備えた国民の創出が不可欠とされる。

[195] **palimpsestic:** < palimpsest: 書いたものを消した上にまた書けるようになっている古代の羊皮紙。palimpsestic transnationalisms は「幾重にも重ね書きされてきた結果，多層構造をもっているトランスナショナリズム」。トランスナショナリズムとは，近代国民国家の枠をこえた様々な運動や現象。

[196] **in colonialism's wake:**「植民地主義の後に」。in the wake of... または in ...'s wake は「…の後に」「…の結果として」(e.g. A rescue operation was underway *in the wake of* the earthquake.)。

## Campus Wide

2006年7月31日　初　版
2012年8月31日　第5刷

[検印廃止]

編　者　東京大学教養学部英語部会
発行所　財団法人　東京大学出版会
代表者　渡辺　浩

113-8654　東京都文京区本郷7-3-1　東大構内
電話：03-3811-8814・FAX: 03-3812-6958
振替：00160-6-59964

印刷所　研究社印刷株式会社
製本所　株式会社島崎製本

© 2006 Department of English, The University of Tokyo, Komaba
ISBN 978-4-13-082119-3 Printed in Japan

R 〈日本複製権センター委託出版物〉
本書の全部または一部を無断で複写複製（コピー）することは，
著作権法上での例外を除き，禁じられています．本書からの複
写を希望される場合は，日本複製権センター（03-3401-2382）に
ご連絡ください．

## On Campus

東京大学教養学部英語部会 編

本書 Campus Wide の姉妹編．東大発「発信型英語運用能力」を目指したユニヴァース・シリーズのエッセンスを受け継ぎながら全面改訂．本書とあわせてさらにバラエティー豊かな学習に！（英文の難易度は同等）

**B5 判・204 頁 / 定価（本体価格 1700 円＋税）**

## 東大英単

東京大学教養学部英語部会 編著

アカデミックな英語の基本を構成する語を厳選，珠玉の例文と例題で学ぶ．On Campus, Campus Wide とも連動．

**A5 判・272 頁 / 定価（本体価格 1800 円＋税）**
**［CD ブック］CD 4 枚付 / 定価（本体価格 3200 円＋税）**

## 自分の英語を組み立てる〈最初の一手（ファースト・ムーブス）〉！
## First Moves: An Introduction to Academic Writing in English

ポール・ロシター＋東京大学教養学部英語部会

「和文英訳」から英語による思考の構成へ．精選されたトピックスとランゲージワークによる画期的ライティング教科書．

**B5 判・192 頁 / 定価（本体価格 2400 円＋税）**

## The Universe of English II

東京大学教養学部英語部会 編

ベストセラーになった東大駒場の1年生用統一テキストが全章新しくなった．最新の英文で語られる知の宇宙と，味わい深い短編小説世界を豊富な注に導かれて散策する「教養英語」の新・定番テキスト．

**［テキストのみ］菊判・240 頁 / 定価（本体価格 1900 円＋税）**
**［テキスト＋4CD］菊判・函入 / 定価（本体価格 3800 円＋税）**